IMAGES
of America

OAKLAND'S CHINATOWN

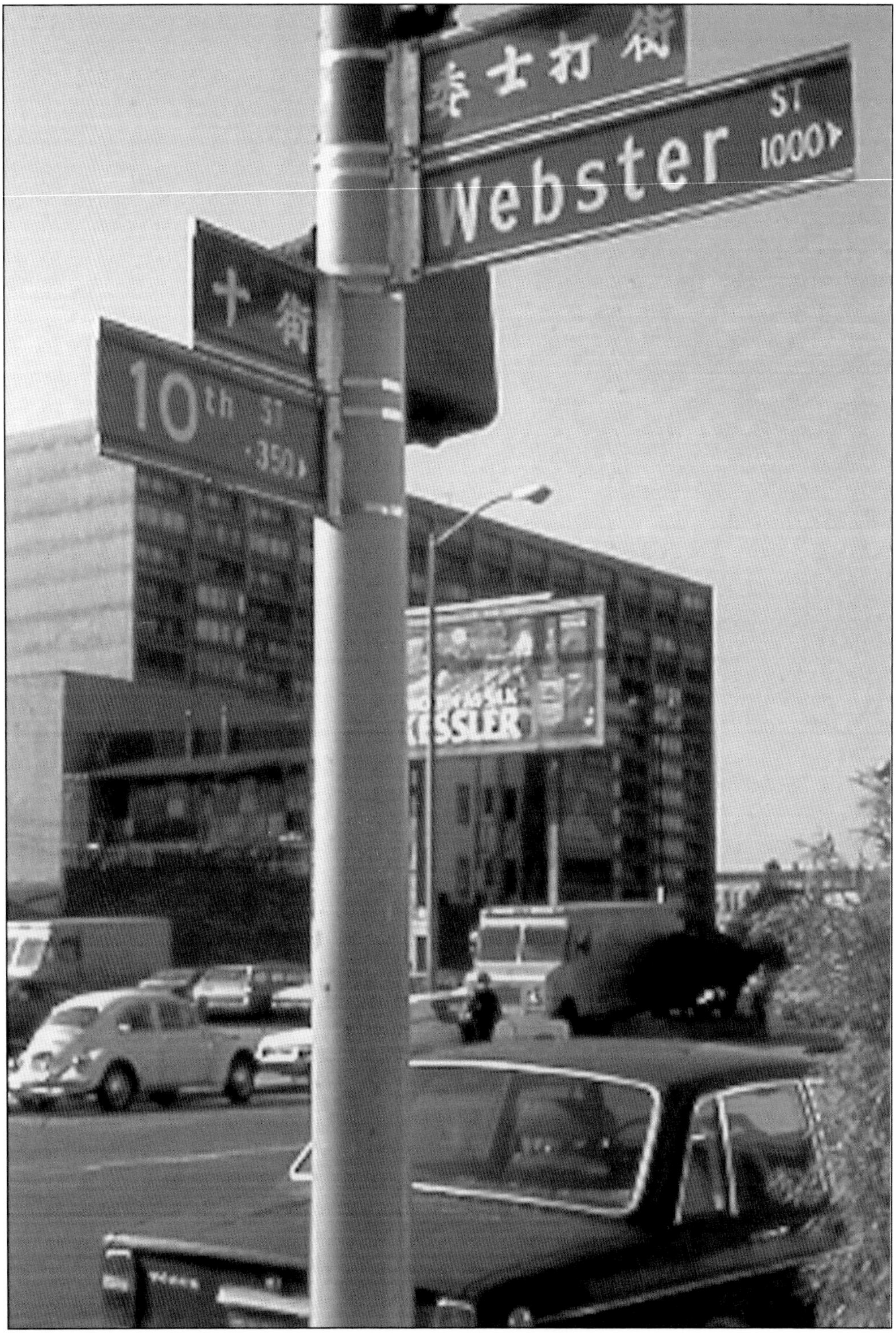

Bilingual street signs signal to residents and visitors alike that they are in Chinatown. (Photo by and courtesy of Russell Lowe.)

IMAGES
of America

OAKLAND'S CHINATOWN

William Wong

ARCADIA
PUBLISHING

ISBN 978-0-7385-2925-7

Published by Arcadia Publishing
Charleston, South Carolina

Printed in the United States of America

Library of Congress Catalog Card Number: 2004110491

For all general information contact Arcadia Publishing at:
Telephone 843-853-2070
Fax 843-853-0044
E-mail sales@arcadiapublishing.com
For customer service and orders:
Toll-Free 1-888-313-2665

Visit us on the Internet at www.arcadiapublishing.com

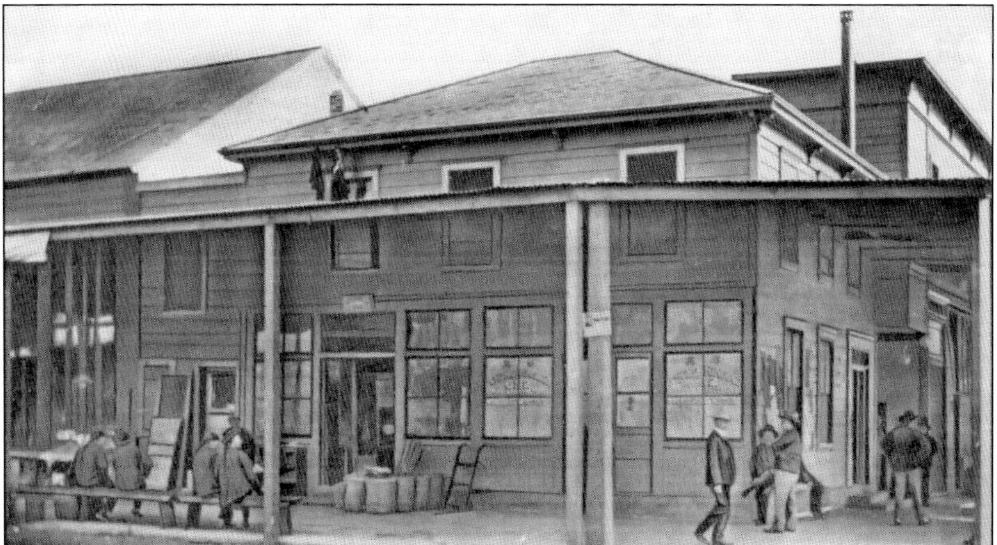

This postcard depicts a typical Oakland Chinatown street scene from the late 1800s. (Courtesy of Ed Clausen.)

CONTENTS

ACKNOWLEDGMENTS

The following people and organizations have been incredibly generous with their help, advice, and counsel:

Asian American Studies Library, University of California at Berkeley (Wei Chi Poon); Evangeline Canonizado Buell, Carl Chan, Linda Yu Chan, Nicole Chan, Henry Chang, Ernest Chann, Serena Chen, Sherlyn Chew, Emily Chow, Ed Clausen, Harvey and Bea Dong, Jeanette Dong, Michael Endo, Tiffany Eng, Weylin Eng, Art Fong, Clifton Fong, George Fong, Wayne Fong, Corinne Jan, Audee Kochiyama-Holman, Rev. Peter Lau, Darlene Lee, George and Mary Lee, Homer Lee, Dr. Janet Lee, Janet Lem, Lee Mun Wah, Kathleen Leung, Sam Chu Lin, Julia Liou, Jean Moon Liu, Rev. Alvin Louie, Jeanie Low, Russell Lowe, Doris Lum, Mary Mar, Luella Mak, Sam Mende-Wong, Linda Montecillo, Oakland Cultural Heritage Survey (Betty Marvin), Oakland Museum of California (Dennis Power, Marcia Eymann, Diane Curry, Stacey Zwald), The Oakland Public Library (Steve Lavoie), George Ong, James Ong, Mel Orpilla, Eugene Quen, Annie Rowley, Rev. Dr. James Shum, Kathy Sloane, Annie Soo, Ed Sue, Wendi Sue, Art Tom, Christopher Tom, Don Tamaki, Rev. Dr. Fran Toy, Lai Chop Webster, Bob Wing, Laraine Wing, Andrew Wong, Betty Wong, Ed and Flo Oy Wong, June Yamane Wong, Kenneth Wong, Li Keng Wong, Nellie Wong, Henry and Henrietta Woon, Ann Yee, Gary and Caroline Yee, May Young, Edward Yu, Judy Yung, and a special word of thanks to the author's wife, Joyce, who was supportive in ways that words cannot describe.

This book is dedicated to Gee Seow Hong and Gee Suey Ting, who made the brave journey across the Pacific and sacrificed to make a good life for their children, beginning in Oakland's Chinatown.

INTRODUCTION

Chinese came to Oakland in significant numbers in the 1850s, after gold was discovered near Sacramento in 1848. They were primarily from southeastern China near Hong Kong. Chinese started congregating in San Francisco and Oakland after being driven from the gold fields by bigotry and violence.

The first Chinese settlements in Oakland were at First and Castro Streets, Telegraph Avenue between Sixteenth and Seventeenth Streets, and San Pablo Avenue between Nineteenth and Twentieth Streets. These settlements were frequently under siege. One burned down mysteriously. City leaders forced two other Chinese settlements to relocate. By the 1870s, Chinese began setting down roots at Eighth and Webster Streets, the epicenter of today's Chinatown.

More Chinese settled in San Francisco, but Oakland became a viable alternative because of jobs, fertile land, good climate, and proximity to San Francisco. Chinese Oaklanders of this era took mostly low-paying jobs. They built Temescal Dam and Lake Chabot Dam. They worked in canneries, cotton mills, and explosives factories. They were cooks, gardeners, houseboys, and laundrymen. They made cigars, helped develop the shrimp and fisheries industries, and labored in the city's thriving railroad building industry. They grew vegetables and fruits, introducing farming innovations and experimenting with new crops like asparagus. Traveling throughout the East Bay region, Chinese peddled fresh fruits and vegetables from baskets hung from a long pole and later from trucks.

Oakland Chinese often faced hostility. Local politicians passed anti-Chinese legislation of one sort or another. Virulent anti-Chinese sentiments broke out throughout California, including Oakland, in the early 1870s, as the general economy soured. The California-grown anti-Chinese movement moved to Washington, D.C., where Congress passed the Chinese Exclusion Act in 1882, barring new Chinese laborers. The Chinese population in Oakland and elsewhere dropped sharply, but the Eighth and Webster Streets Chinatown survived.

The 1906 San Francisco earthquake and fire provided an unexpected boost to Oakland's Chinatown. Thousands of San Francisco Chinese who fled to Oakland chose to stay in Oakland. Some white Oaklanders, however, pressured the city to restrict the growing Chinese population to the Eighth and Webster Streets neighborhood. Chinatown grew nonetheless, from the waterfront up to Tenth Street along the Webster Street corridor.

Even as Chinatown grew, it became more isolated. But the Chinese developed a complex society, often based upon intricate and ancient traditions. They organized men's and women's sports teams. The Wa Sung Service Club began as a baseball team in the 1920s. Chinese organizations emerged and evolved—family and district associations, business associations, tongs, and civil-rights groups. Some tongs engaged in criminal activities like the Chinese lottery. Patriotic organizations had strong ties to Chinatown. One was the Kuomintang, the political movement founded by Sun Yat-Sen, leader of the Chinese Republic. Another was the Chinese American Citizens Alliance (CACA), which fought for the civil rights and assimilation of Chinese Americans. The Oakland lodge at Eighth and Harrison Streets was the third CACA branch formed.

Oakland Chinese remained largely segregated in the first half of the 20th century. But as family life gradually developed in Chinatown, a process of Americanization began, and Lincoln Elementary School was a principal vehicle of acculturation. Chinatown children also went to Chinese schools. By the early 1930s, there were as many as a dozen such schools in Chinatown. In 1953, the Oakland Chinese Community Center, which included a Chinese school, opened at Ninth and Harrison Streets to great fanfare. Protestant Christian churches have been influential in Chinatown. Chinese Presbyterian, Methodist, Episcopal, and Baptist churches continue to have followings in Chinatown today.

A second cataclysmic event—World War II—began to lift the strict segregation of Chinatown and helped create a new Chinese American middle class. Congress repealed the Chinese Exclusion Act in 1943, reflecting China's status as a U.S. ally in World War II. Shipyards hummed in Oakland, employing many people, including Chinese. Chinatown businesses benefited. The Oakland Chinese population grew 37.5 percent to 5,500 in the 1940s. Some Oakland Chinese fought in the war, while others raised funds to help China battle the invading Japanese. This duality has been a continuing undercurrent in older generations of Chinese Americans.

For the smaller number of Japanese Americans around Chinatown, however, World War II was not a good time. They were shipped off to internment camps in remote areas of the West. The Japanese presence in Oakland has never been quite the same since. Filipinos also found work in Chinatown in the 1930s and 1940s.

In the post-war years, the younger generation of Chinese Americans began getting work and buying homes in other parts of Oakland that once forbade Asians. Ironically, World War II prosperity was short-lived for Chinatown. With the shipyards shut down and its young people moving out, Chinatown suffered. Major public projects—the Nimitz Freeway, the Bay Area Rapid Transit District, Laney College, and the Oakland Museum—gobbled up Chinatown housing. The insulated vibrancy of Chinatown, evident in the decades before and during the war, became muted in the 1950s.

Chinatown's dormant state lasted well into the 1960s, until Congress liberalized laws allowing more immigration from Asia and Latin America. Oakland Chinatown experienced a renaissance beginning in the 1970s. That renaissance was accelerated when the end of the Vietnam War brought over thousands of refugees from Southeast Asia, some of them ethnic Chinese.

Oakland's Chinatown showed new life. Shuttered storefronts became restaurants and shops. Gasoline stations were transformed into multi-use buildings. Property values soared. More banks opened Chinatown branches. Redevelopment, a dream of Chinatown leaders since the somnambulant 1950s, resulted in the multi-purpose Pacific Renaissance Plaza on Ninth Street, at Franklin and Webster Streets. This project attracted Hong Kong money, as have other smaller developments.

This growth brought greater ethnic diversity to Chinatown and a continuing cycle of immigrant adaptation issues. The Chinese were the first Asian presence in Oakland, followed by Japanese, Filipinos and Koreans. After 1965, the community exploded with immigrants and refugees from all over Asia. Traditional Chinatown's resurgence and the creation of a new Asian district southeast of Lake Merritt are attributable in part to a Southeast Asian influx.

Perhaps Chinatown is now a misnomer, because the traditional Asian district at Eighth and Webster, while still very Chinese, is much more than that today. The ebb and flow of the Asian communities in Oakland have been, and will continue to be influenced by immigration policies and geopolitical and globalization trends. With multiple generations of Chinese and other Asians living all over the city, and a population of at least 60,000, the Chinese American and Asian American presence in Oakland is now deeply rooted.

One

A Sense of Place

Chinese lived in different parts of Oakland from the 1850s to the 1870s, when the corner of Eighth and Webster Streets became the center of Chinatown. This intersection continues as its center today. Photos in this chapter show street scenes, significant buildings, and families in front of their homes or in a community setting. Even though hostile outside forces made life difficult for early Oakland Chinese, they managed to set down roots.

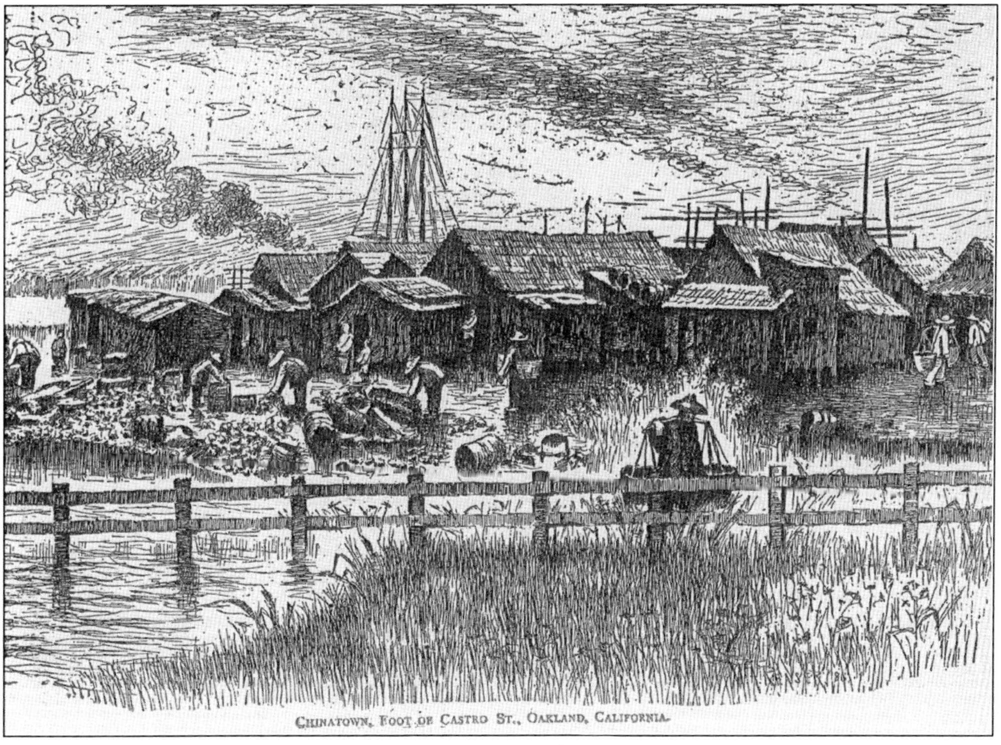

This line drawing depicts an early Chinatown at the foot of Castro Street in what is now West Oakland in the mid- to late 1800s. (Courtesy of the Oakland Cultural Heritage Survey, City of Oakland.)

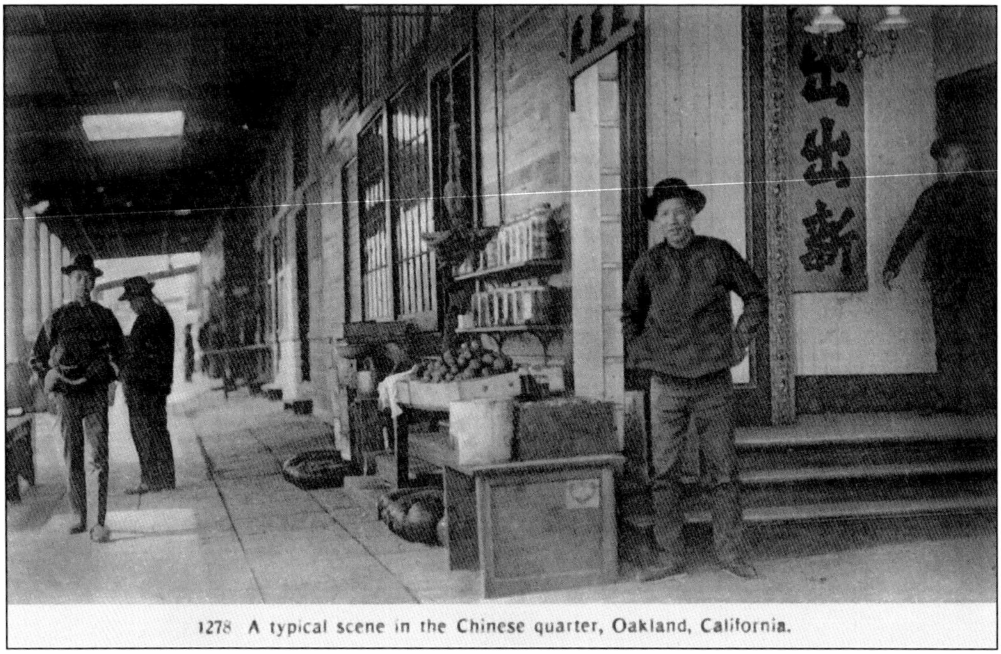

This postcard's caption reads, "A typical scene in the Chinese quarter, Oakland, California." The scene is most likely from the late 1800s. (Courtesy of Ed Clausen.)

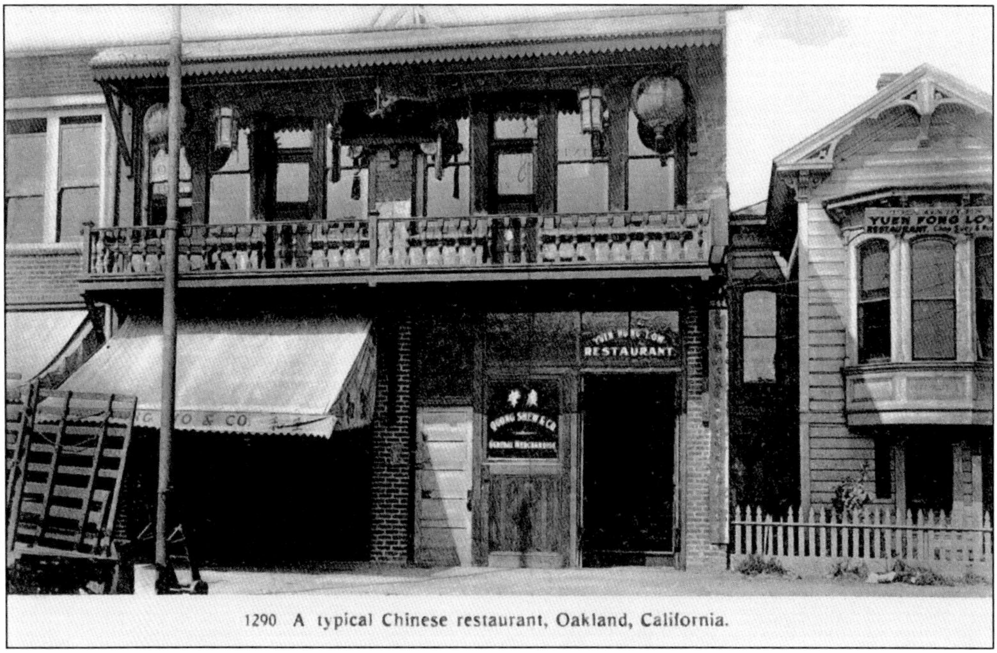

Pictured here is "A typical Chinese restaurant, Oakland, California," according to this postcard. The date is probably from the late 1800s. (Courtesy of Ed Clausen.)

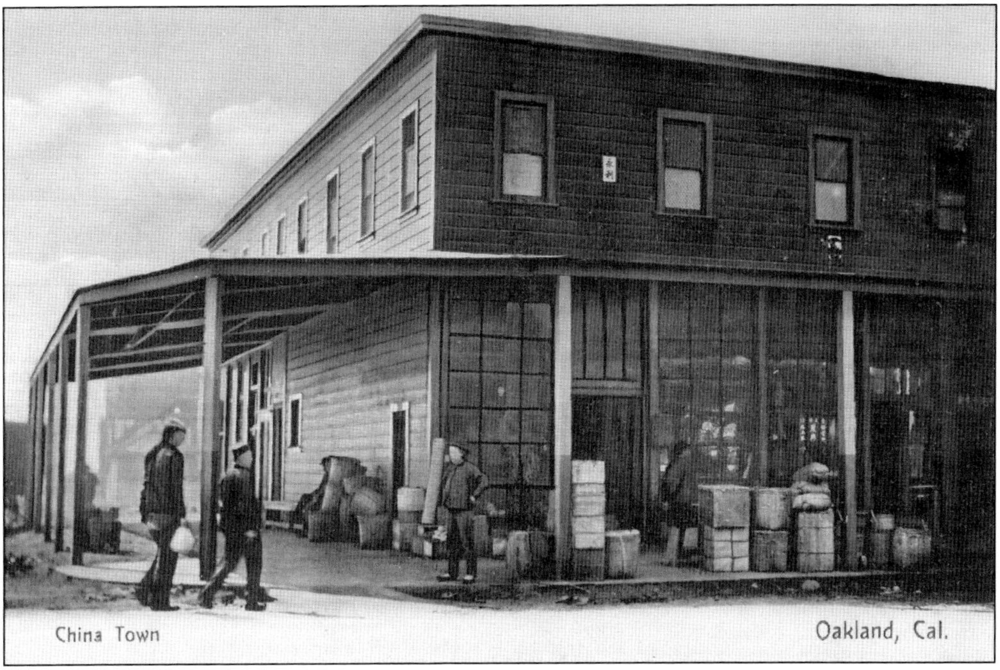

Here is another postcard depicting an Oakland Chinatown street scene from the late 1800s. (Courtesy of Ed Clausen.)

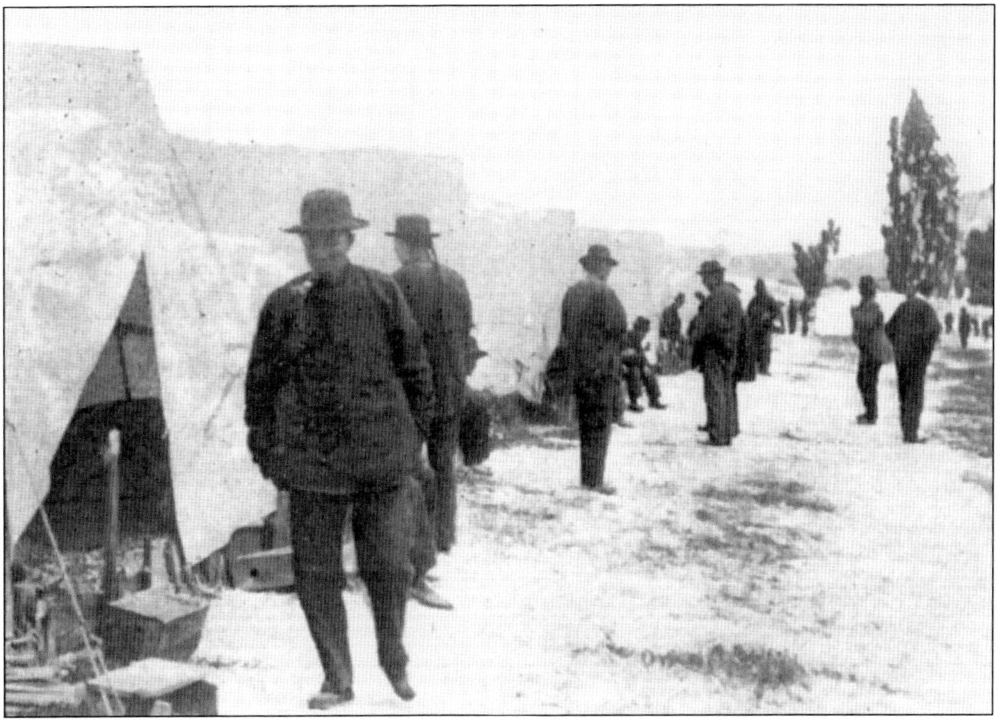

A Chinese refugee camp developed in Oakland in 1906, right after the San Francisco earthquake. The quake and fire drove many San Francisco Chinese across the Bay to Oakland, and many stayed there. (Courtesy of the Oakland Public Library.)

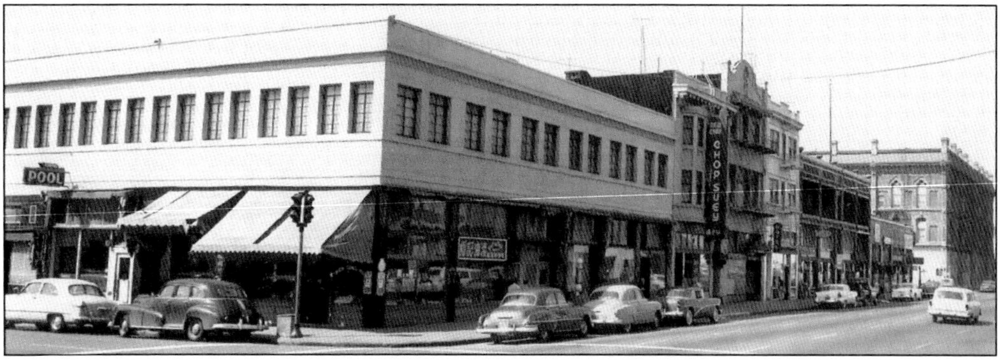

The epicenter of Chinatown is Eighth and Webster Streets. It dates back to the 1870s as the center of the Chinese community in Oakland and is busier than ever now. This is a 1958 view, looking west. (Photo by the Downtown Property Owners Association, courtesy of the Oakland Public Library.)

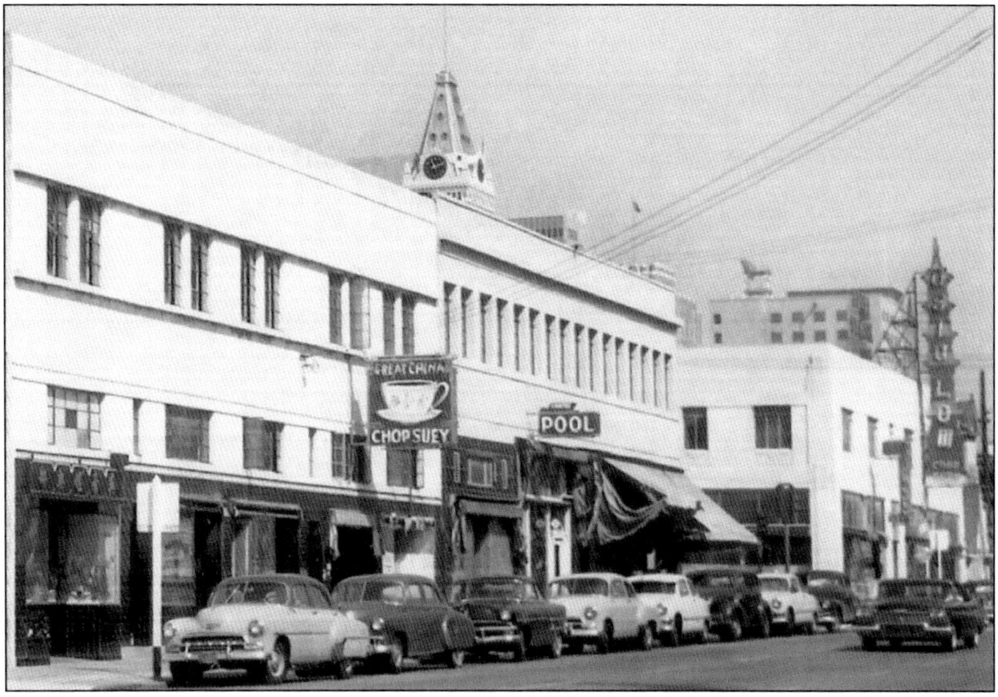

A 1958 view of Webster Street looking north toward Eighth Street shows the Great China restaurant, a pool hall, and the Asia Low restaurant. In the background is the *Oakland Tribune* tower at Thirteenth and Franklin Streets. (Photo by the Downtown Property Owners Association, courtesy of the Oakland Public Library.)

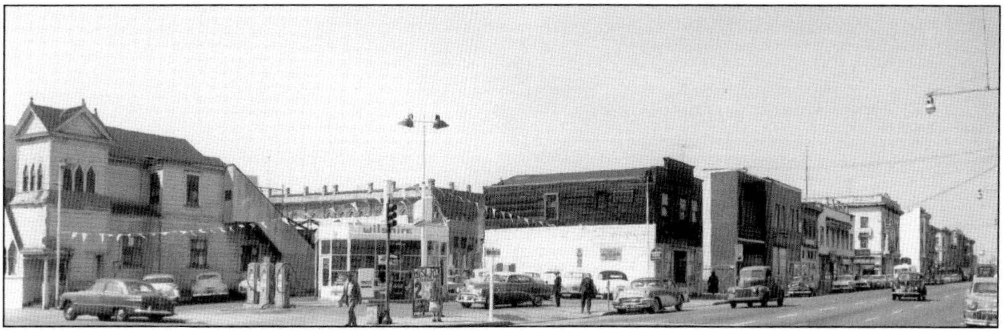

This is the corner of Ninth and Webster Streets, looking west, in 1958. The building at left is the Chinese Independent Baptist Church. (Photo by the Downtown Property Owners Association, courtesy of the Oakland Public Library.)

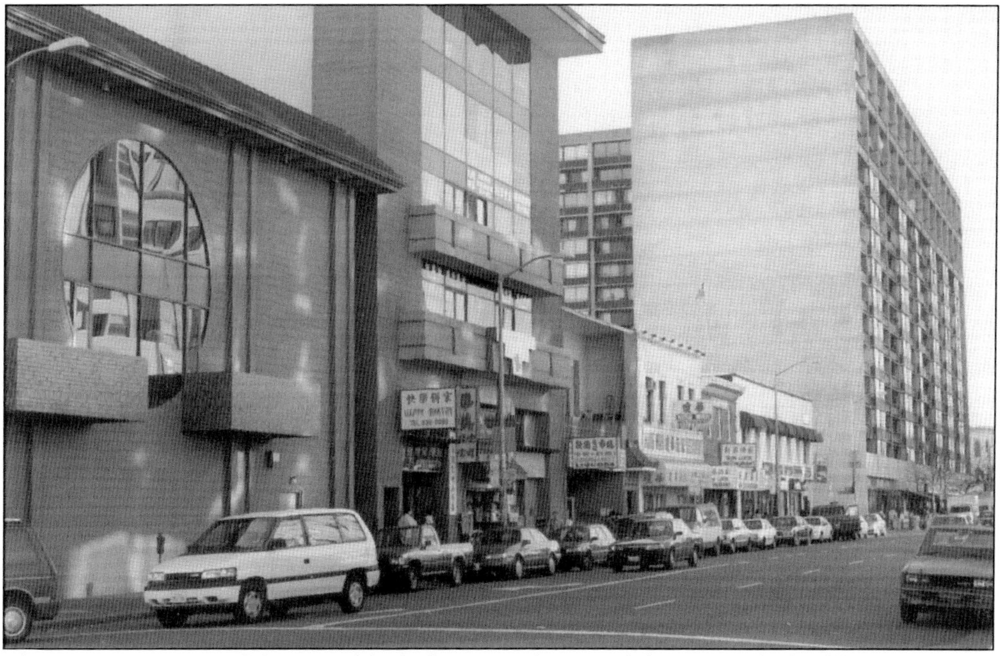

This is a 1990s view of the same block shown at the top of the page. The building on the left with a round window is the Silver Dragon restaurant. The tall edifice in the right background is City Center Towers, built in the 1970s as a condominium apartment building with retail stores on the street level. (Courtesy of Family Bridges Inc.)

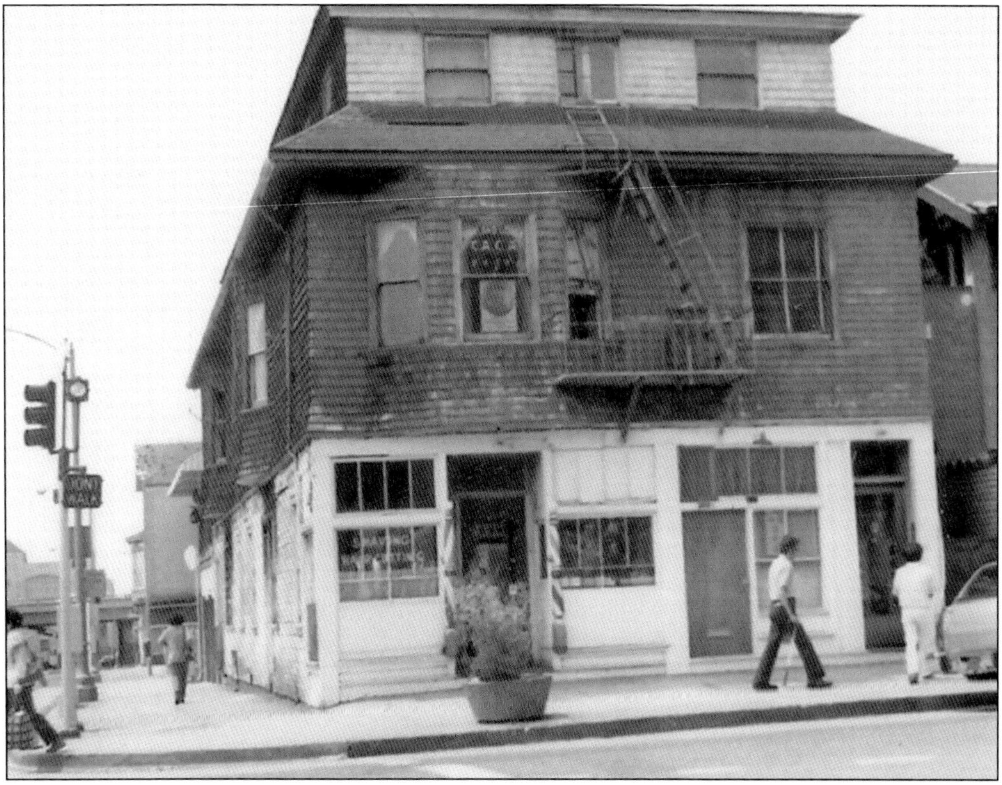

The building at Eighth and Harrison Streets is a Chinatown landmark. On the ground floor was the famous barbershop of Fong Get Moo. On the second floor is the Oakland Lodge of the Chinese American Citizens Alliance. Dr. Charles Lee, a pioneering Oakland Chinese American dentist, financed the construction of this building. (Photo by W. Chin, courtesy of Mary Mar.)

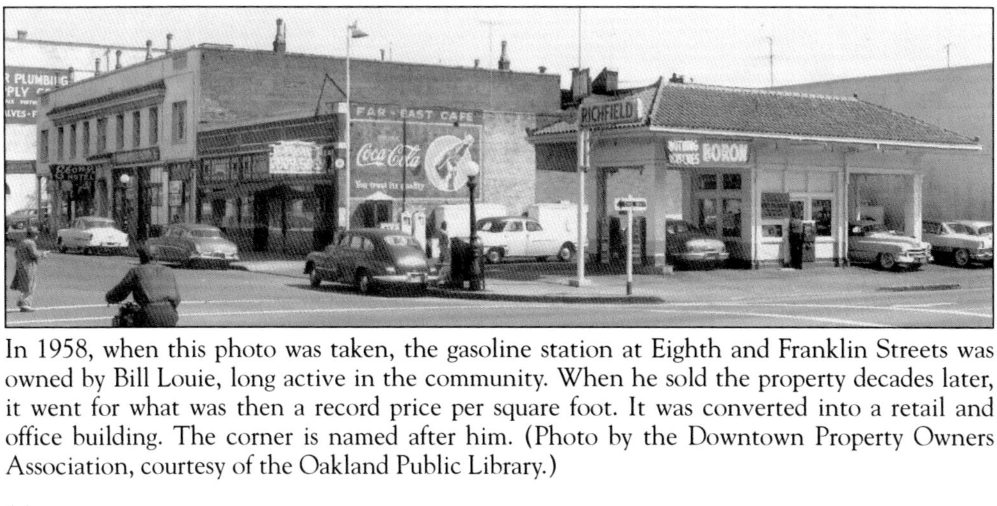

In 1958, when this photo was taken, the gasoline station at Eighth and Franklin Streets was owned by Bill Louie, long active in the community. When he sold the property decades later, it went for what was then a record price per square foot. It was converted into a retail and office building. The corner is named after him. (Photo by the Downtown Property Owners Association, courtesy of the Oakland Public Library.)

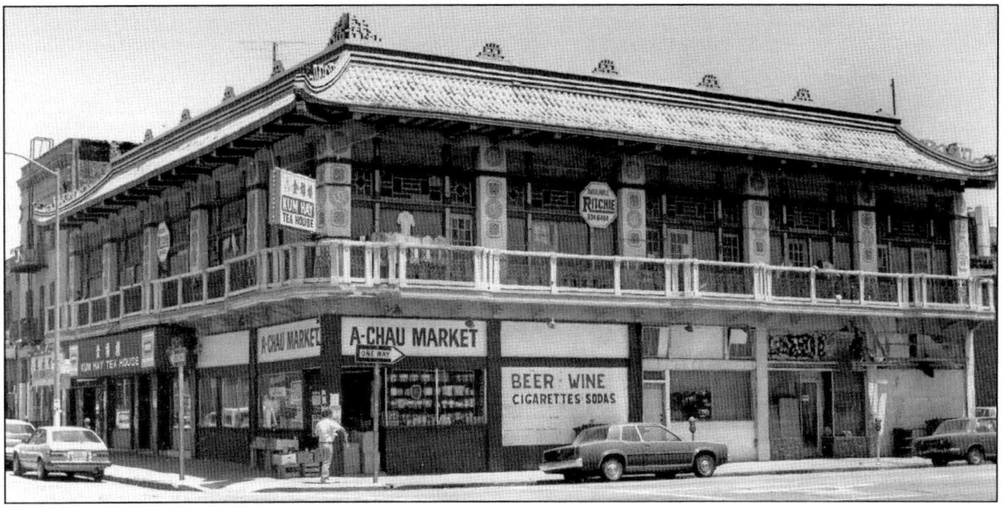

Another Chinatown landmark, this building at Seventh and Franklin Streets, shown here in the 1980s, was constructed in 1927 and has been a nightclub, low-rent housing, and now a Hong Kong-style restaurant, the Legendary Palace. In the early 1990s, it was at the center of a dispute between social service providers and business interests over the best use for the building. (Courtesy of George Ong.)

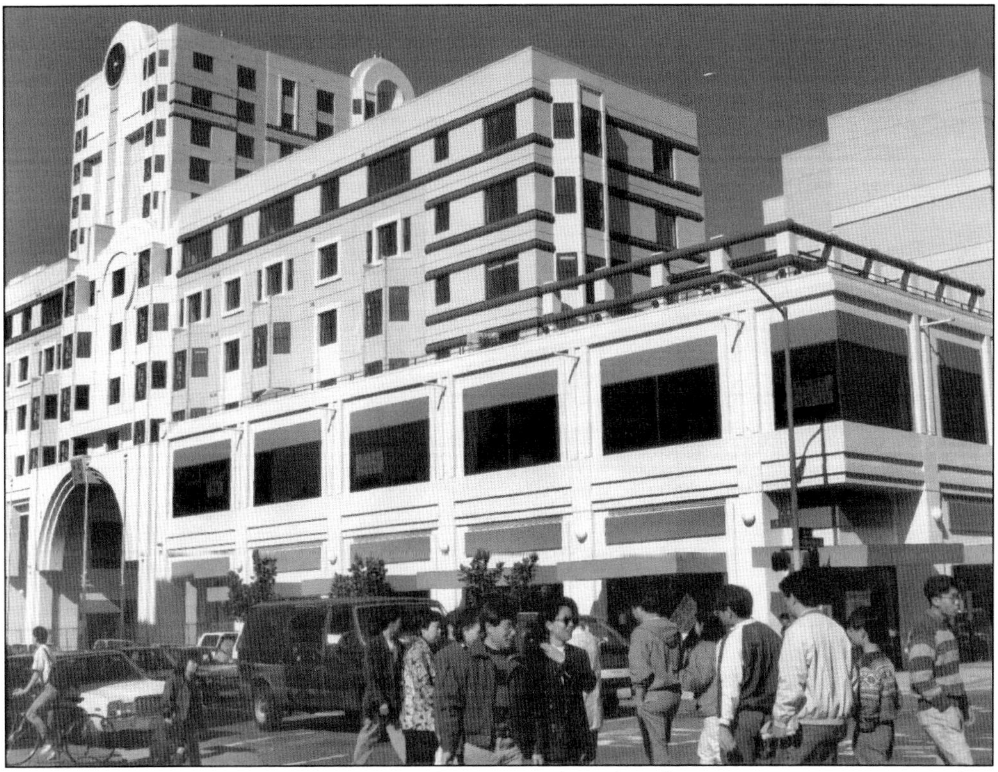

The multi-purpose Pacific Renaissance Plaza at Ninth and Webster Streets was constructed in the early 1990s by a Hong Kong-based developer, C&L Financial. Built on land targeted in the 1960s for Chinatown redevelopment, the plaza has become a hub of Chinatown. (Courtesy of Sue Associates Architecture and Planning.)

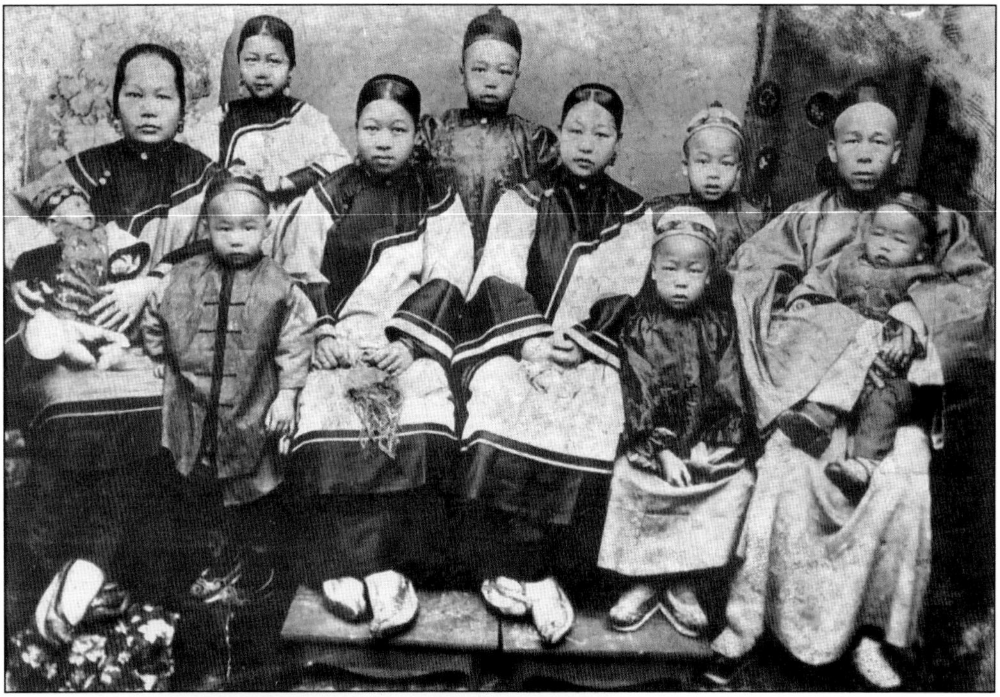

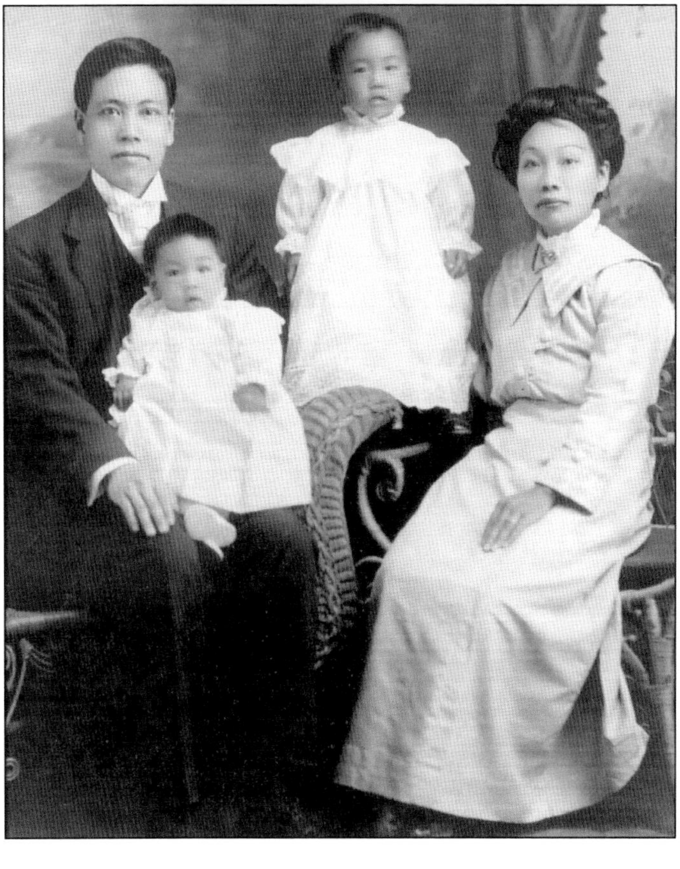

This 1891 photo shows a 10-year-old Charles Lee (back row, middle) with his family. He was the first Chinese dentist in California, practicing for 34 years in Oakland before retiring in 1940. He helped start the Oakland Lodge of the Chinese American Citizens' Alliance and was active in other community groups. His son, Lester, became an Oakland dentist too. (Courtesy of Mary Mar.)

Fong Wan, shown with his young family in the early 1900s, became a well-known and controversial herbalist and businessman near Chinatown. State and federal authorities questioned his advertising claims, but he was never convicted. (Courtesy of the Oakland Museum of California.)

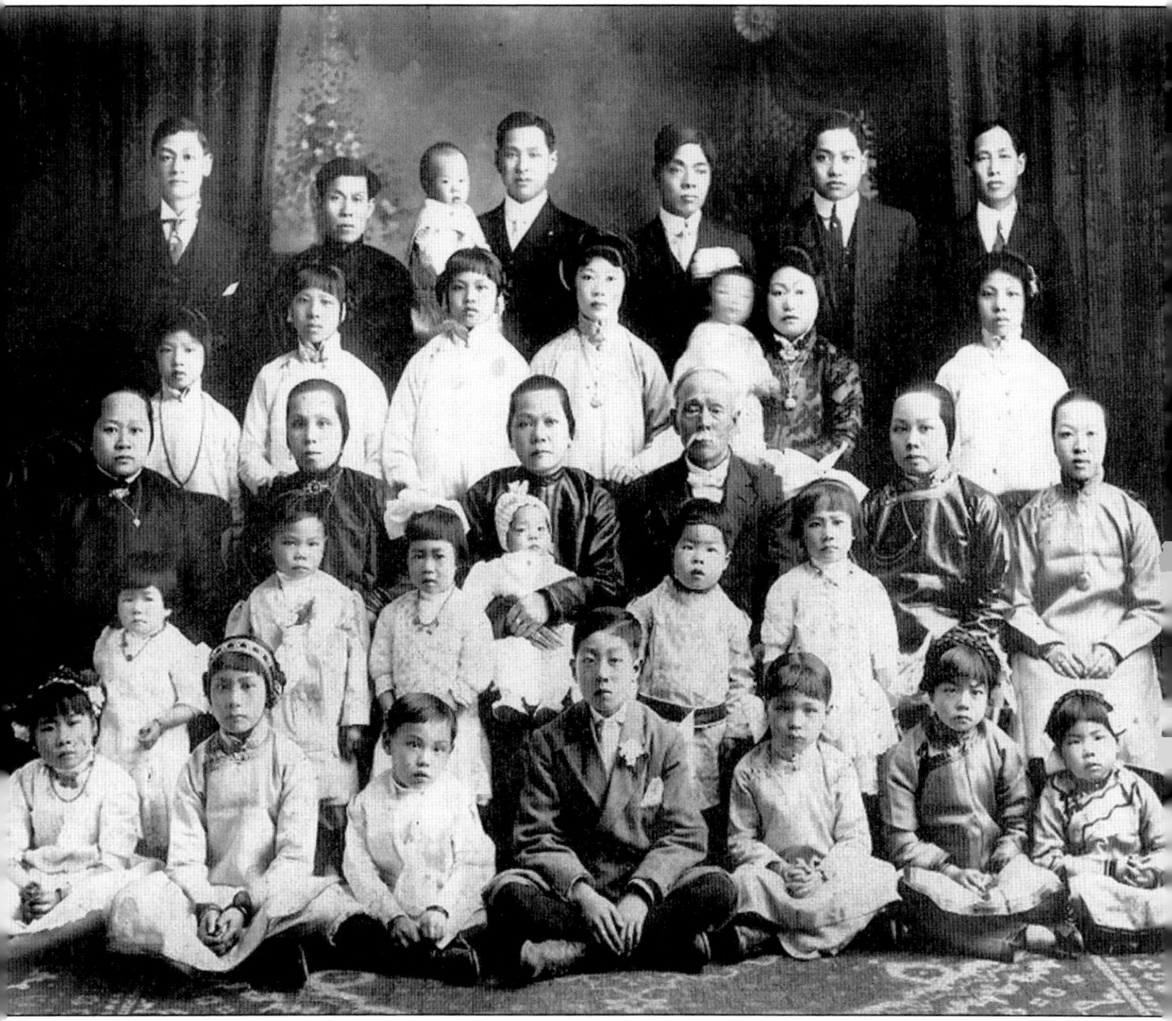

Lee Bo Wen (third row, fourth from left), celebrating his 70th birthday in this 1912 photo, was the patriarch of a remarkable Oakland Chinese family, which now carries the Bowen and Wing surnames, among others. Dating back to the 1850s in California, the family now has been in America for six generations. Lee's wife, Mary Wong Ching, is to his right, holding a baby. Their descendants have broken color lines in education, housing, and employment; organized men's and women's sports teams; and became vaudeville performers and political, civil rights, and labor activists. (Courtesy of Laraine C. Wing.)

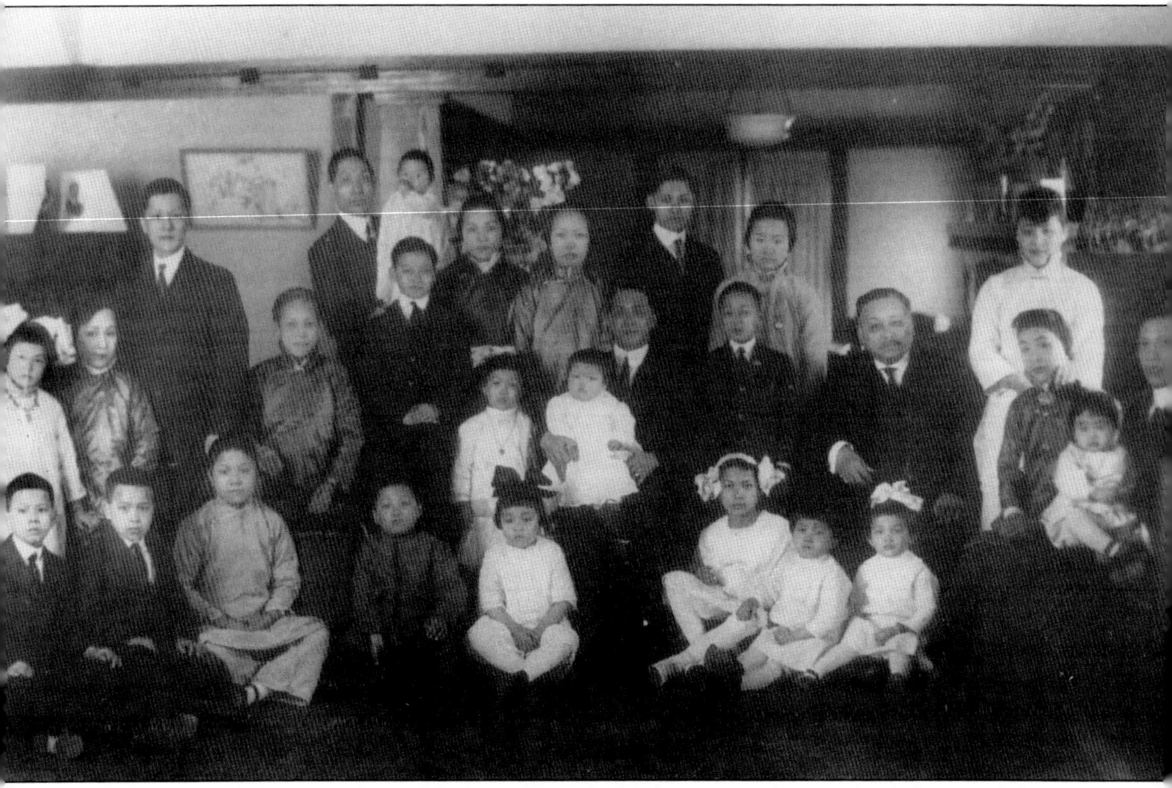

Pioneering Oakland industrialist Lew Hing (seated in second row, third from right) poses with his extensive family in 1916 in his home near Lake Merritt. Lew was remarkable for his time, having started a cannery in West Oakland as early as 1904. The youngest descendants of his family are sixth-generation Americans, and many still reside in the Oakland area. One descendant, Carol Liu, is in the state assembly. (Courtesy of Jean Moon Liu.)

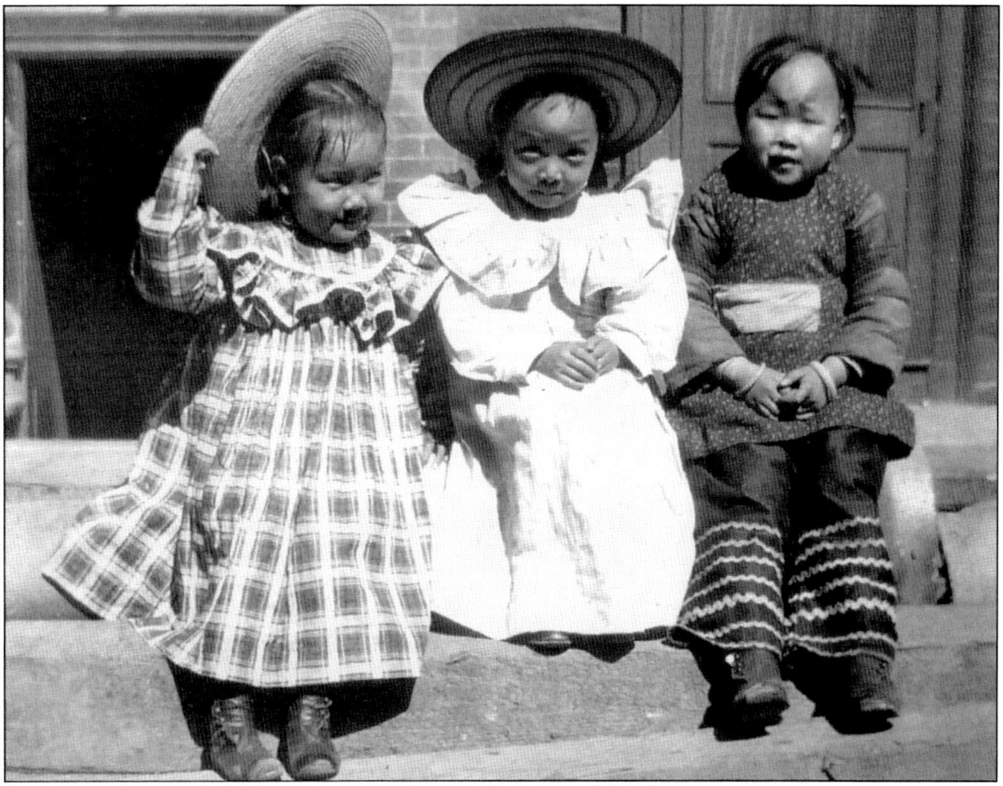

Three unidentified children sit for a photo taken in Oakland in the early 1900s. (Courtesy of the Chinese Independent Baptist Church, Oakland, Gift of Janie S. Chu.)

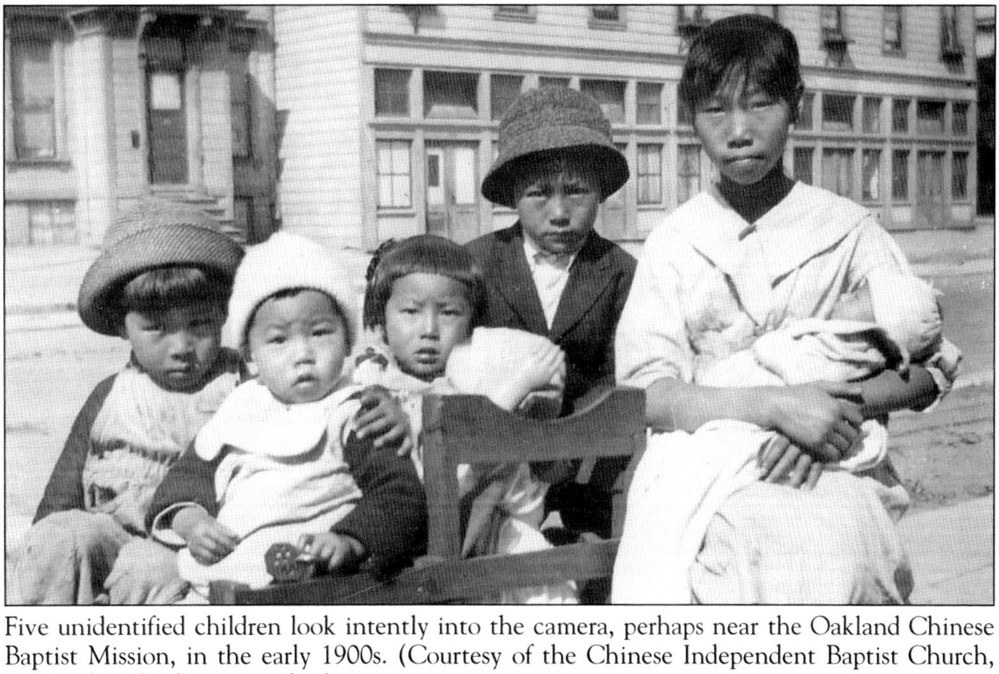

Five unidentified children look intently into the camera, perhaps near the Oakland Chinese Baptist Mission, in the early 1900s. (Courtesy of the Chinese Independent Baptist Church, Oakland, Gift of Janie S. Chu.)

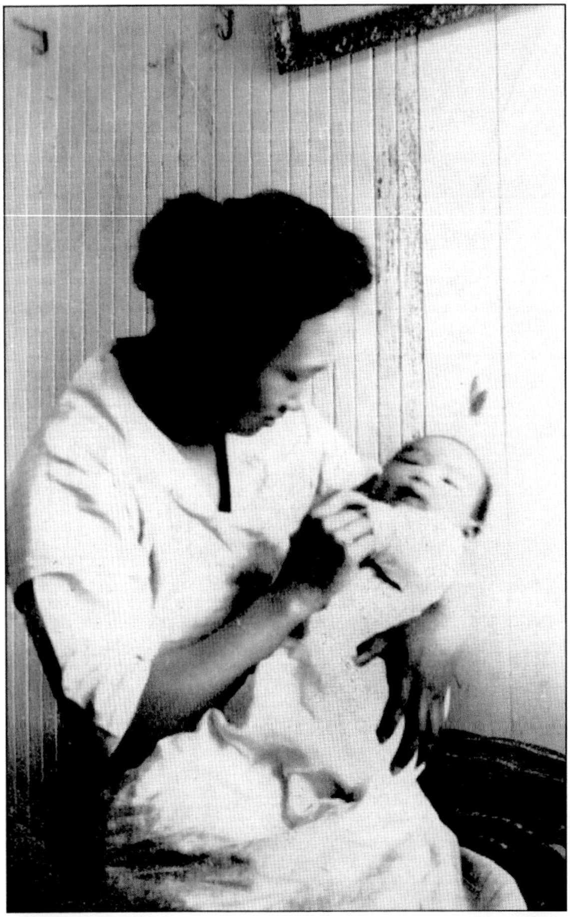

Lon Yoke Fong, later to be known as Fong Get Moo, nurtures her infant son Clifton in her husband's barbershop at Eighth and Harrison Streets, around 1917. (Courtesy of Clifton Fong.)

Elizabeth Hoo (left) is with three unidentified babies in this photo from the 1910s. (Courtesy of Art Tom.)

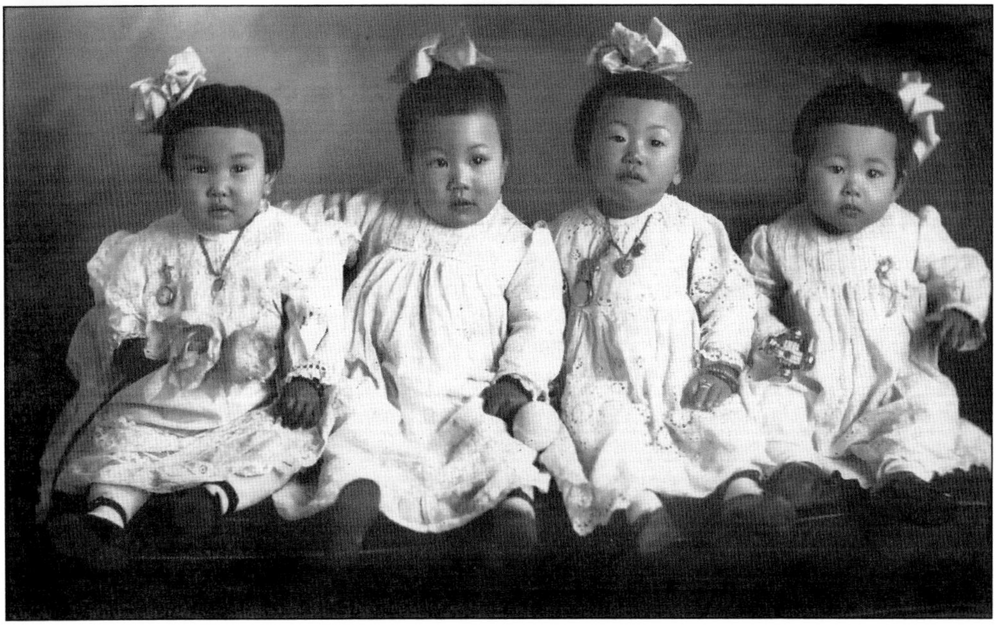

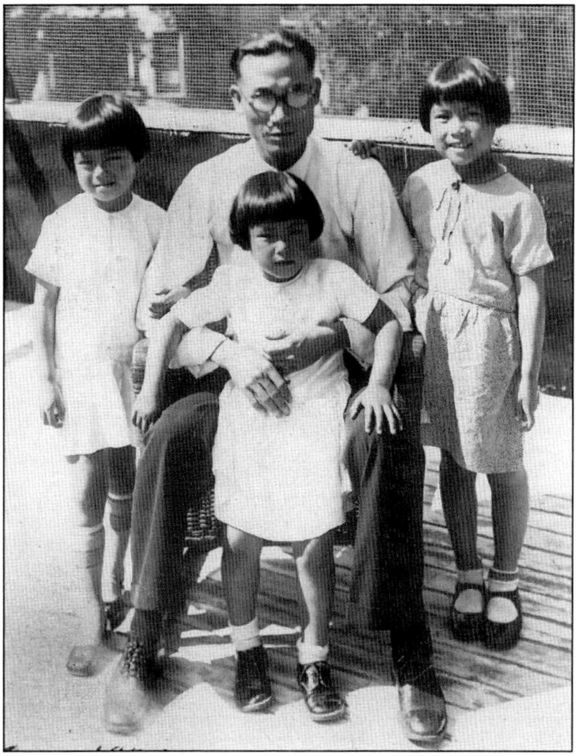

The Lee sisters, shown from left to right, are Fran, age seven, Flo, six, and Jayne, nine. They welcome their uncle Dock Young, who had just emigrated from Canton, China, in this 1932 photo. The group assembled on the roof of their home at 731 Madison Street, owned by the Lee sisters' parents, Mr. and Mrs. G.Y. Lee. (Courtesy of Bea Dong.)

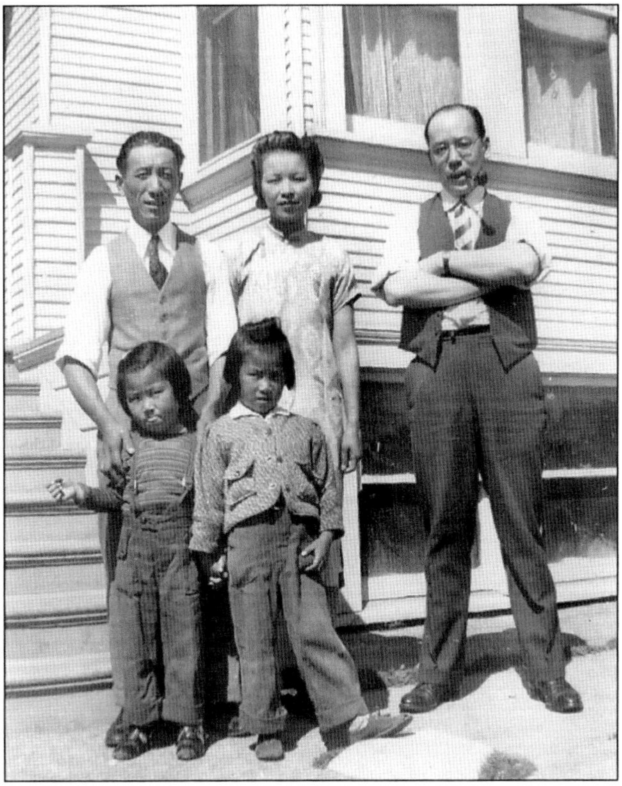

Ruby Lum, age five (front row at left), and her sister, Peggy, six, are outside the family home at Fifth and Alice Streets in this early 1940s photo. In the back row, from left to right, are the girls' father, Henry Lum; their mother, Chan Lin Lum; and uncle Kwai Fong Chan, editor of the *Chinese Times*. (Courtesy of May Young.)

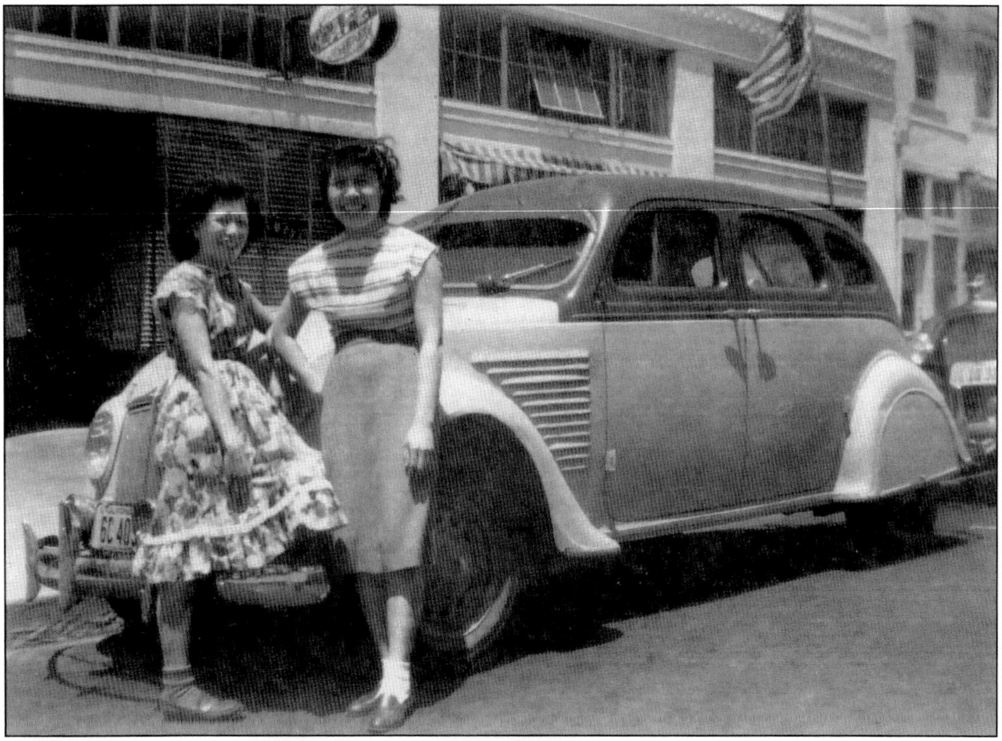

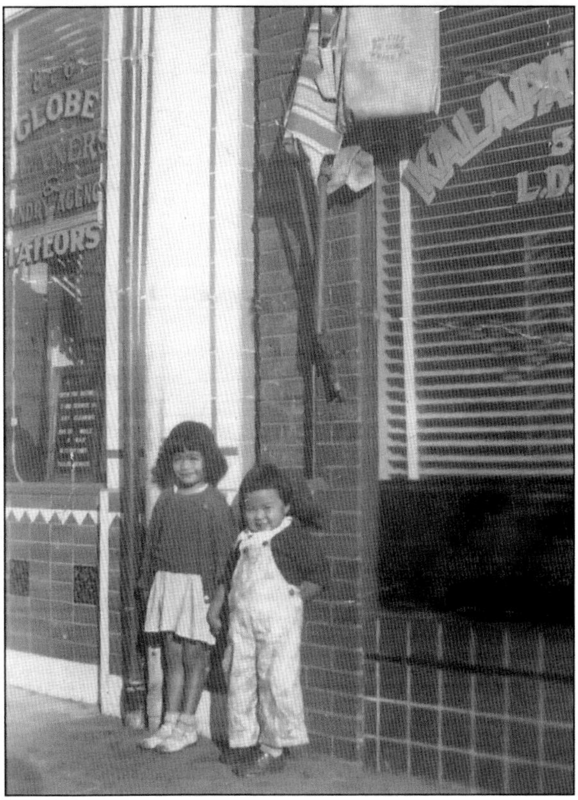

Cleope (Oping) Montecillo, left, shares a happy moment with her cousin Basilia Montecillo at Ninth and Franklin Streets in the early 1950s. The Chevy belonged to Basilia. Filipino Americans lived and worked in Chinatown in the decades before and just after World War II. (Courtesy of Linda Montecillo.)

Linda Montecillo, left, and the unidentified daughter of the owner of the Far East Café down the street played on the east side of Franklin Street between Eighth and Ninth Streets in the late 1940s. (Courtesy of Linda Montecillo.)

Ed Sue at age 16 rests on a truck in front of his family's grocery store, Key's Market, in West Oakland in 1947. He stands with a neighborhood youngster named "Junior." Sue's uncle had purchased the market from a Japanese American family that was interned during World War II. Sue went on to become a successful architect and contractor. (Courtesy of Ed Sue.)

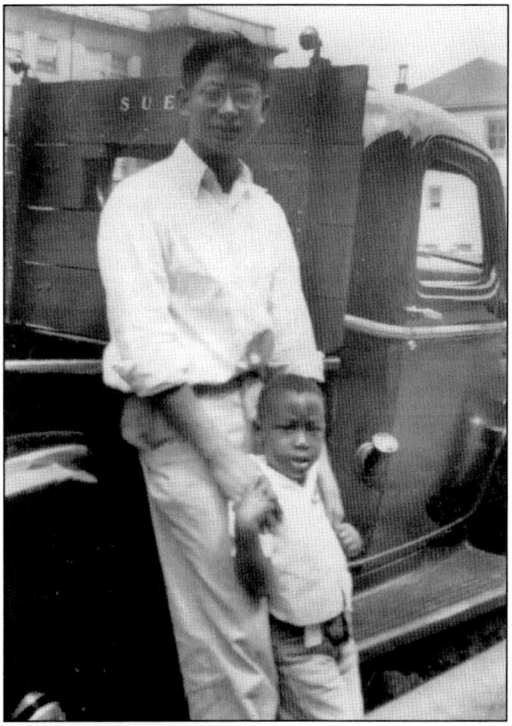

Bowen/Wing family members gathered at Grayce Bowen Wye's Oakland home at 564 Sixty-second Street in the 1950s. From left to right are (front row) Rally Eng, Rhetta Wing Ah-Tye, and Wendell Wye; (second row) John Won; (third row) Joyce Wye Mar, Mary Bowen Wing, Elsye Bowen Won, and Janie Wing Dang; (top row) Grayce Bowen Wye, Florence Bowen Eng, and Pauline Wing Lou. (Courtesy of Laraine C. Wing.)

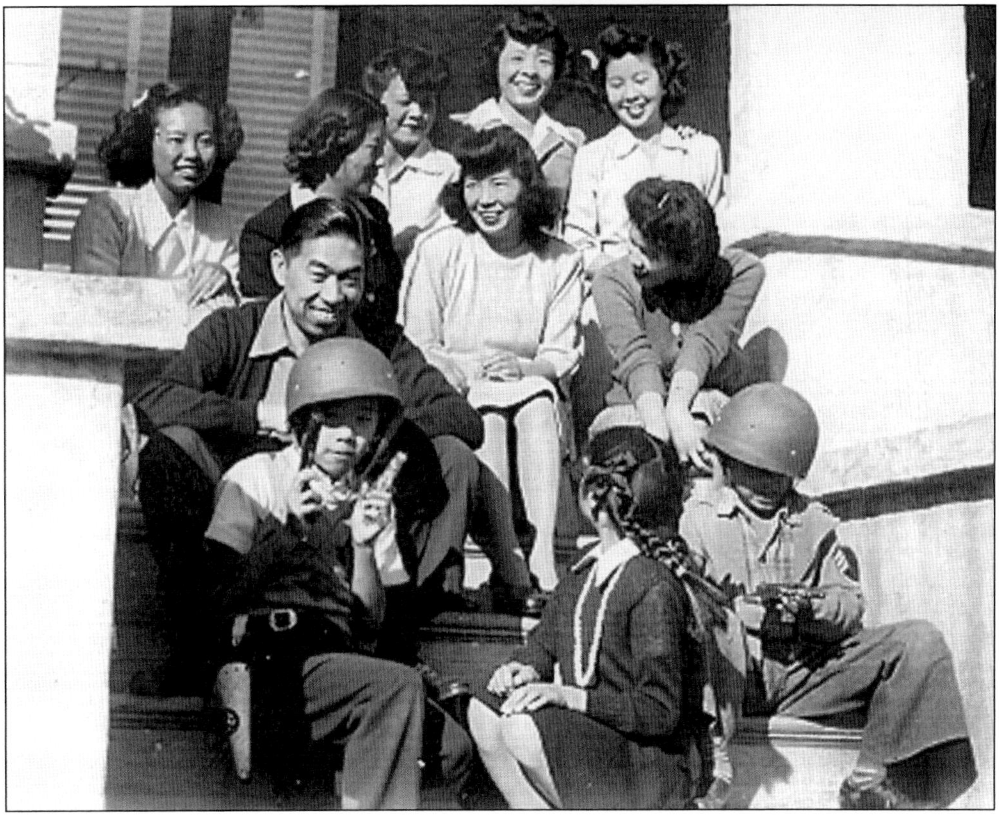

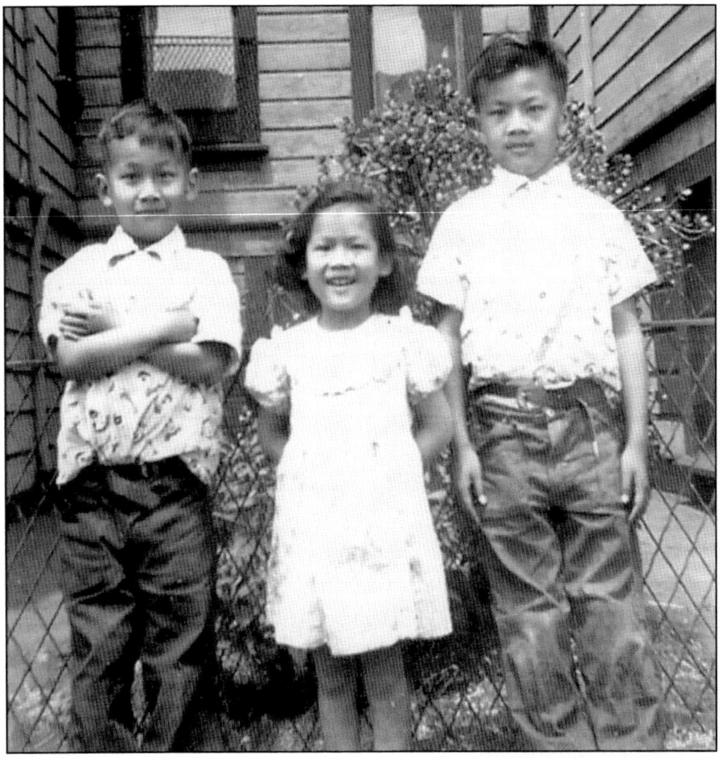

From left to right, Ben, Shirley and Barry Fong-Torres pose in front of their family's home at 206 Eighth Street in the late 1940s. Their parents operated several restaurants in Chinatown and other parts of Oakland. Barry, a youth counselor in San Francisco, was killed in 1972 in a gang-related incident. Shirley became a professional chef and San Francisco Chinatown tour guide, while Ben became a celebrated journalist, author, and radio personality. (Courtesy of Ben Fong-Torres.)

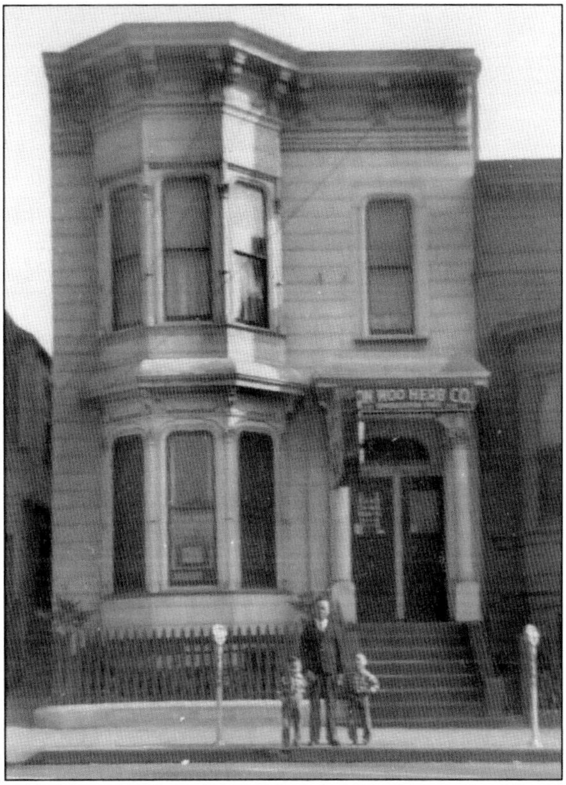

Young Tung Dang clutches the hands of his sons, Ted (right), and Lucas, at the family home at 708 Jefferson Street, just west of Chinatown, in this 1955 photo. Ted Dang went on to a distinguished career in business, real estate development, and community leadership. (Courtesy of Ted Dang.)

Sisters Gee Li Keng, left, and Gee Lai Wah show off fancy new outfits at their family's new home near Lake Merritt in 1950. This scene illustrates the movement of a struggling working class family before World War II to an emerging middle class. Li Keng was the first Chinese American teacher in southern Alameda County. Lai Wah married and moved with her young family to Santa Clara County, later known as Silicon Valley, in the early 1960s. (Courtesy of Li Keng Wong.)

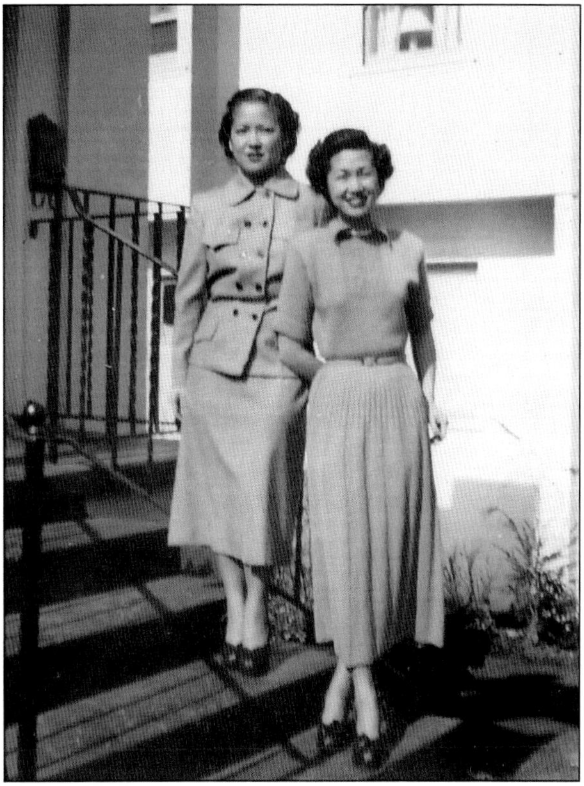

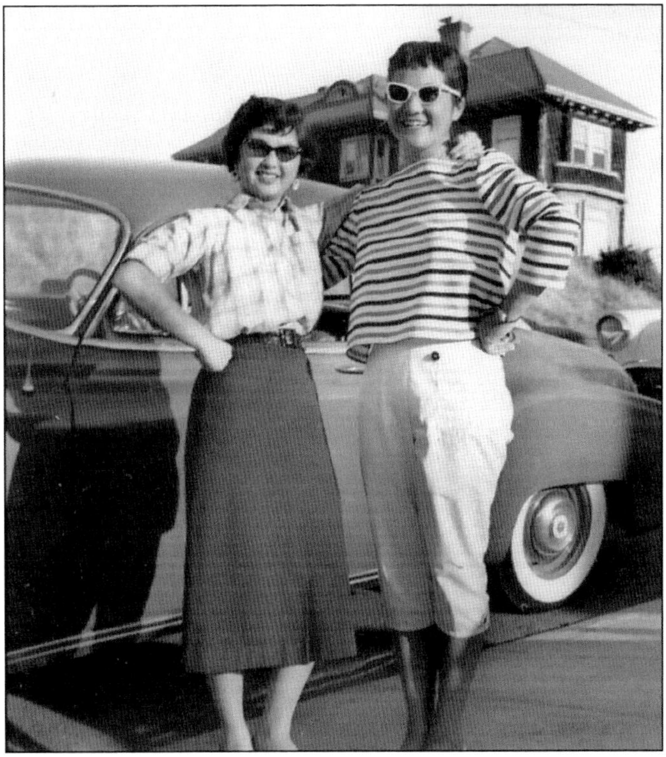

Sisters Leslie Yee, left, and Nellie Wong preen in their cool, casual outfits in front of their family's China Hill home in the early 1950s. This photo, like the one above, illustrates an Oakland Chinese family's move into the middle class after World War II. Nellie worked as a secretary and administrator in the public and private sector, while blossoming as a poet and political activist. Leslie raised three children while working in the Oakland public schools. (Courtesy of Nellie Wong.)

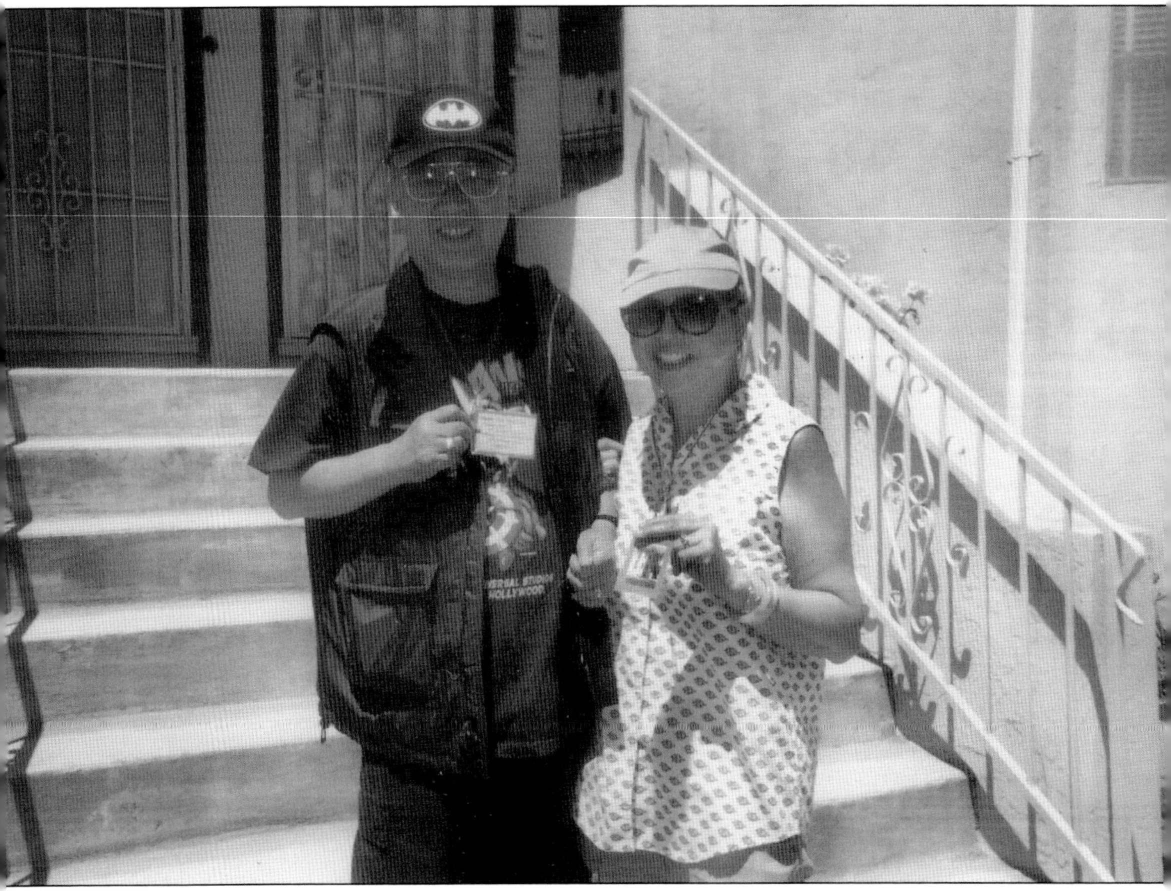

Paul and Darlene Lee stand happily in front of 703 Jackson Street, three blocks from the heart of commercial Chinatown, their home since 1965, when they were married. They are among the few people born in Chinatown who remain residents. As children, they were neighbors. Paul worked for the U.S. Postal Service and Darlene has been a teacher, community historian, and works as a Lincoln Square supervisor. (Courtesy of Darlene Lee.)

Two

Working Hard

A propensity for hard work is a stereotype that is often applied to Chinese Americans. Oakland Chinese are no different. Railroad barons of the 19th century imported Chinese workers to build the transcontinental railroad. The earliest Chinese in Oakland came seeking fortune in the California hills where gold was discovered. They first referred to California in Cantonese as *Gum Saan*, or "Gold Mountain," where they clustered together in cities like Oakland to protect themselves from violent bigotry. Wherever they or their descendants settled in Oakland, they worked hard, first as low-skilled labor, then in higher skilled jobs, and eventually owning their businesses or gaining professional positions. This chapter depicts working Chinese in Oakland, past and present.

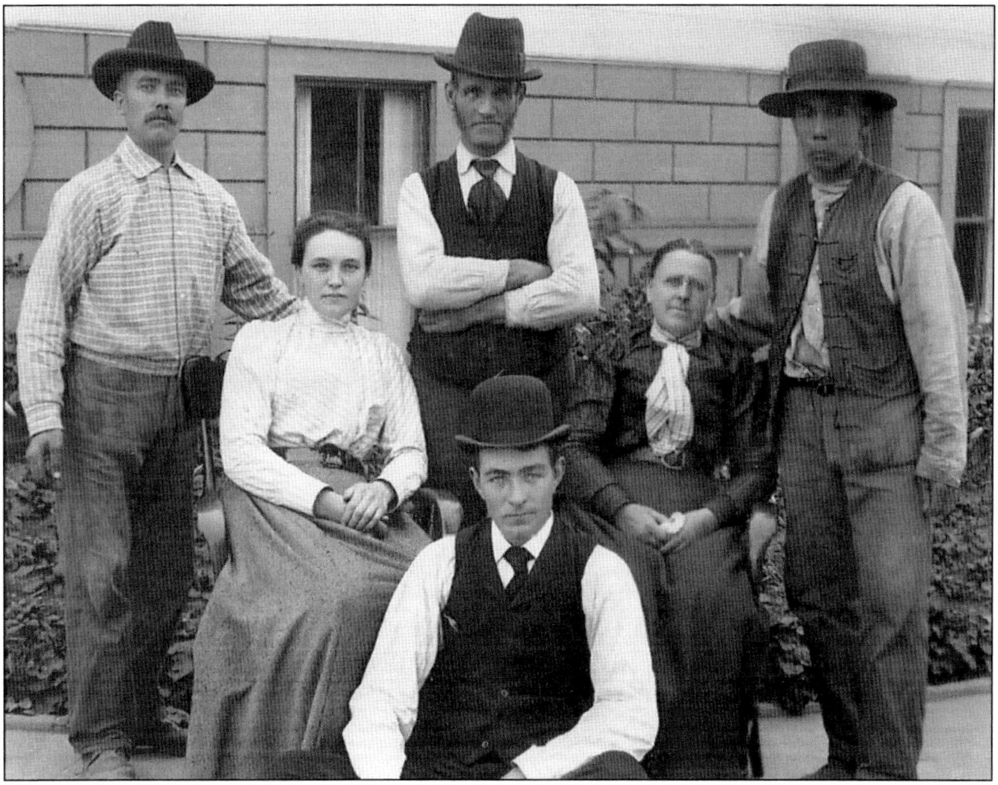

An unidentified Chinese gardener, standing at right, worked on the Delger family estate, located on their extensive grounds between Telegraph and San Pablo Avenues, around 1900. (Gift of Frank Moller, courtesy of the Oakland Museum of California.)

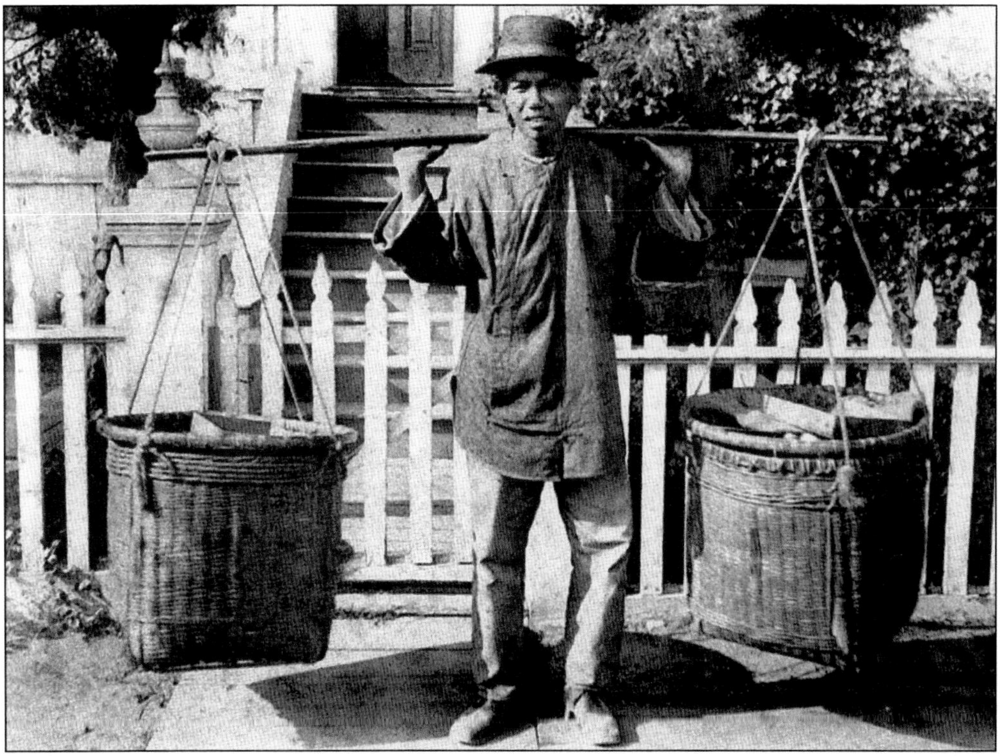

This unidentified Chinese vegetable peddler balanced a long pole with baskets suspended from either end. Peddlers sold fresh produce throughout the East Bay. This photo was taken around 1890. (Gift of the Berkeley Firefighter Association Historical Commission, courtesy of the Oakland Museum of California.)

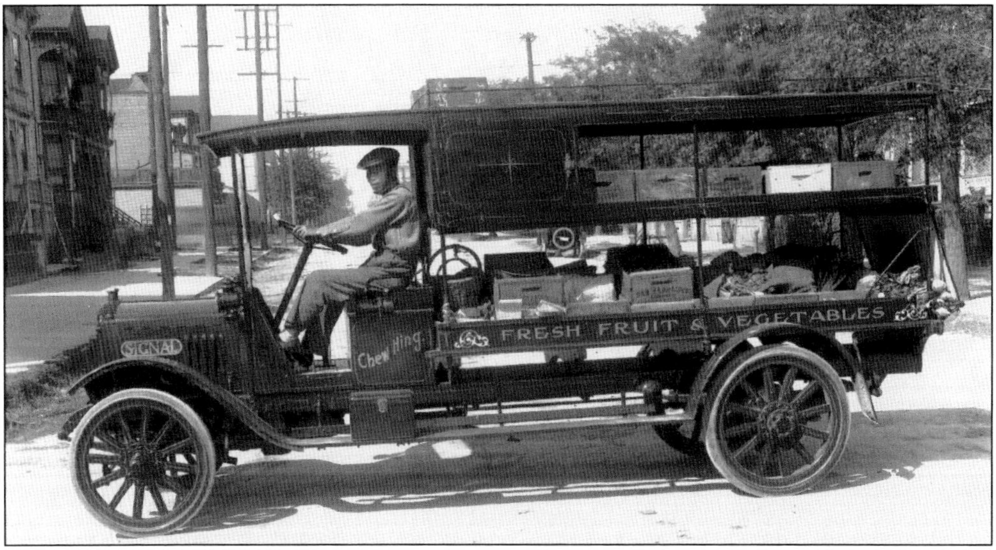

Delivery trucks like this one belonging to the Chew Hing Company in 1915 advanced the sale and delivery of Chinese-grown fresh produce throughout Oakland and nearby communities. (Courtesy of the Oakland Tribune Collection, the Oakland Museum of California, Gift of Alameda Newspaper Group.)

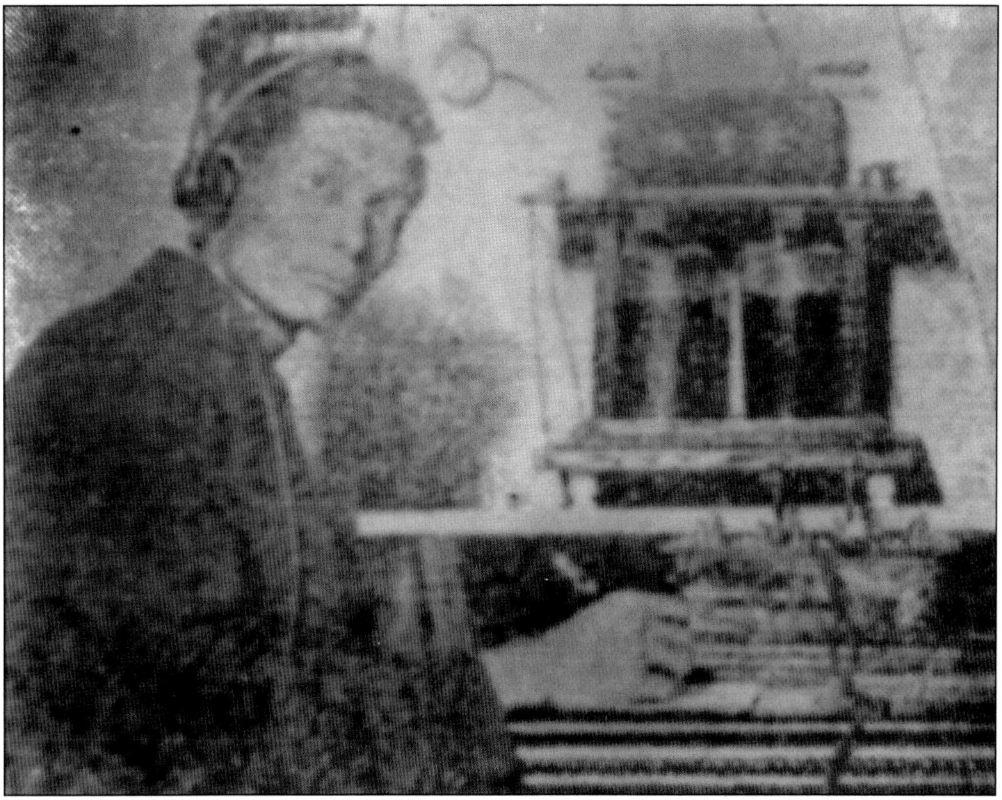

China-born Fong Joe Guey moved to Oakland in 1906 after the San Francisco earthquake and started an airplane manufacturing shop at 359 East Ninth Street. Fong test flew his own plane twice over Oakland, crashing both times, but remaining aloft for 20 minutes in his second attempt. He went home to build planes to defend China, but was killed in a 1912 crash. (Courtesy of Mary Mar.)

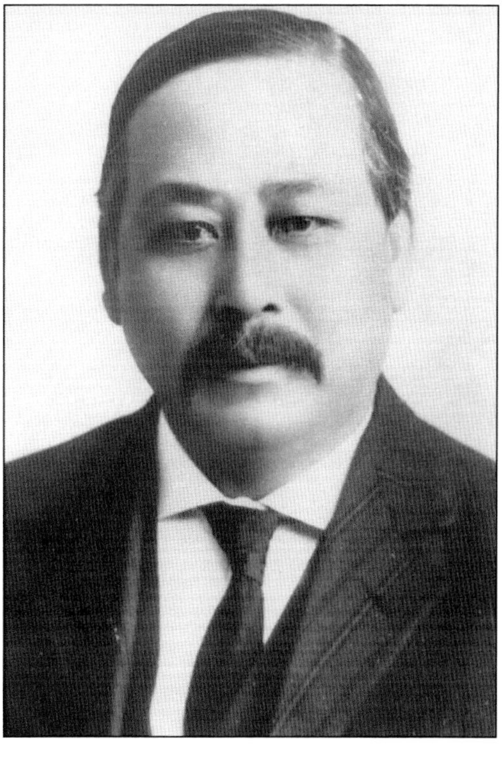

After perfecting techniques in San Francisco, Lew Hing established the Pacific Coast Canning Company at Twelfth and Pine Streets in West Oakland in 1904, employing as many as 1,000 workers at peak season. The cannery shipped goods all over the country and supported U.S. troops during World War I. Lew also had extensive business interests in San Francisco. (Courtesy of Jean Moon Liu.)

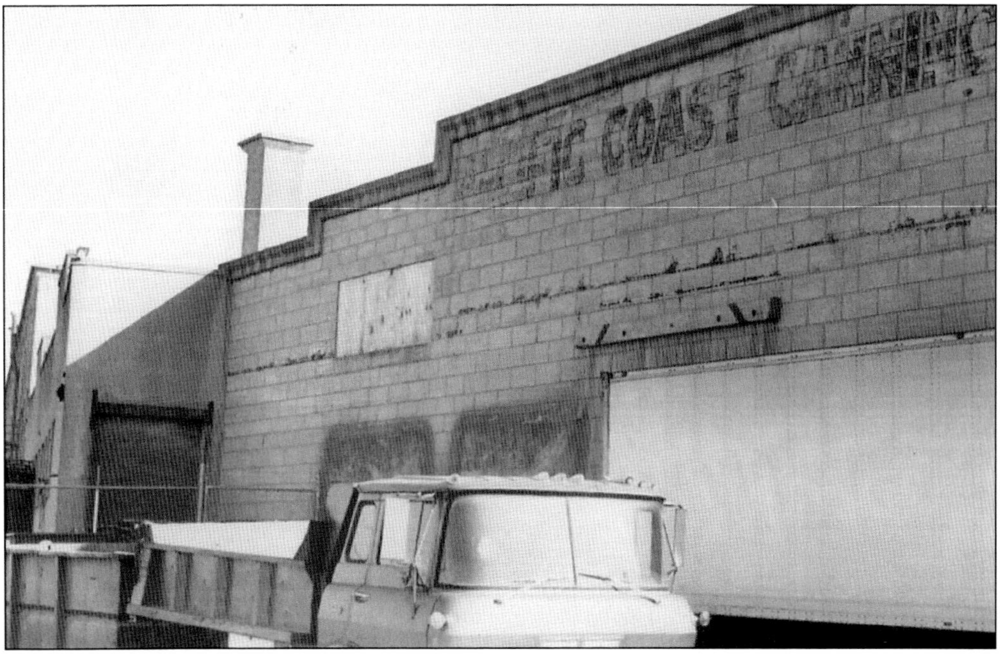

The Pacific Coast Canning building at Twelfth and Pine Streets survives to the present, but is used for other purposes. The company was owned and operated by Lew Hing. (Courtesy of Mary Mar.)

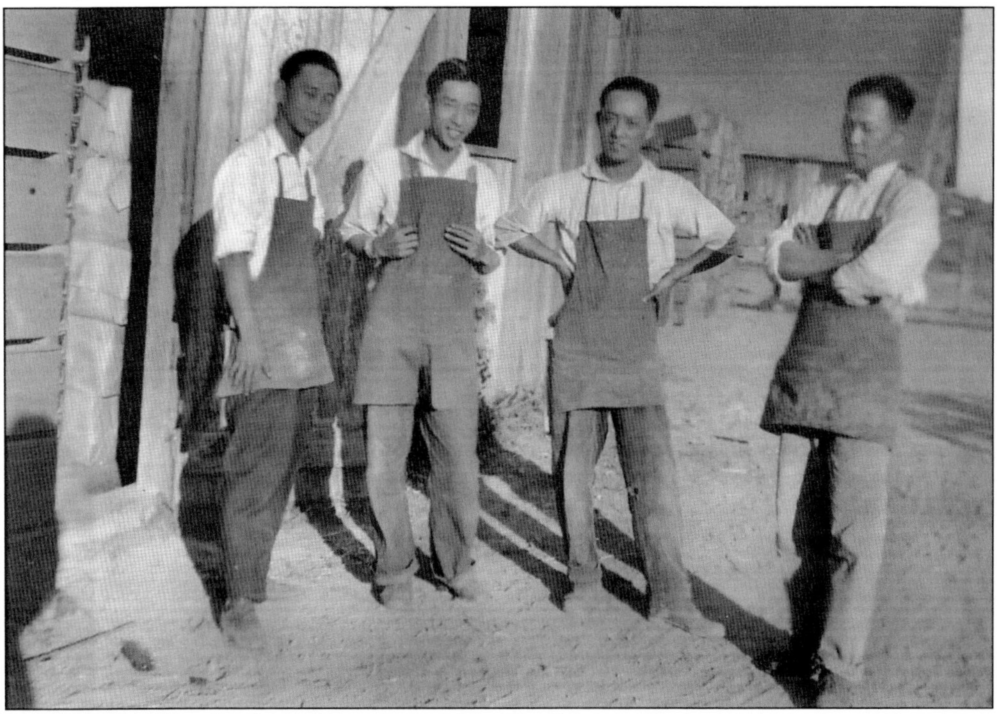

Four workers take a break on the grounds of the Pacific Coast Canning Company in this 1920s photo. The cannery also employed Italian, Portuguese, and perhaps Greek workers. (Courtesy of Jean Moon Liu.)

The flamboyant China-born Fong Wan sold herbs to customers of all ethnic backgrounds in Oakland. State and federal authorities investigated his advertising claims for his herbs, but he was never convicted of any crimes. Many satisfied customers testified on his behalf. He parlayed his herbal profits into real estate, nightclubs. and restaurants. (Courtesy of the Oakland Tribune Collection, Gift of Alameda Newspaper Group.)

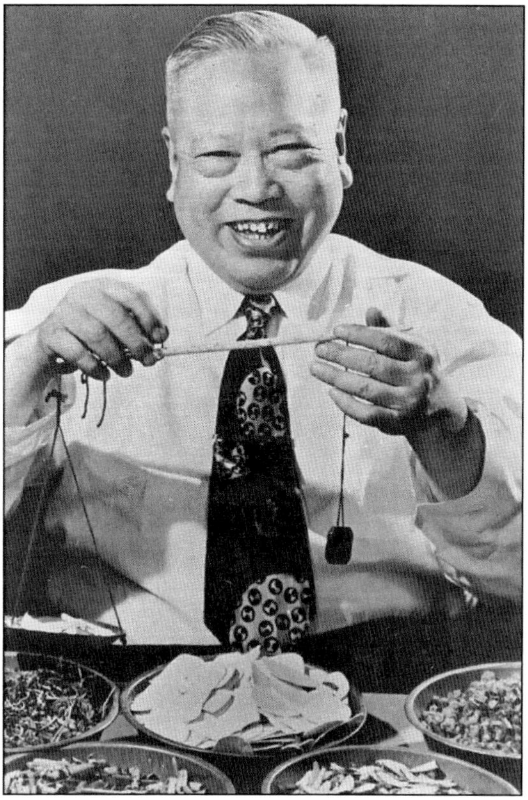

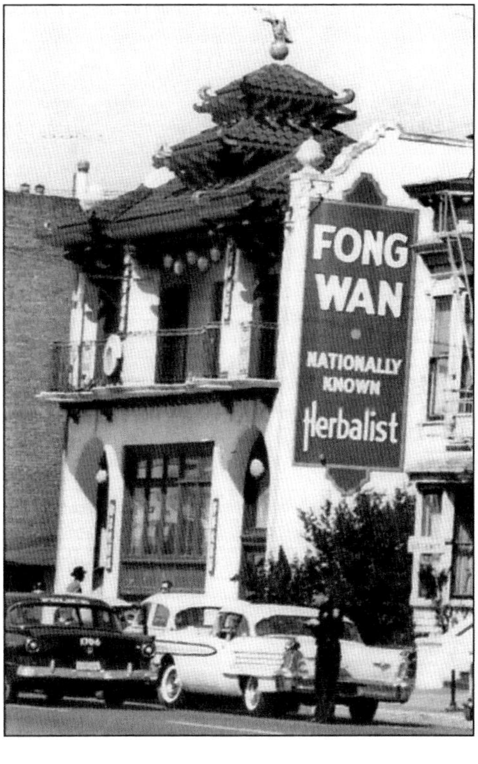

The legendary Fong Wan Building is shown in this 1958 photo at 576 Tenth Street between Clay and Jefferson Streets. The police activity depicted here was not related to Fong Wan's business. (Photo by Downtown Property Owners Association, courtesy of the Oakland Public Library.)

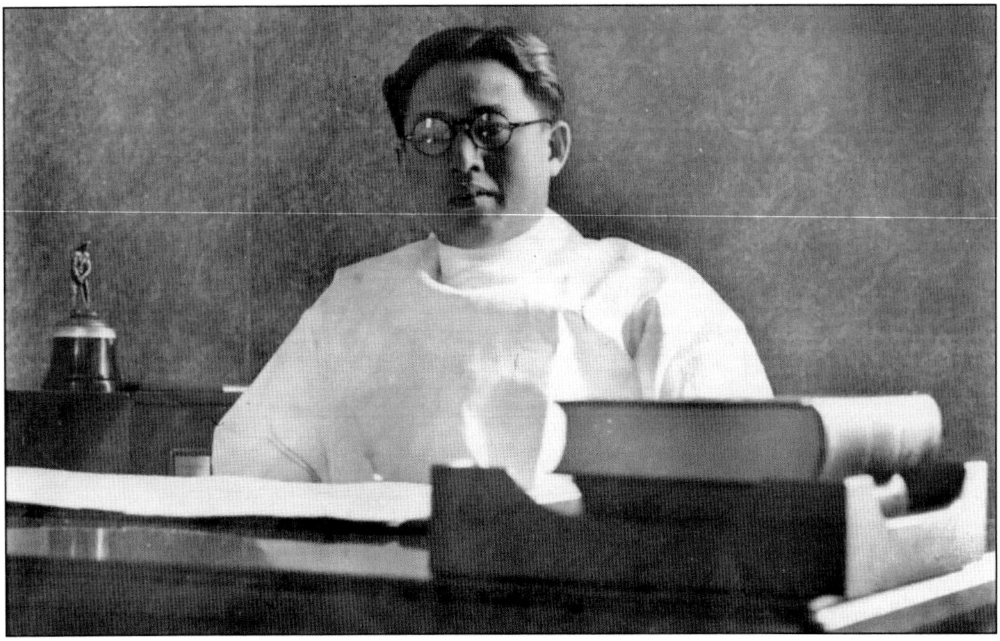

Born in Sacramento, Dr. Jacob Yee became a local legend because he was the first bilingual doctor to practice Western medicine when he opened a Chinatown office in 1931. He retired in 1970. He was inspired to become a doctor when some young friends died of a flu epidemic without the benefit of Western medical practices. He was also active in Chinatown community life. (Courtesy of Mary Mar.)

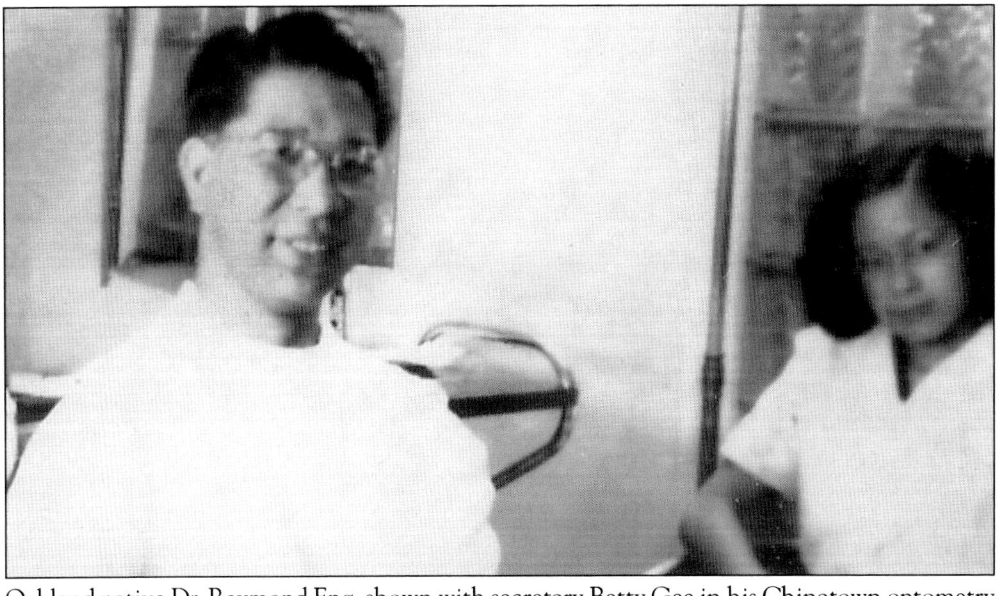

Oakland native Dr. Raymond Eng, shown with secretary Betty Gee in his Chinatown optometry office, worked well outside his ethnic community. He was the first Chinese American on the Oakland City Council. He was active in many community activities, including the Chinese American Citizens Alliance, the Oakland Chinese Community Center, the Boy Scouts, Lion's Club, and United Crusade. He also led a dance band during his college years. (Courtesy of Weylin Eng.)

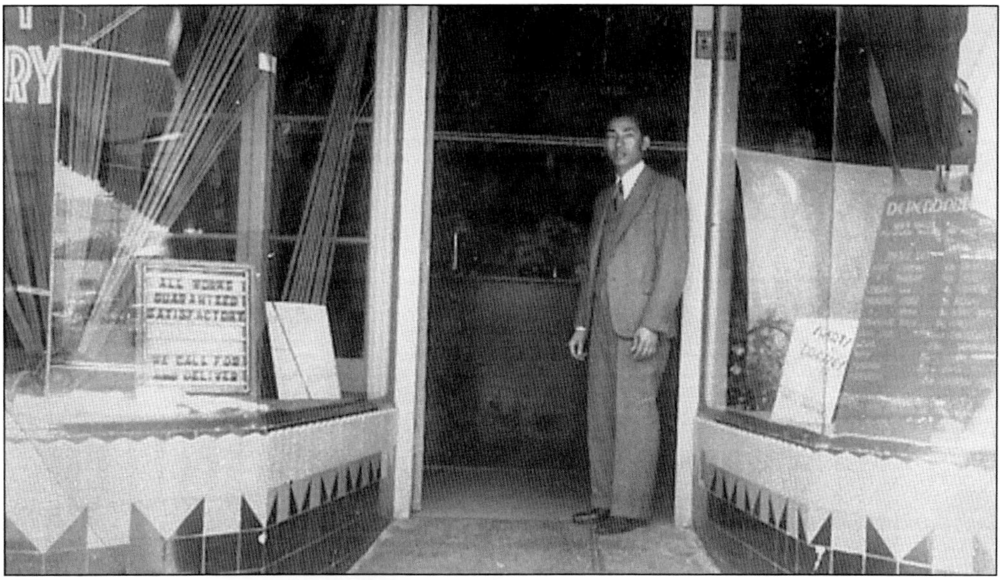

Yee Quon Wah, also known as Byron Yee Mark, shown in this 1930s photo, was a laundry owner outside Chinatown who defended the rights of Chinese laundrymen. In the mid-1930s, he challenged an Oakland ordinance restricting the working hours of Chinese laundries, and won. His victory helped advance the cause of racial equality in the U.S. (Gift of Carolyn Yee, courtesy of Mary Mar.)

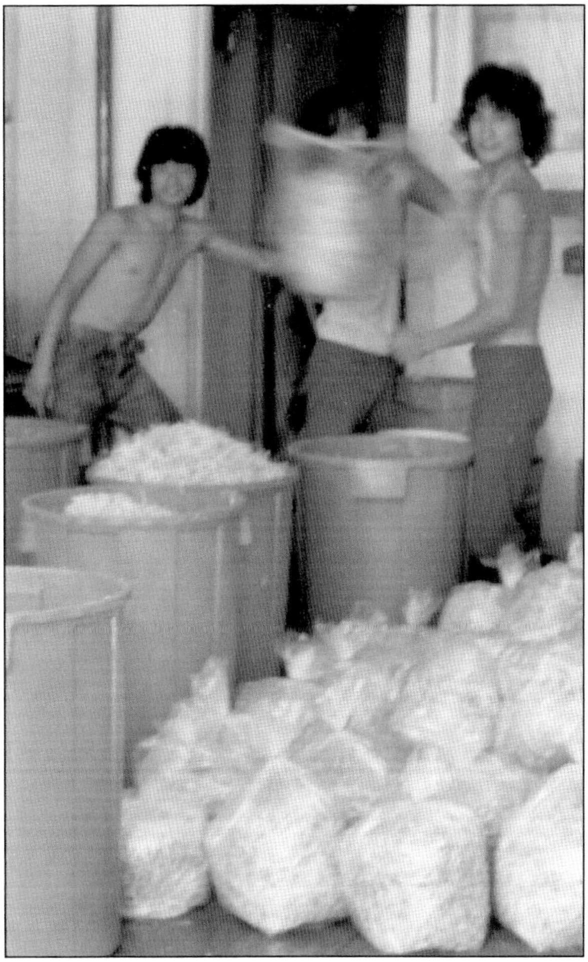

Workers bag bean sprouts in the 1970s grown at Yuen Hop, a Webster Street Chinatown business begun in 1931 by Quong Pon and still operating today. Yuen Hop sold bean sprouts to big supermarket chains, and sold noodles to the Berkeley Coop Stores. In 1998, the store expanded into a full-service produce store. It moved its noodle-making operation a few blocks away. (Courtesy of Sylvia Quan.)

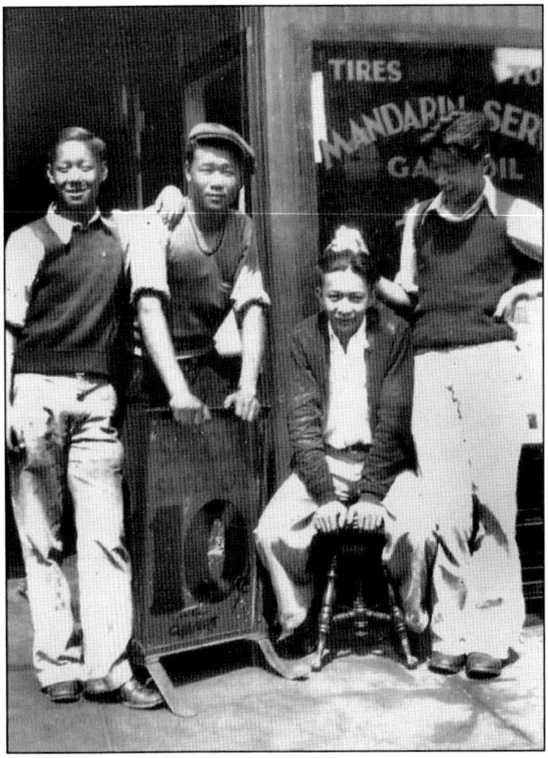

Art Tom (seated) and Harry Chin (not pictured) started the Mandarin Service gasoline station on Eighth Street between Webster and Harrison Streets in the 1930s, the first Chinese-owned gasoline retailer in Oakland. The other young men in this 1933 photo are, from left to right, Hugh Chin, "Buckshot" Louie, and an unidentified man. (Courtesy of Art Tom.)

In this 1950s photo, Art Tom, the first Chinese American to work for the California Department of Motor Vehicles (since 1935) demonstrates a camera that takes pictures of driver applicants. A Chinatown native, Tom worked for the DMV for 37 years and headed up the agency's Oakland and San Leandro offices. Long after retirement, he remains active in the Masonic Order. (Courtesy of Art Tom.)

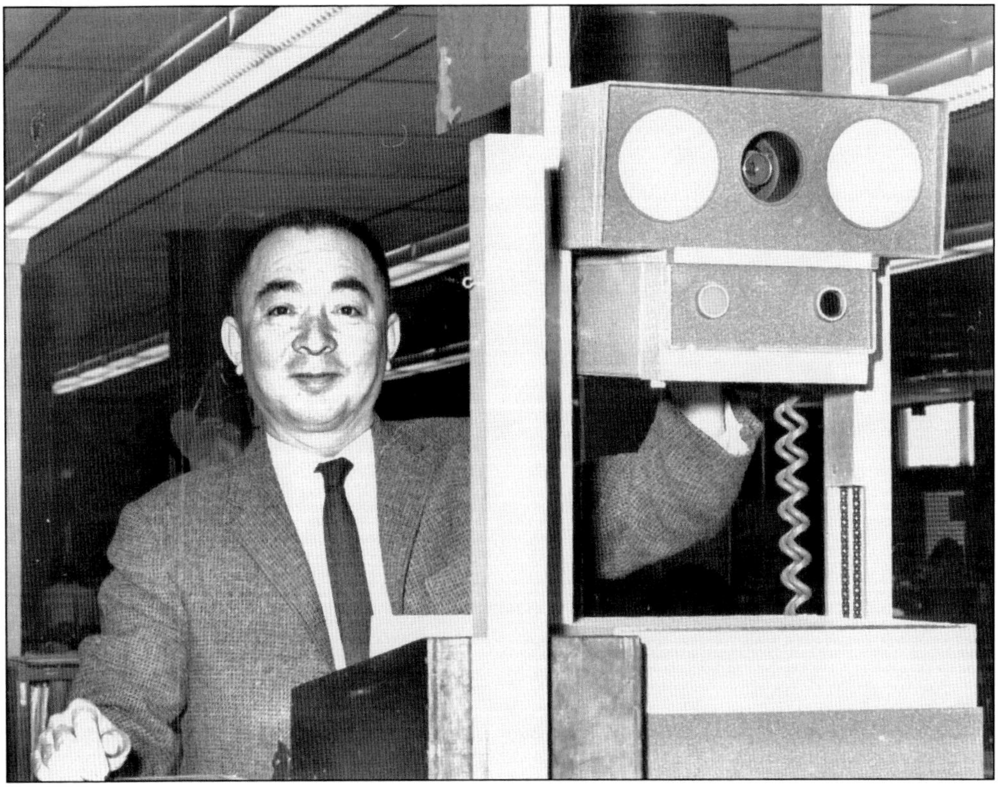

George Wong, an Oakland chef, elaborately decorates a cake in this 1935 photo. (Courtesy of the Oakland Tribune Collection, the Oakland Museum of California, Gift of Alameda Newspaper Group.)

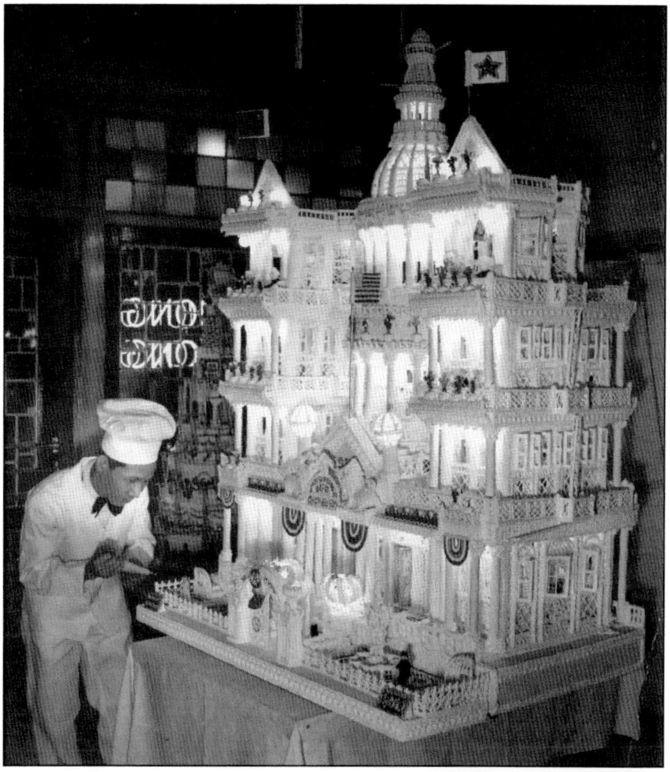

The Chinese-owned Ninth Street Market, in this 1955 photo, served a Chinatown and non-Chinese clientele in the 1940s through about the 1970s. It was on Ninth Street between Broadway and Washington Streets. (Photo by Downtown Property Owners Association, courtesy of the Oakland Public Library.)

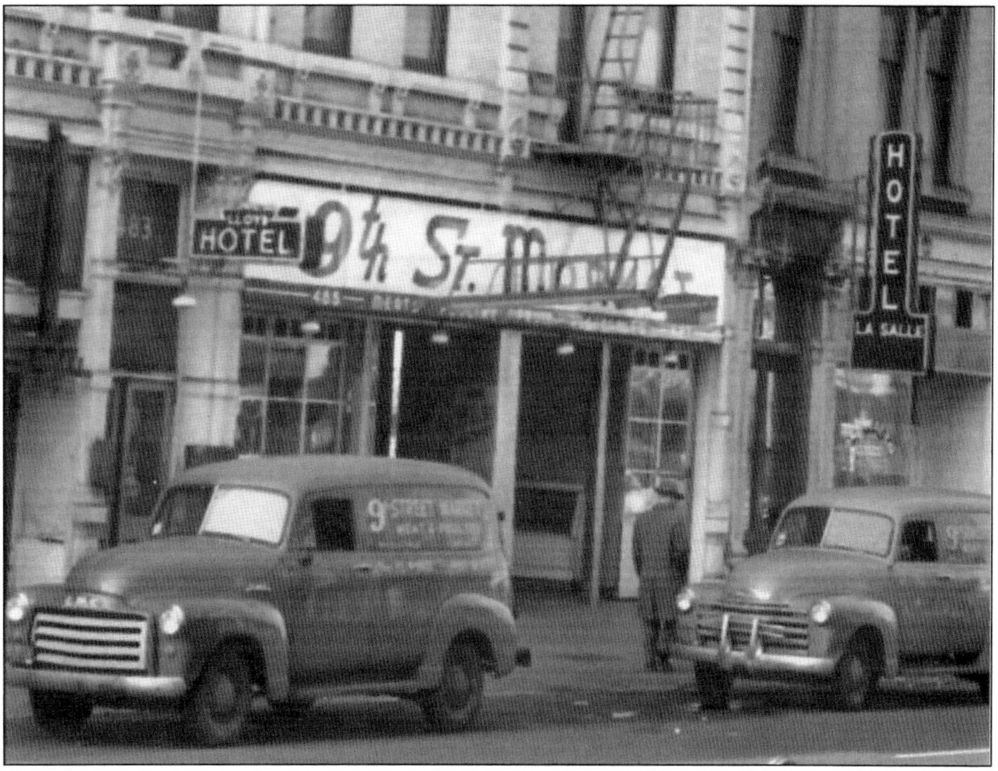

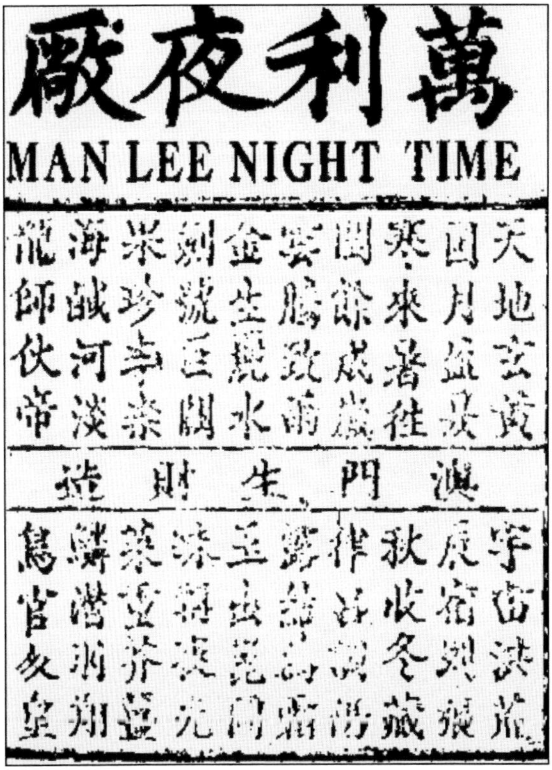

萬利夜廠

MAN LEE NIGHT TIME

天地玄黃 日月盈昃 寒來暑往 閏餘成歲 雲騰致雨 金生麗水 劍號巨闕 果珍李柰 海鹹河淡 龍師火帝

澳 門 生 財 造

宇宙洪荒 辰宿列張 秋收冬藏 律呂調陽 露結為霜 玉出崑岡 珠稱夜光 菜重芥薑 鱗潛羽翔 鳥官人皇

This lottery ticket is typical of ones used by Chinatown companies in the first half of the 20th century. The game, a precursor of today's California lottery, was illegal in its Chinatown heyday, and bribery of government officials was common. About a dozen companies operated the Chinatown lottery. Players came from all over the city. Children worked as runners and counters. It was one way for struggling families to make ends meet. (Courtesy of Laraine C. Wing.)

The lottery business in Chinatown had its dangers. This diary entry describes the injuries suffered by Gee Seow Hong, father of the author of this book, as a result of being shot in an illicit gambling dispute. Gee survived the shooting and lived another 21 years, operating the Great China restaurant on Webster Street. The doctor treating Gee wrote this entry. (Courtesy of William Wong.)

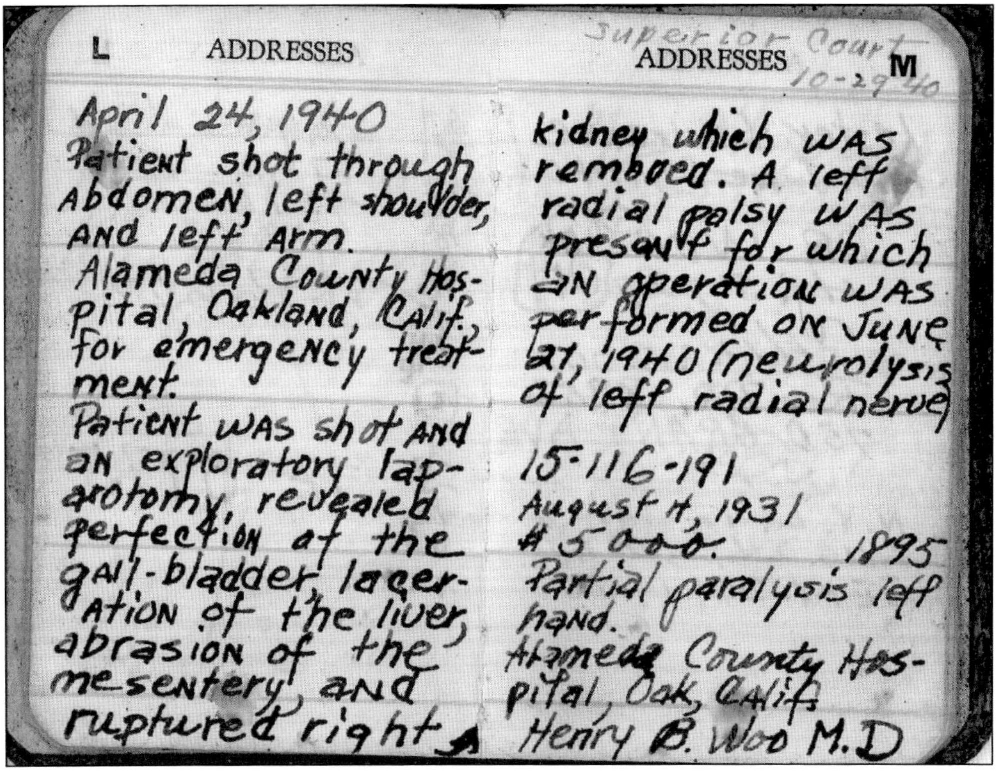

L ADDRESSES

April 24, 1940
Patient shot through Abdomen, left shoulder, and left arm.
Alameda County Hospital, Oakland, Calif., for emergency treatment.
Patient was shot and an exploratory laparotomy revealed perfection of the gall-bladder, laceration of the liver, abrasion of the mesentery, and ruptured right

ADDRESSES M

Superior Court 10-29-40

kidney which was removed. A left radial palsy was present for which an operation was performed on June 27, 1940 (neurolysis of left radial nerve)

15-116-191
August 4, 1931
#5000. 1895
Partial paralysis left hand.
Alameda County Hospital, Oak, Calif.
Henry B. Woo M.D

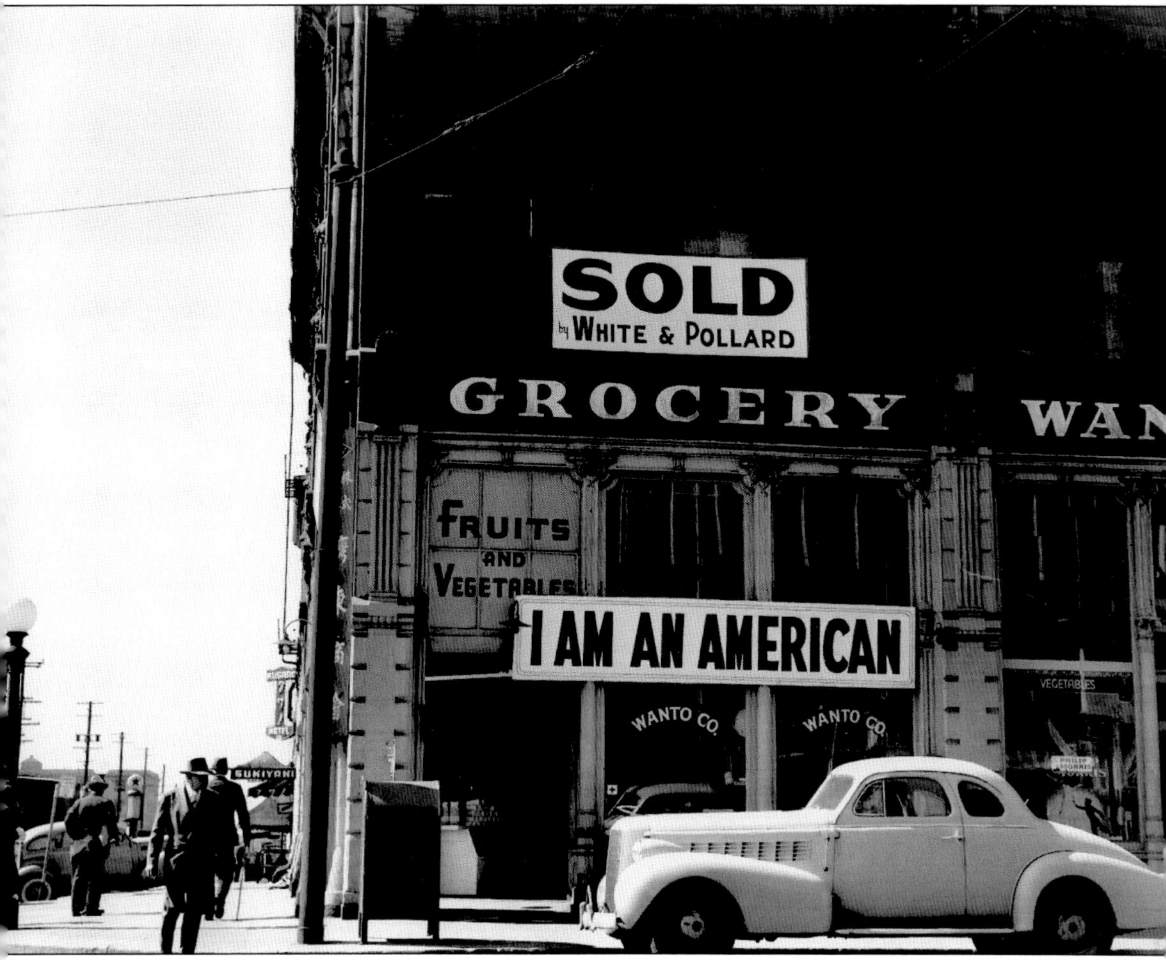

An unidentified Japanese American owned this grocery store at 401 Eighth Street at Franklin Street at the time of the Pearl Harbor attack. He told photographer Dorothea Lange, who took this picture in early 1942, that he had paid for the "I Am An American" sign to put up the day after Pearl Harbor. A few months later, he joined other West Coast Japanese Americans evacuated to remote internment camps. Four Chinese families purchased the store. (Copyright, the Dorothea Lange Collection, the Oakland Museum of California, Gift of Paul S. Taylor.)

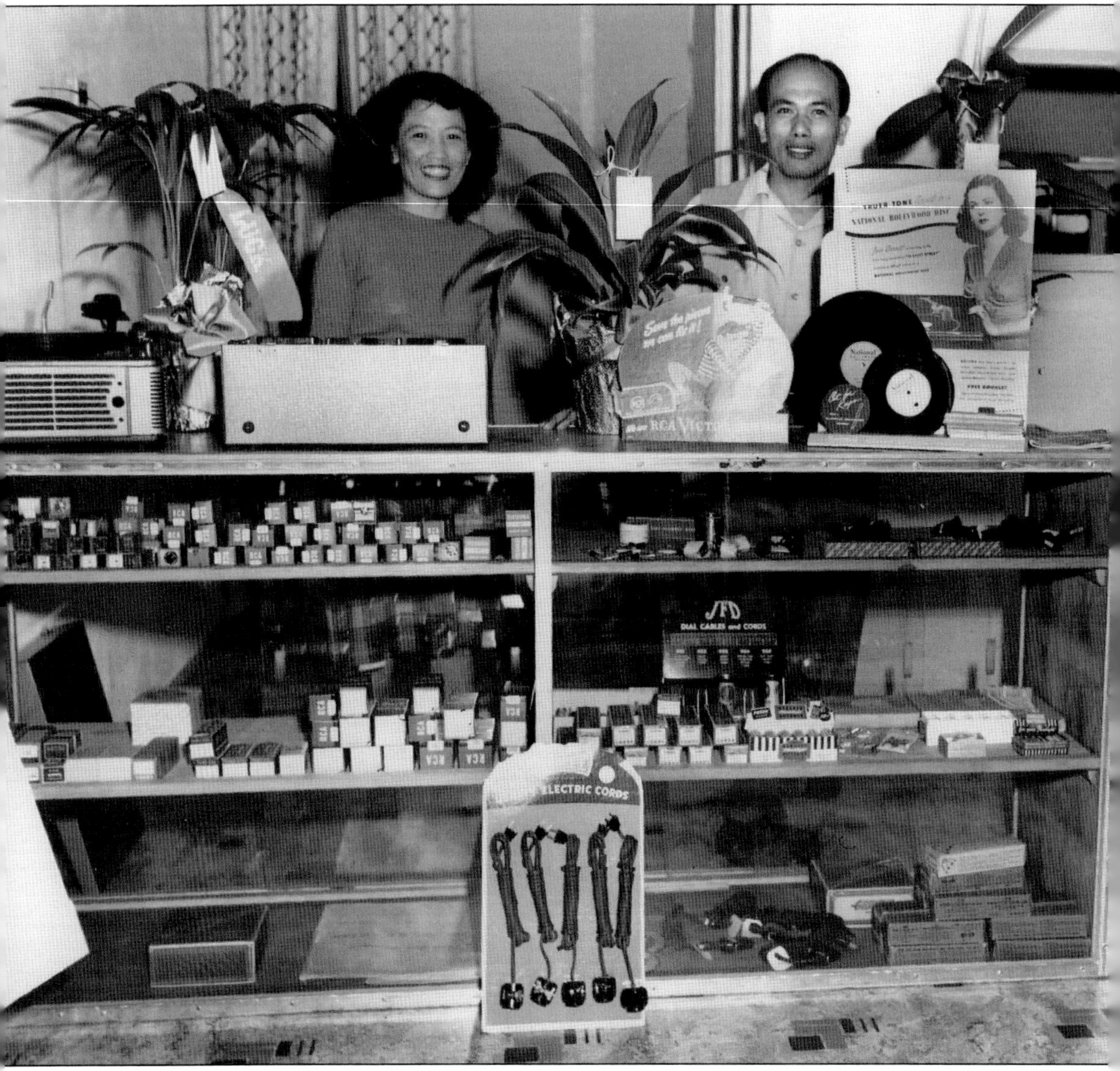

Filipino Americans lived and worked in Chinatown too, especially in the 1930s and 1940s. Here, in this late 1940s photo, are Cleope (Oping) and George Montecillo at their "New Radio Shop" near the corner of Ninth and Franklin Streets. It operated until the early 1950s. (Courtesy of Linda Montecillo.)

Marie Rivera stands in the doorway of a cleaning business at 816 Franklin Street. Marie's mother purchased it from a Japanese American proprietor uprooted by the U.S. government's internment of West Coast Japanese Americans in 1942. Her mother had the shop until 1947. Marie, about eight years old here, went to Lincoln School and worked at the Oakland Naval Supply Center and for Alameda County until retirement. (Courtesy of Marie Rivera-Yip.)

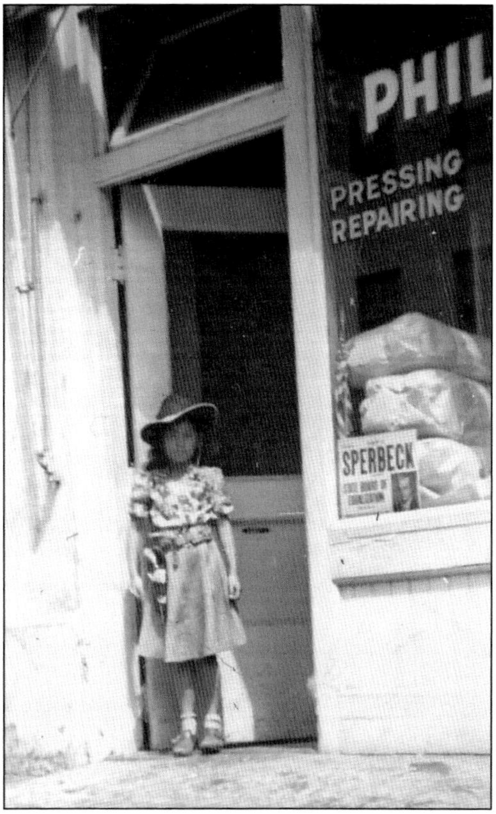

George Catambay, cutting hair here in the early 1990s, owned the legendary George's Movieland Barber Shop on Seventh Street between Webster and Franklin Streets since the early 1940s. During the early days, he served a fashion-conscious, multicultural clientele drawn to his innovative "razor cut" techniques. When he wasn't cutting hair, Catambay, a Filipino immigrant, loved ballroom dancing and fishing. (Photo by and courtesy of Mel Orpilla.)

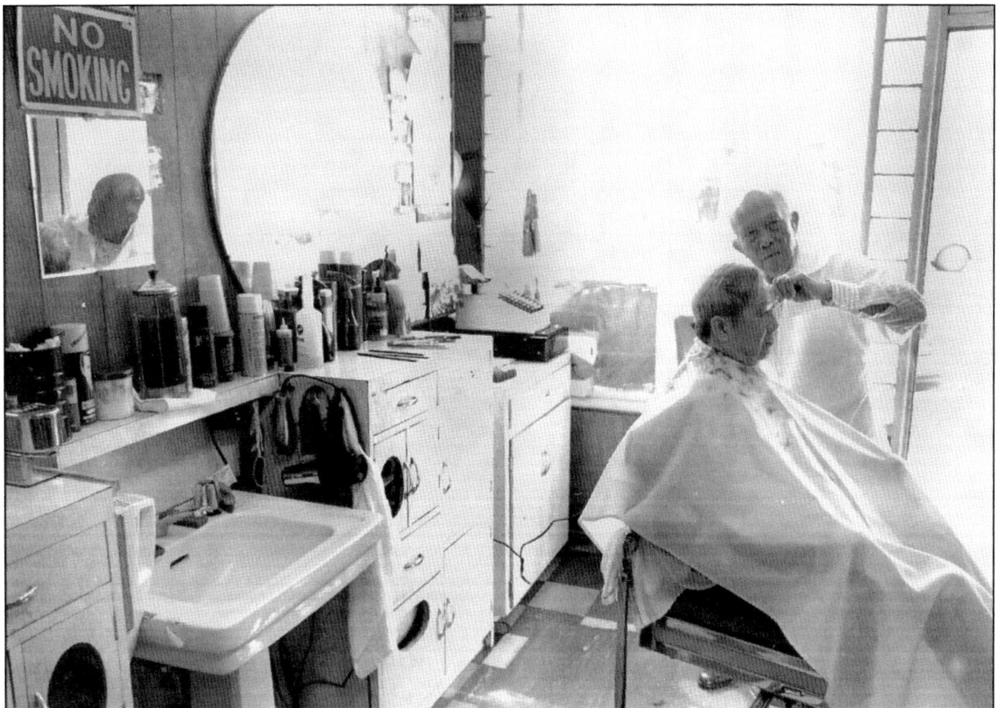

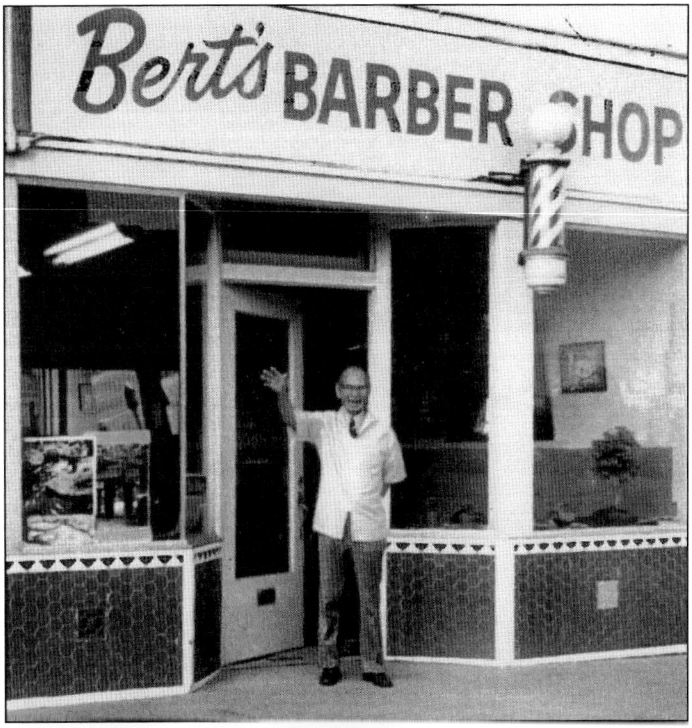

Bert Yamane, shown here in the late 1940s, operated with his wife, Haruko Jean Yamane, a barbershop on Franklin Street between Eighth and Ninth Streets before and after World War II. The Yamanes were relocated to the Tule Lake internment camp from 1942 to 1945. Bert gave free haircuts at the camp. Jean was Oakland Chinatown's second female barber, the first being Fong Get Moo. (Courtesy of June Yamane Wong.)

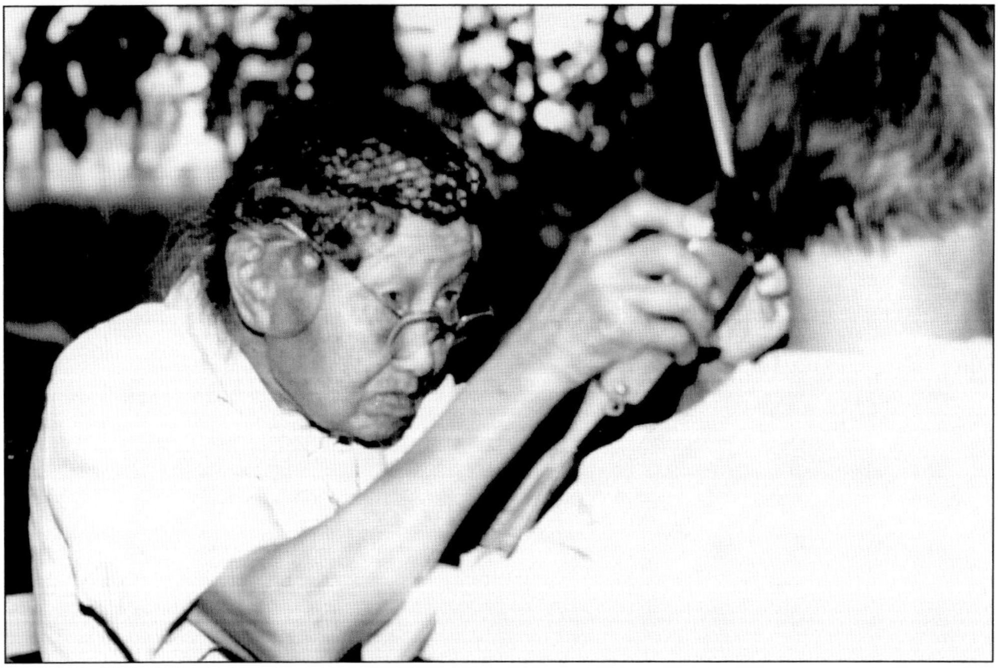

Lon Yoke Wong, better known as Fong Get Moo, was a rarity—a Chinese female born in the United States in the 19th century (1894). She was the first Chinese woman barber in Oakland. Her customers got more than a haircut; they also got candy and a place to hang out. In her later years, her shop was a meeting place for families shopping in Chinatown. She lived to be 95 years old. (Courtesy of Clifton Fong.)

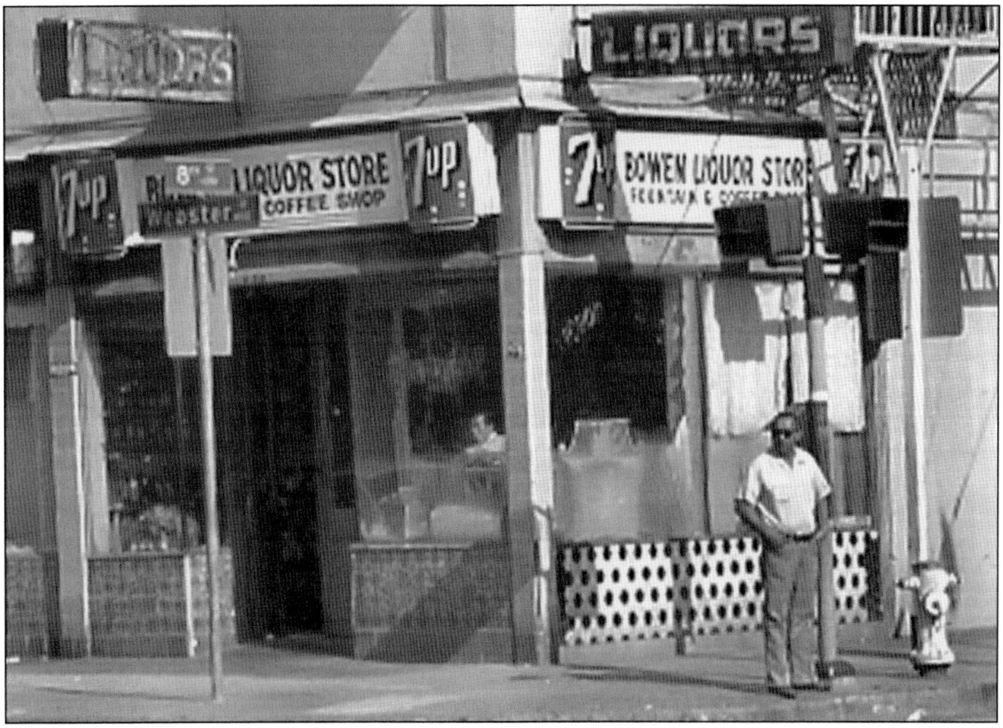

Bowen Liquor Store at Eighth and Webster Streets was a mainstay in the decades before and after World War II. It was owned by Ed Bowen, a member of the pioneering Bowen/Wing family. (Photo by and courtesy of Russell Lowe.)

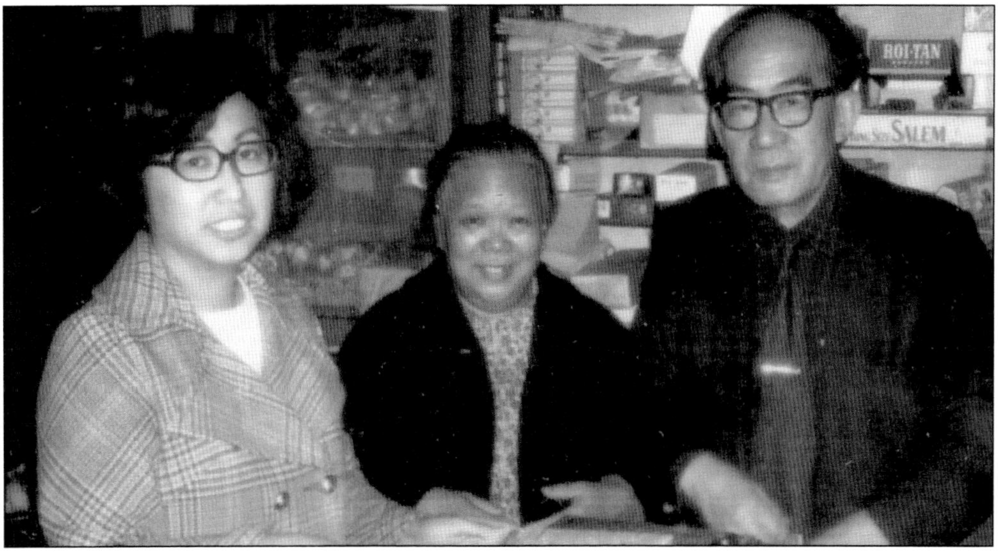

Gee Guey, right, owned and operated Man Sing Wo, the anchor business at Eighth and Webster Streets, from 1925 until 1989. This 1971 photo shows one of his daughters, Mary Soo Hoo, and his wife, Gee Hom Shee, inside the store that served as a community gathering place. It sold Chinese newspapers, candies, cigarettes, and pastries baked by Mrs. Gee. Gee Guey was active in the Oakland Chinese Community Center and other organizations. (Courtesy of Mary Soo Hoo.)

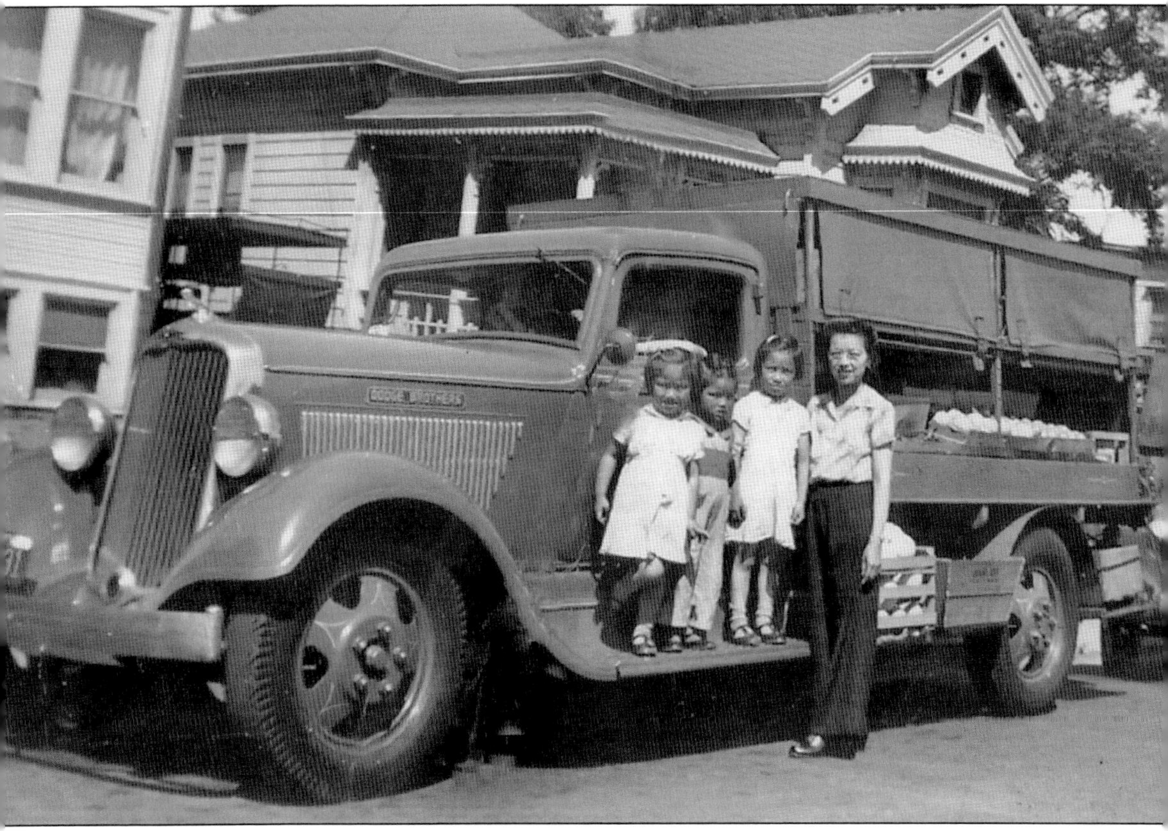

Henry Lum's produce truck delivered fresh produce to the Oakland and Berkeley hills in the early 1940s. Pictured, from left to right, are Ruby Lum, May Lum, Peggy Lum, and Chan Lin Lum, mother of the three girls and wife of Henry. (Courtesy of May Young.)

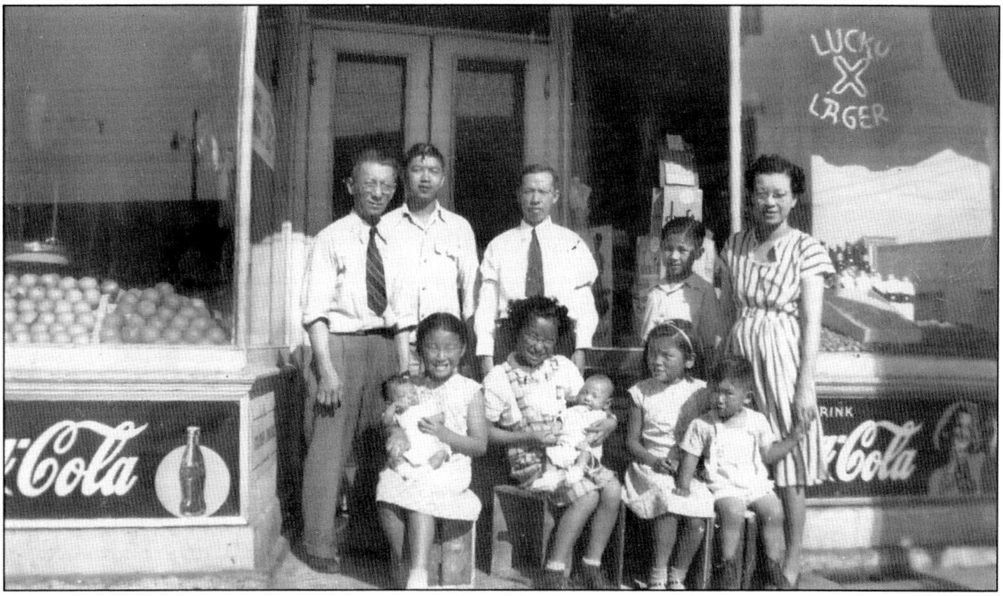

Chinese merchants operated outside of Chinatown too. The Star Market was owned and operated by Henry Lum at Thirtieth and Market Streets, shown here in this 1947 photo. From left to right are (front row) Ruby, holding Jeannie Lum; Peggy, holding Johnnie Lum; May, and Ray; (standing) Henry Lum, Bun Lum, Chun Gut Mon and his son Bob, and Chan Lin Lum. (Courtesy of May Young.)

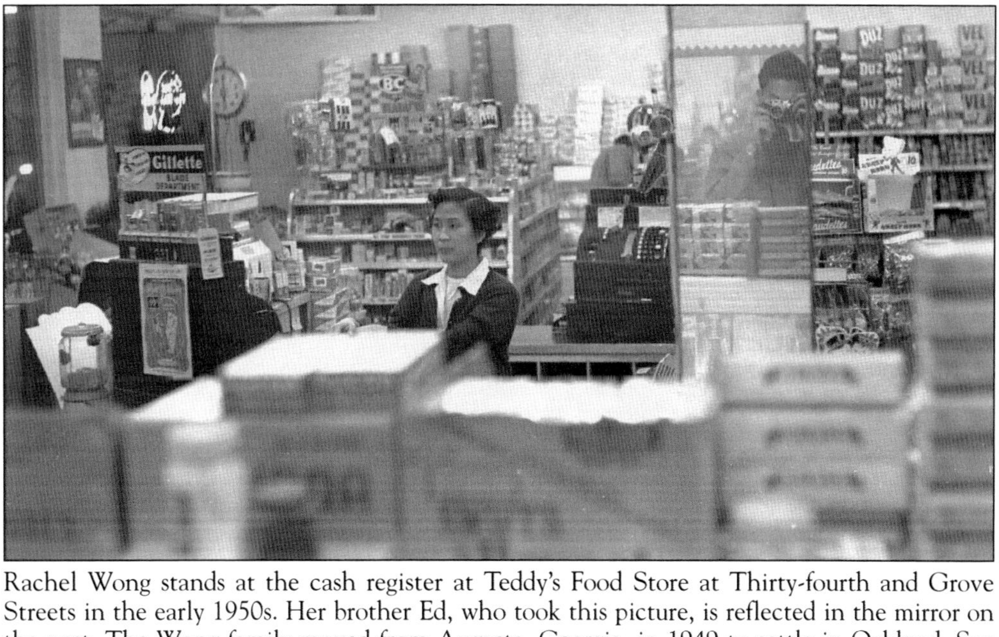

Rachel Wong stands at the cash register at Teddy's Food Store at Thirty-fourth and Grove Streets in the early 1950s. Her brother Ed, who took this picture, is reflected in the mirror on the post. The Wong family moved from Augusta, Georgia, in 1949 to settle in Oakland. Sue Shee Wong was the matriarch and older brother Ted was the manager. (Photo by and courtesy of Edward K. Wong.)

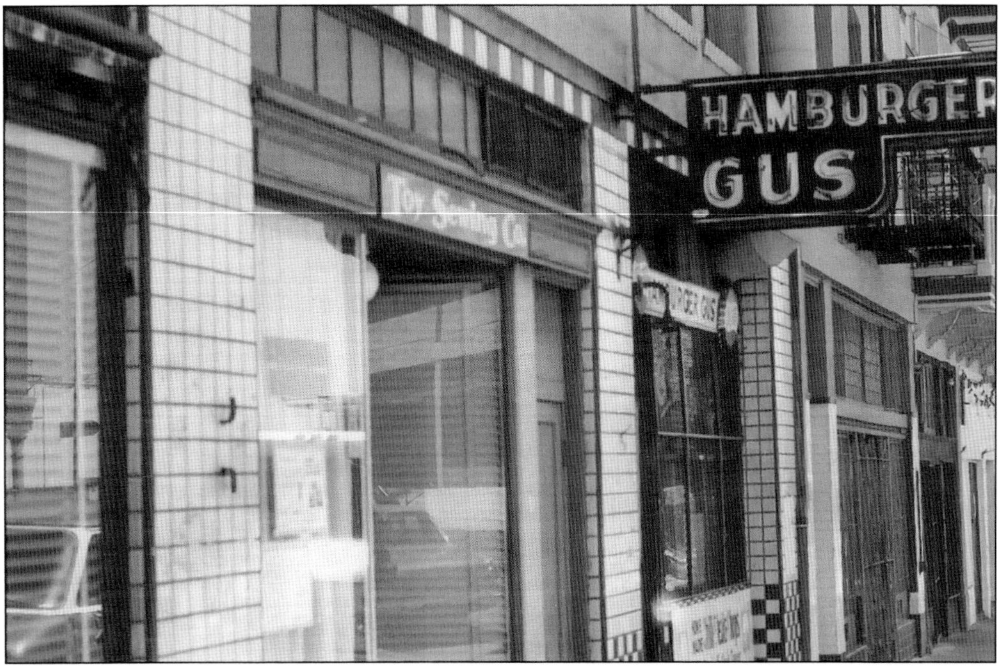

Not all Chinatown businesses during World War II were operated by Chinese. Greek Americans owned Hamburger Gus, shown in this 1970s photo, on Franklin Street between Seventh and Eighth Streets. Chinatown kids used to patronize it and Greek-owned Hamburger Joe's at Eighth and Franklin Streets. (Photo by and courtesy of Russell Lowe.)

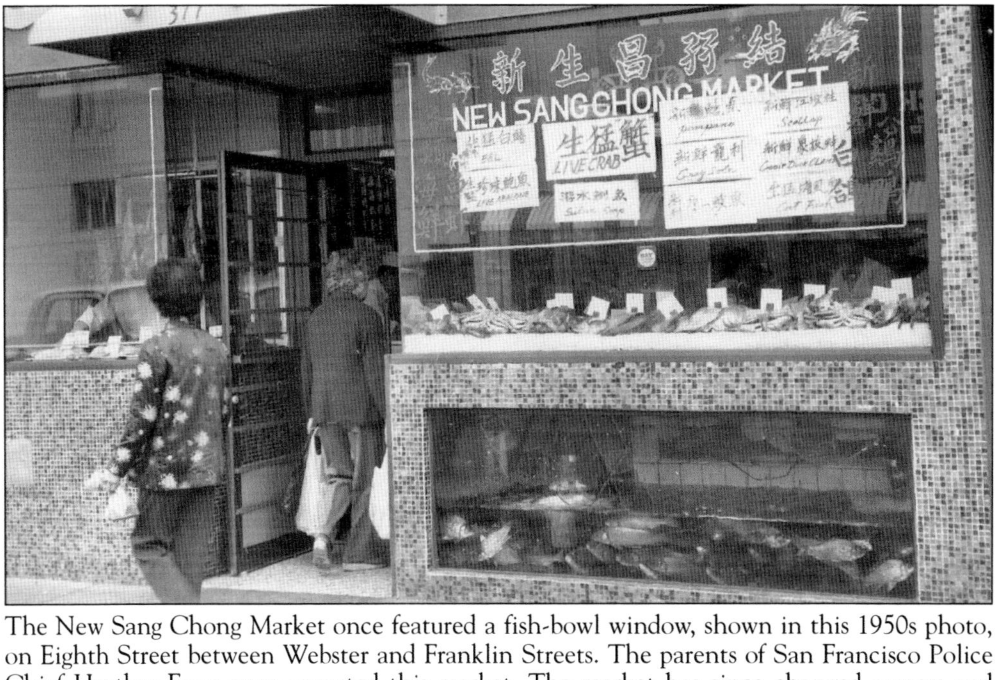

The New Sang Chong Market once featured a fish-bowl window, shown in this 1950s photo, on Eighth Street between Webster and Franklin Streets. The parents of San Francisco Police Chief Heather Fong once operated this market. The market has since changed owners and its appearance, but is as busy as ever dispensing fresh seafood, pork, chicken, and produce. (Courtesy of George Ong.)

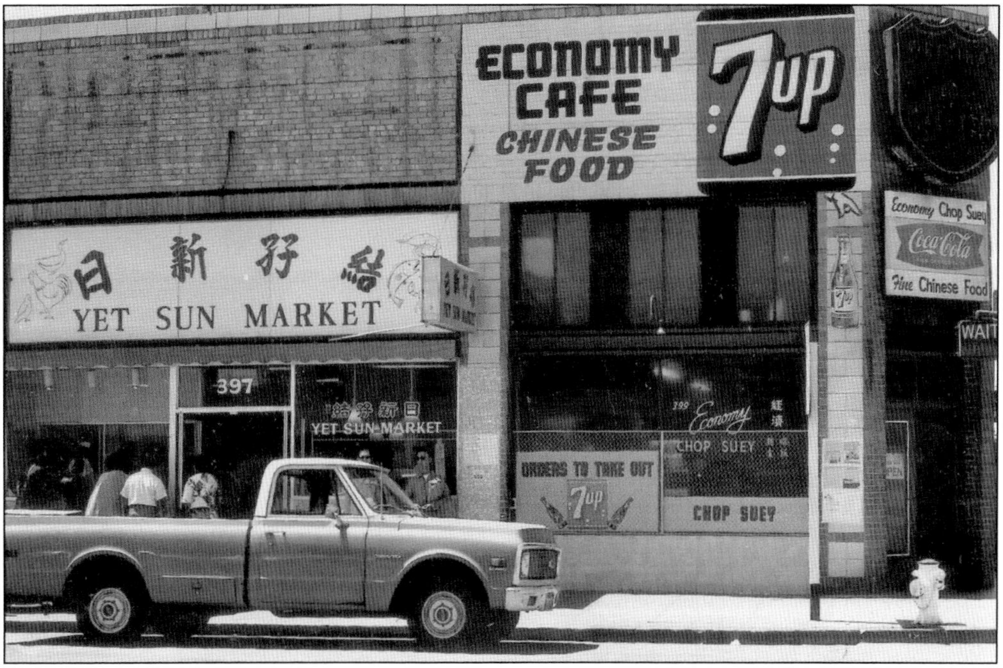

Two more businesses, Yet Sun and Economy Cafe, on Eighth Street near or at Franklin Streets, endured for many decades in the last half of the 20th century. Yet Sun remains at that site, mostly as a fresh seafood purveyor. Economy, however, changed a few years ago to a mostly take-out delicatessen. (Photo by and courtesy of Russell Lowe.)

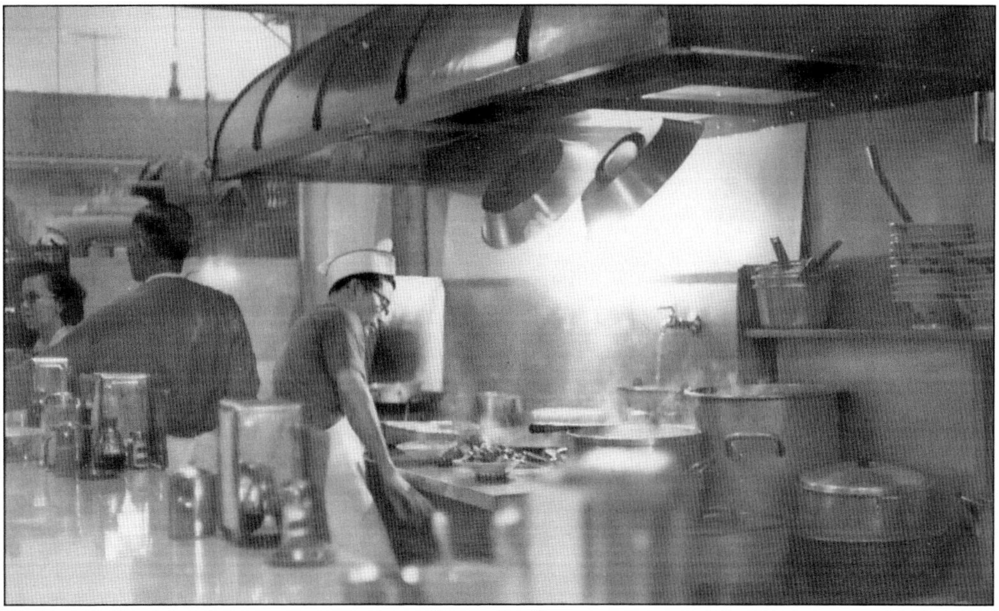

This photo, taken perhaps in the 1980s, shows the former owners of the Economy Cafe, the Soo Hoos, presiding over their open kitchen and serving customers. This was one of the distinctive features of the Economy Cafe, where customers got inexpensive hot rice plates and noodles, in as little time as it takes a so-called American fast-food restaurant to serve. (Photo by and courtesy of Henry Woon.)

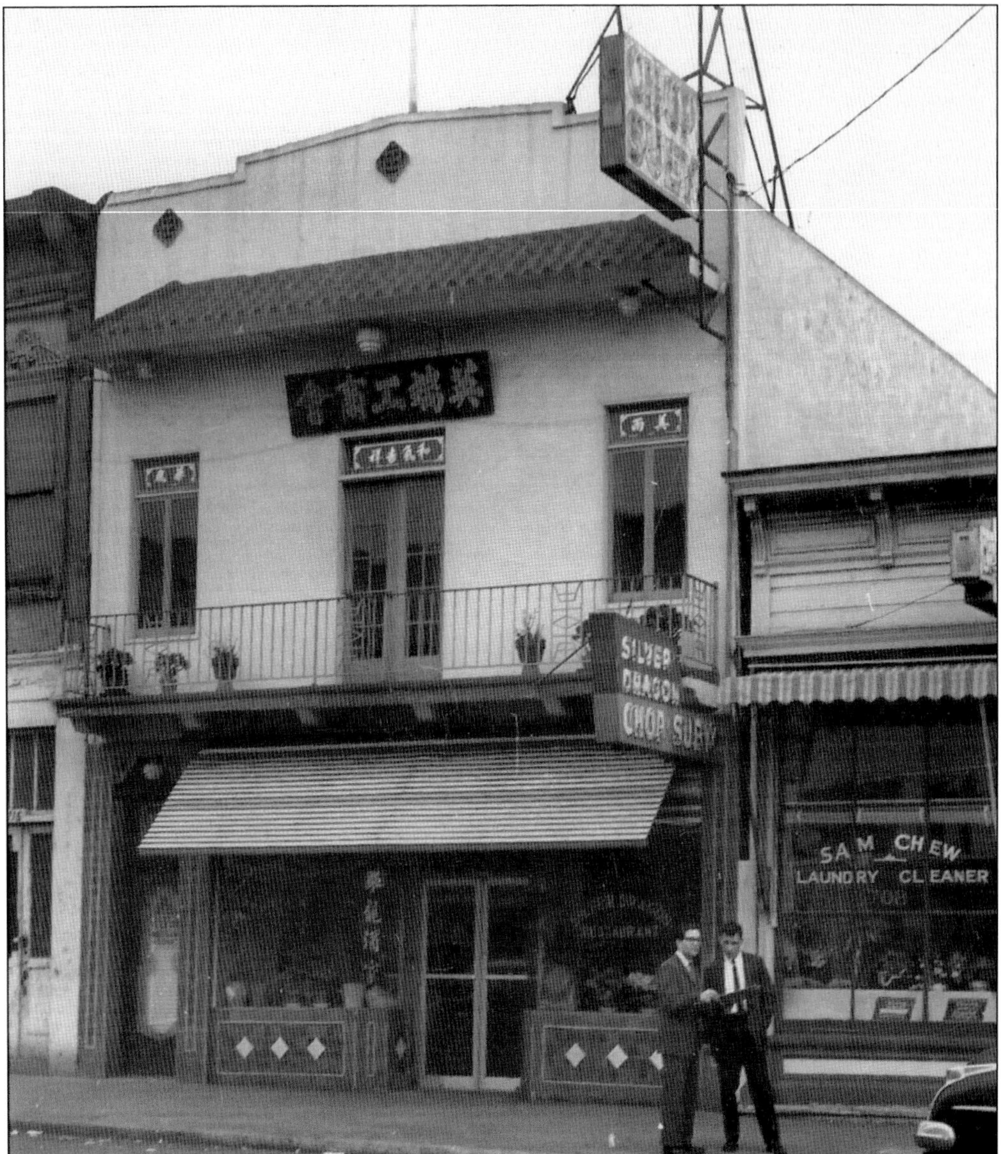

Wah Quon Chee opened the original Silver Dragon restaurant, shown here, on the east side of Webster, between Seventh and Eighth Streets, in the 1950s. It succeeded the New Eastern restaurant, owned by the Fong-Torres family. Chee moved the Silver Dragon, popular for big weddings and community banquets, to its current site at Ninth and Webster Streets in 1972. Chee got his training at Sun Hang Heung, a well-known San Francisco Chinatown restaurant, and he brought to Oakland some of its signature dishes. Upstairs at the original site is the Ying On Association. (Courtesy of George Ong.)

Florence Wong wipes off a table in her family's restaurant, the Great China, on Webster Street between Seventh and Eighth Streets, in the 1950s. Typical of Chinatown family experiences at that time, she and her siblings worked at the restaurant when not in school. She later became a mother, schoolteacher, and later in life, an installation artist. (Courtesy of Flo Oy Wong.)

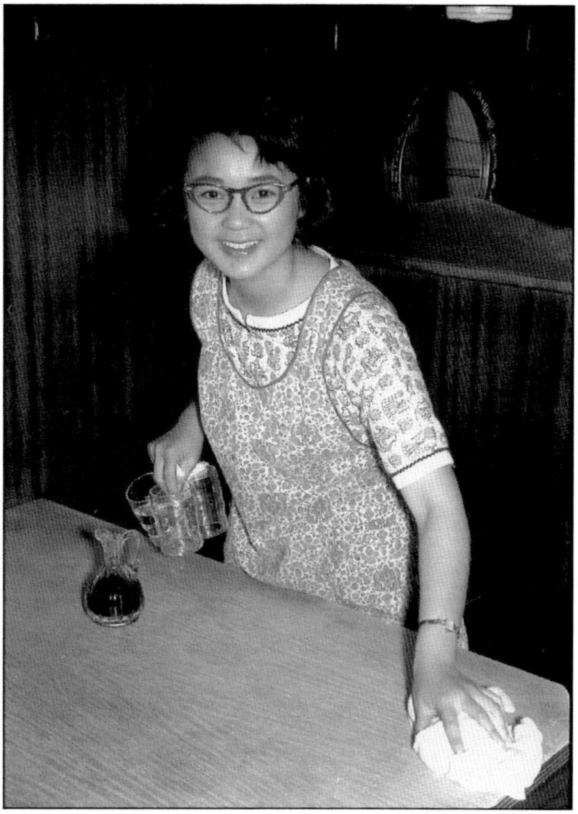

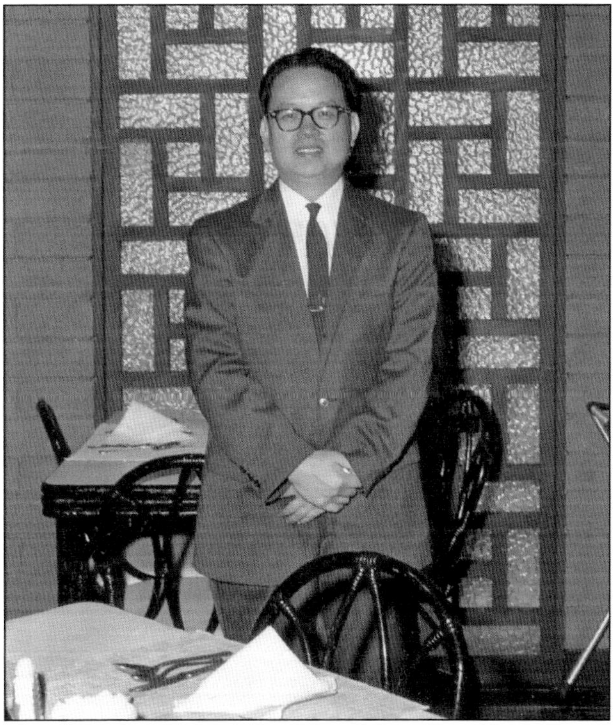

Richard Lee owned and operated the House of Lee restaurant outside of Chinatown in the 1950s and 1960s. He pioneered an upscale Chinese restaurant model, was active in Oakland Chinese community activities, and later ran a tour bus operation to Reno and Lake Tahoe. (Courtesy of Lee Mun Wah.)

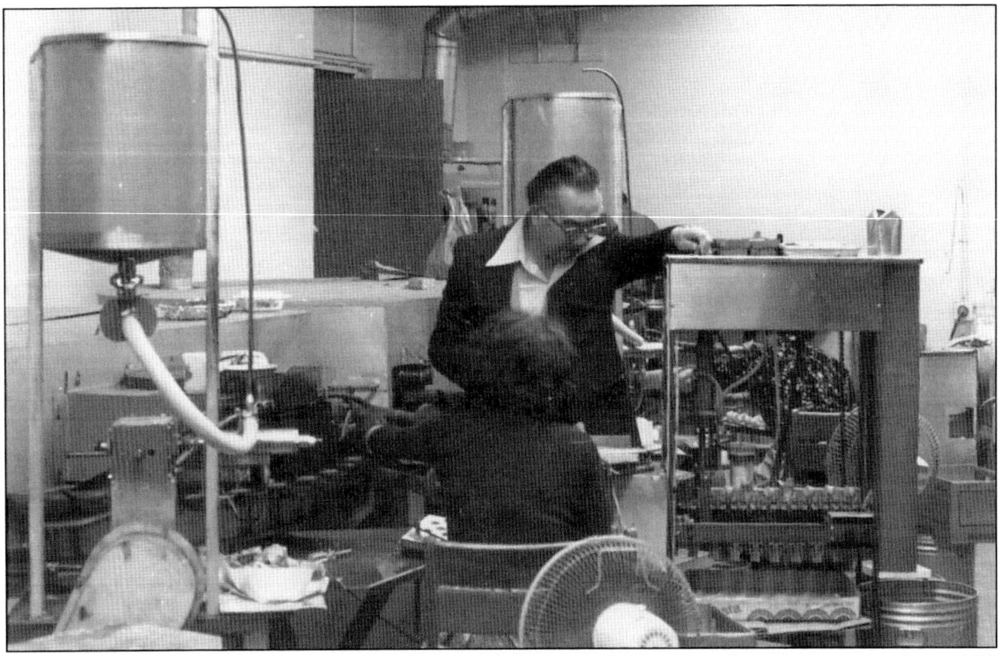

Shuck Yee, in this undated photo, inspects an automatic folding machine he invented in 1973 to make fortune cookies. Some Chinatown bakeries continue to use that machine, and Yee's son maintains them. Yee got his mechanical engineering degree from the University of California at Berkeley in 1943 after coming to the United States from China in 1928. He still resides in Oakland. (Courtesy of Mary Mar.)

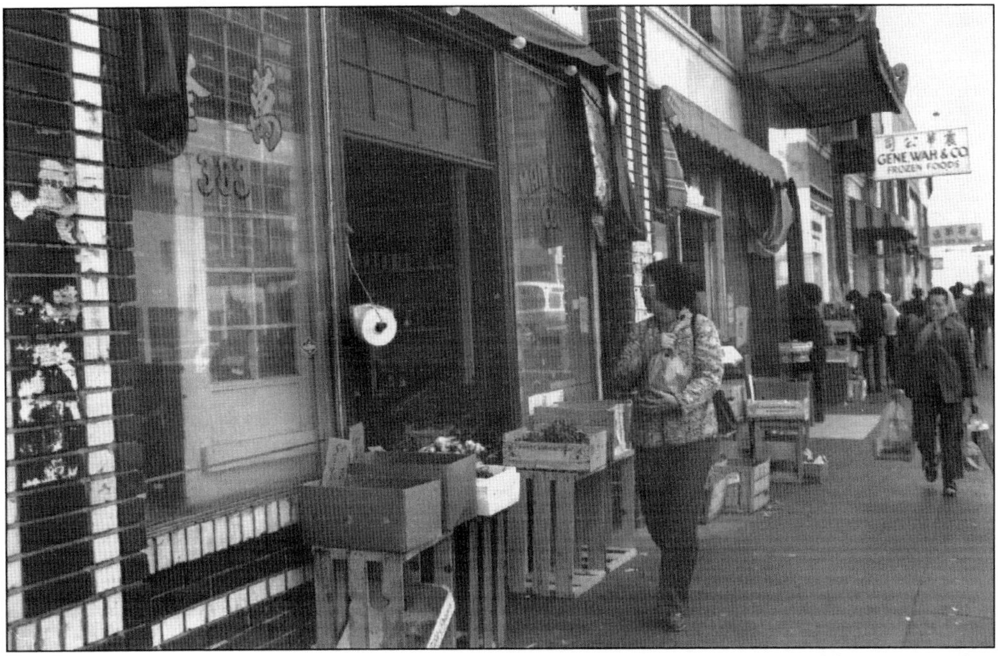

Man Lung was a grocery store on Eighth Street between Webster and Franklin Streets that operated from 1936 into the 1970s. It was owned and operated by the Hong/Tom family in that era. (Photo by and courtesy of Edward K. Wong.)

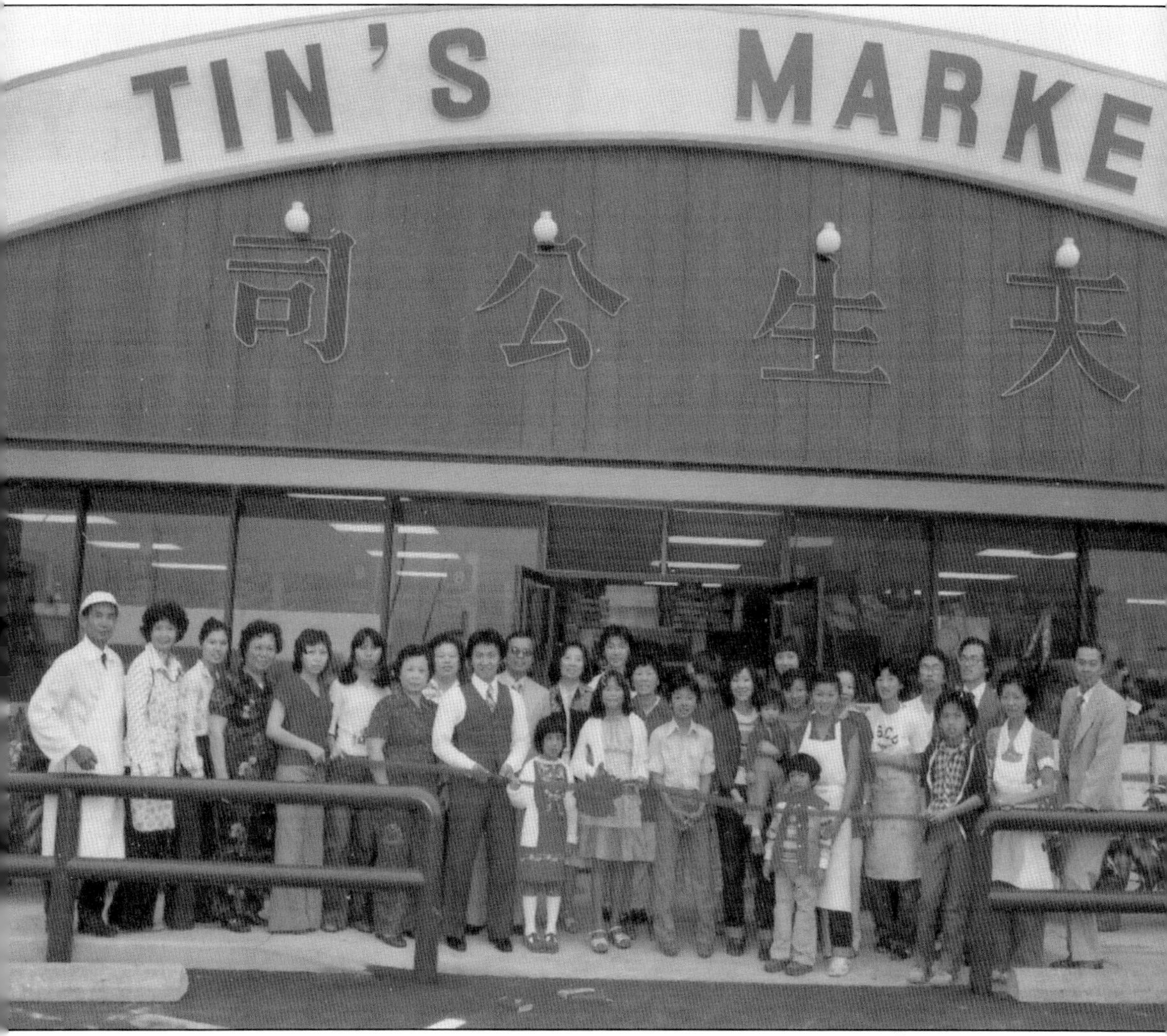

Tin's Market had a grand opening in July 1979 at Seventh and Harrison Streets. Owner and patriarch Tin Wah Yu is on the far left. His oldest son, Vincent (in the middle in a white long-sleeved shirt, tie, and vest), became the manager. Others in the photo are family and friends. Yu practiced Western medicine in Hong Kong and moved to Oakland in 1964. Language and cultural barriers and racial bias kept him from practicing medicine here. Instead, he started a market to support his large family, first in East Oakland, then in Chinatown at Seventh and Webster Streets in 1972. When Tin's Market moved to Harrison Street, he converted the Webster Street store into a dim sum restaurant. Yu passed away in 1997, and the market and restaurant were leased out, but the family still owns the properties. (Courtesy of Linda Yu Chan.)

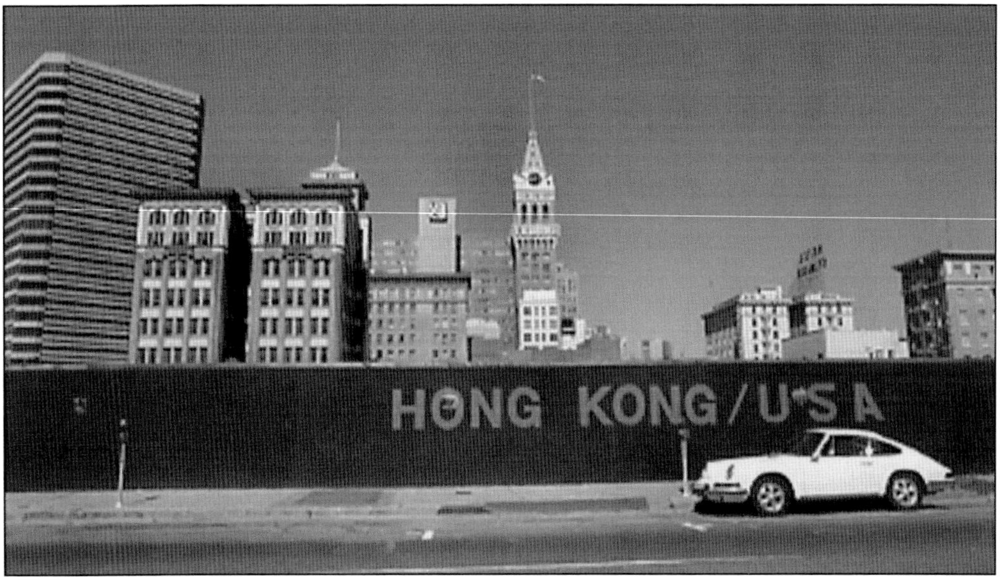

In 1980, the City of Oakland tried to persuade a Hong Kong businessman to construct a building at Eleventh Street and Broadway. The businessman wanted to build an 82-story tower, but his plans imploded when he ran into legal problems in Hong Kong. The city settled for the six-story Trans Pacific Center, pictured below. Despite its thwarted ambitions, Chinatown is a place Asian business interests find attractive for investment. (Photo by and courtesy of Russell Lowe.)

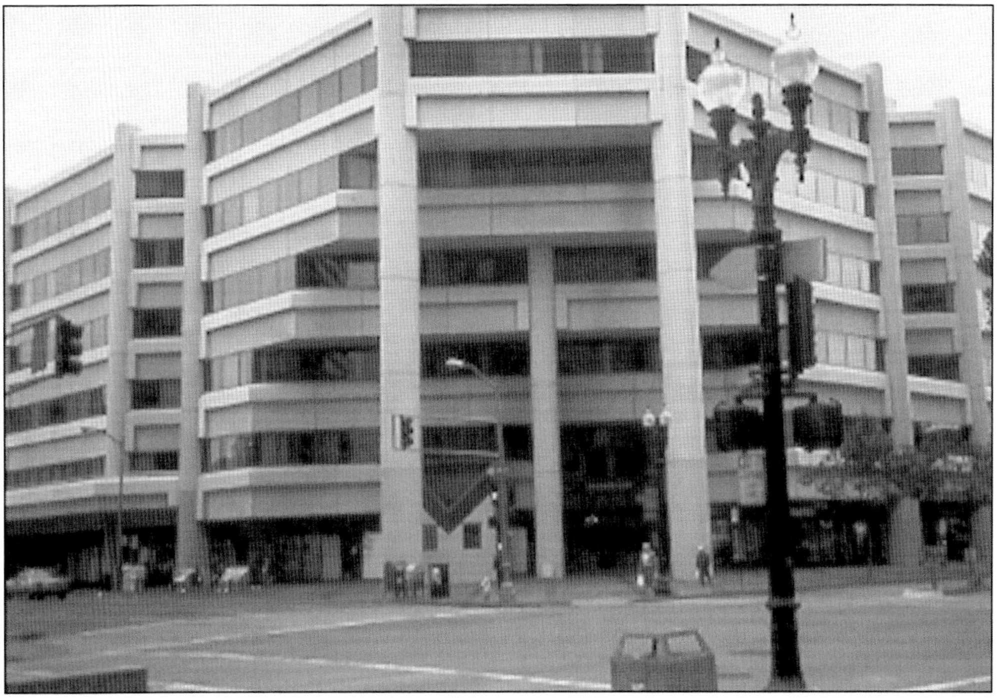

This is the Trans Pacific Center at Eleventh Street and Broadway that replaced the ambitious 82-story tower once proposed by a Hong Kong businessman who ran into legal problems in the early 1980s. (Photo by and courtesy of Ernest Chann.)

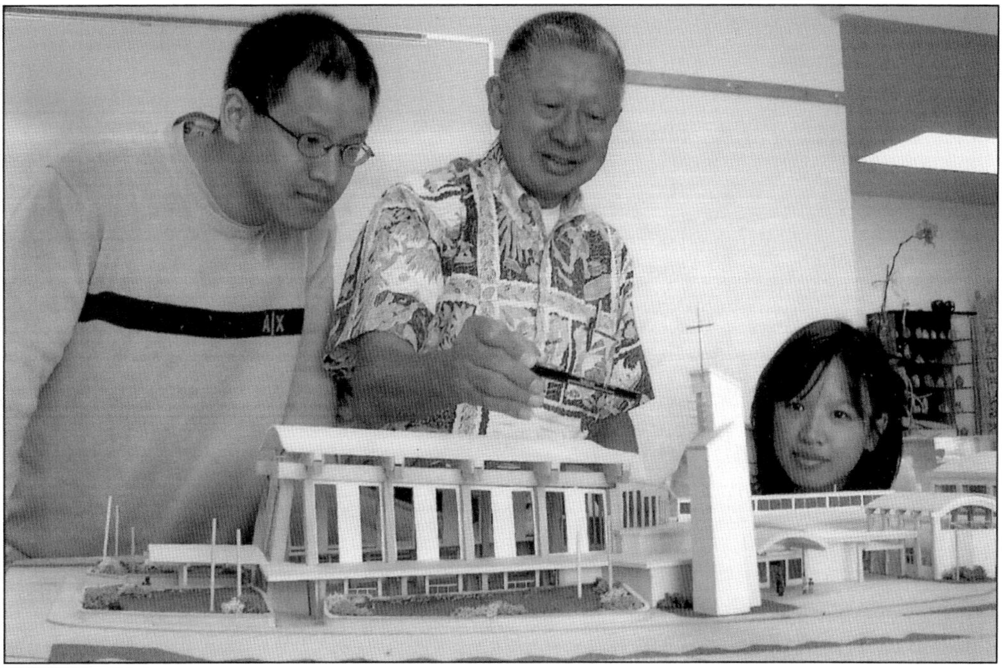

Architect Ed Sue and his children, Jonathan and Wendi, look over a model of a project they are designing. Sue has been an Oakland architect and contractor for many years. Among his many projects are the Pacific Renaissance Plaza, the East Bay Municipal Utility District headquarters, the Oakland Asian Cultural Center, and the Milton Shoong Building, all in Chinatown, (Courtesy of Ed Sue.)

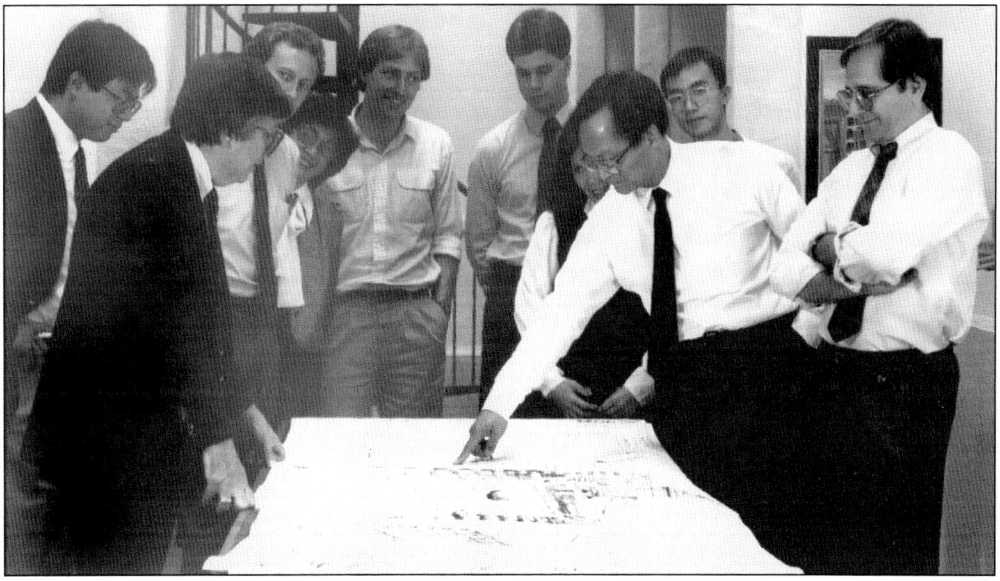

Architect Yui Hay Lee (pointing) discusses the winning design for the Frank Ogawa Plaza project with colleagues, outside City Hall in 1984. Other identifiable people are Bob LaRocca (second from left), Suzie Lee (fourth from left), Robert Lindley (fifth from left), and Mike Pyatok (far right). Yui Hay and Suzie Lee have long been active in Oakland and Chinatown civic and political affairs. (Courtesy of YHLA Architects.)

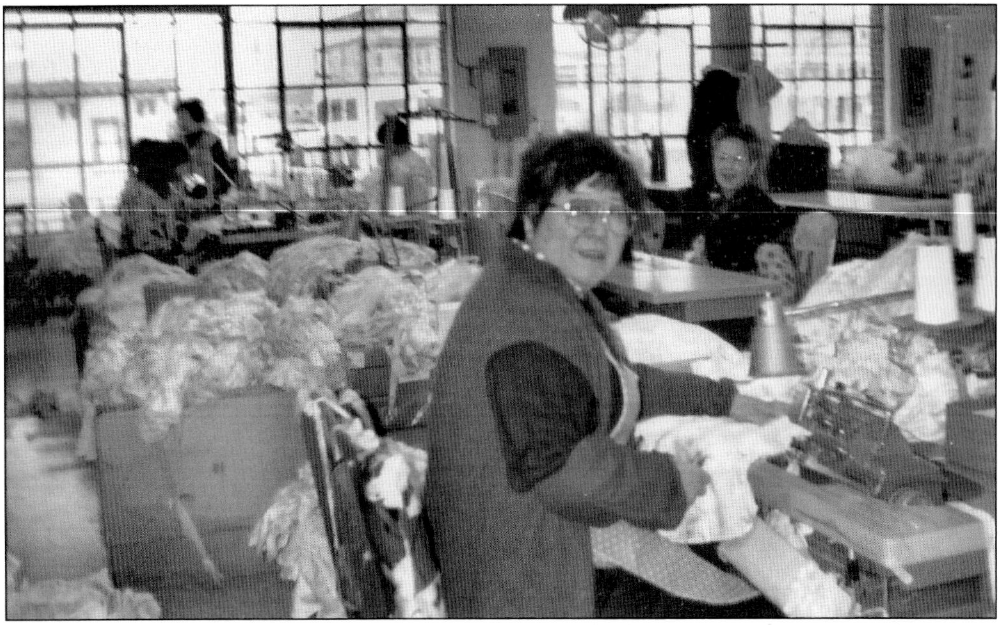

A popular, if controversial, place of work for Chinese and other immigrant women is the sewing factory. Here, in this undated photo, unidentified Oakland Chinese women sew garments in a Chinatown factory. (Courtesy of Asian Immigrant Women Advocates.)

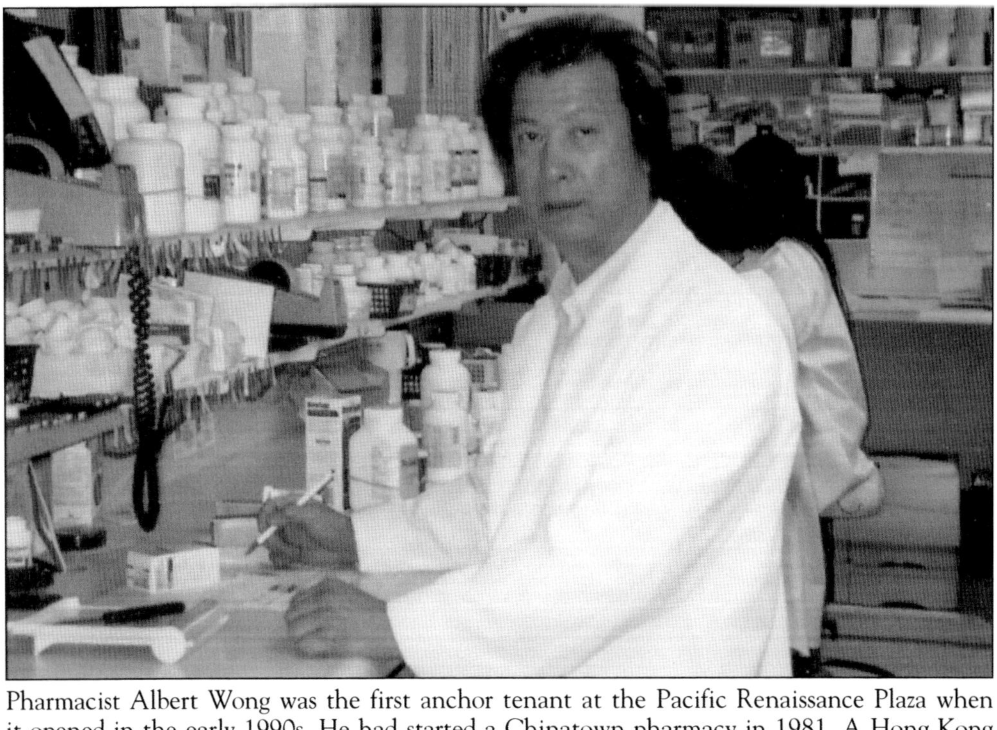

Pharmacist Albert Wong was the first anchor tenant at the Pacific Renaissance Plaza when it opened in the early 1990s. He had started a Chinatown pharmacy in 1981. A Hong Kong immigrant, Wong came to Oakland in 1964. He has been active in Chinatown political and cultural matters, actively supporting Jerry Brown's mayoral campaigns. He offers a free lunch for Chinatown seniors on the Sunday of StreetFest. (Courtesy of Albert Wong.)

Three

COMMUNITY AND COUNTRY

Generations of Oakland Chinese managed to create a largely internalized and complex network of social interactions and relationships in response to the legal discrimination and bigotry of other Oaklanders, from the 1850s through World War II. They went to schools, which taught in Chinese and, separately, in English. They formed social, fraternal, and business associations. They went to Christian churches on Sunday. They established sports teams. After the turbulent 1960s, with changes in U.S. immigration laws that allowed more immigrants from Asia, and the end of the Vietnam War, Oakland Chinese expanded their horizons and continued to help one another through social service agencies and organizations. This chapter reflects the multi-faceted self-help and socialization process.

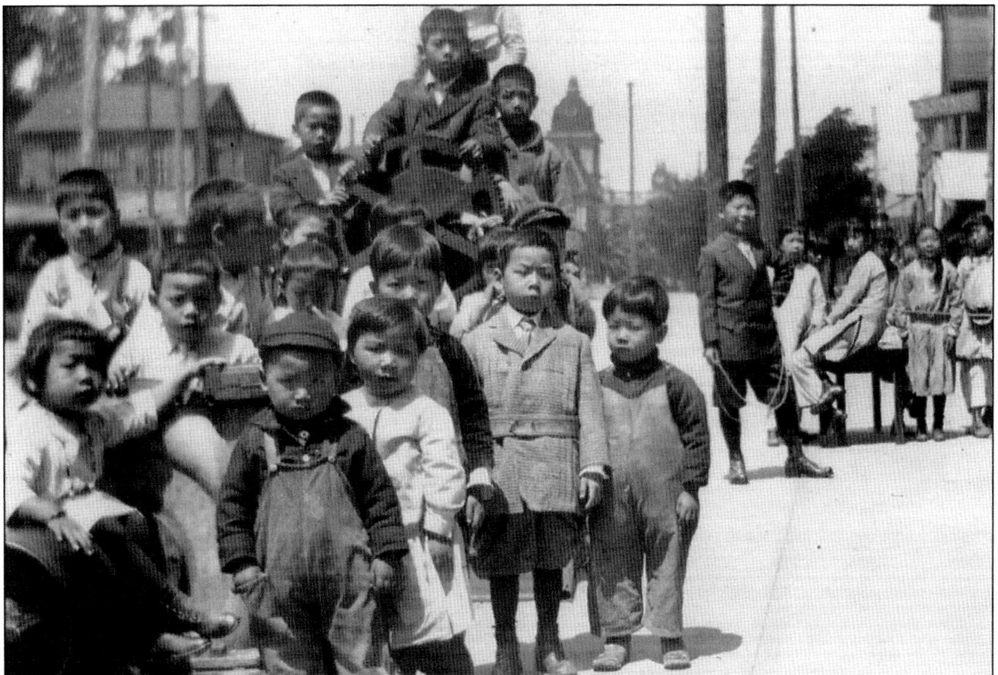

Children of Chinatown gather outside the Chinese Baptist Mission school on Third Street near Harrison Street in 1912. (Courtesy of Darlene Lee.)

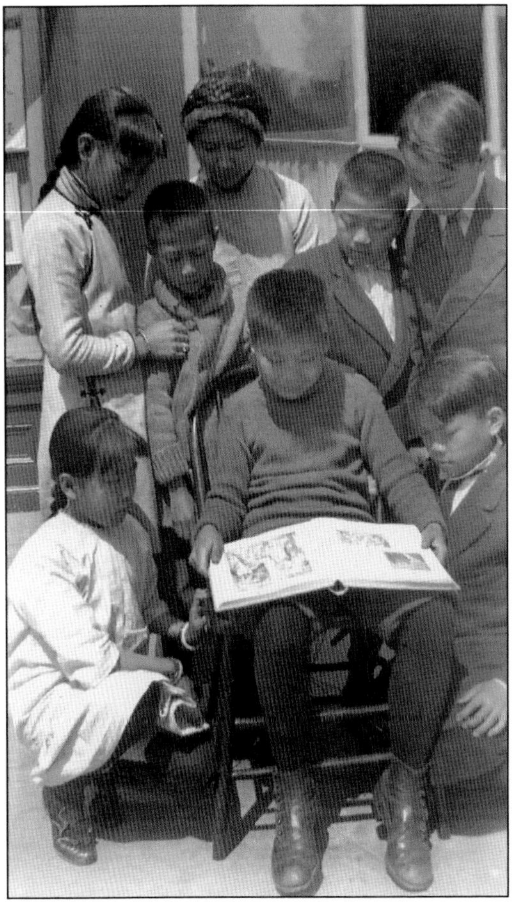

Sarah Leong Joe, standing at left, and other Chinatown children take a break from the Chinese Baptist Mission class in this 1912 photo. The Baptist Mission was then on Third Street near Harrison Street. (Courtesy of Darlene Lee.)

This is a 1911 third-grade class at Lincoln Elementary School, the main "American" school for Chinatown. (Photo by Hugo Weitz, courtesy of Janet Lem.)

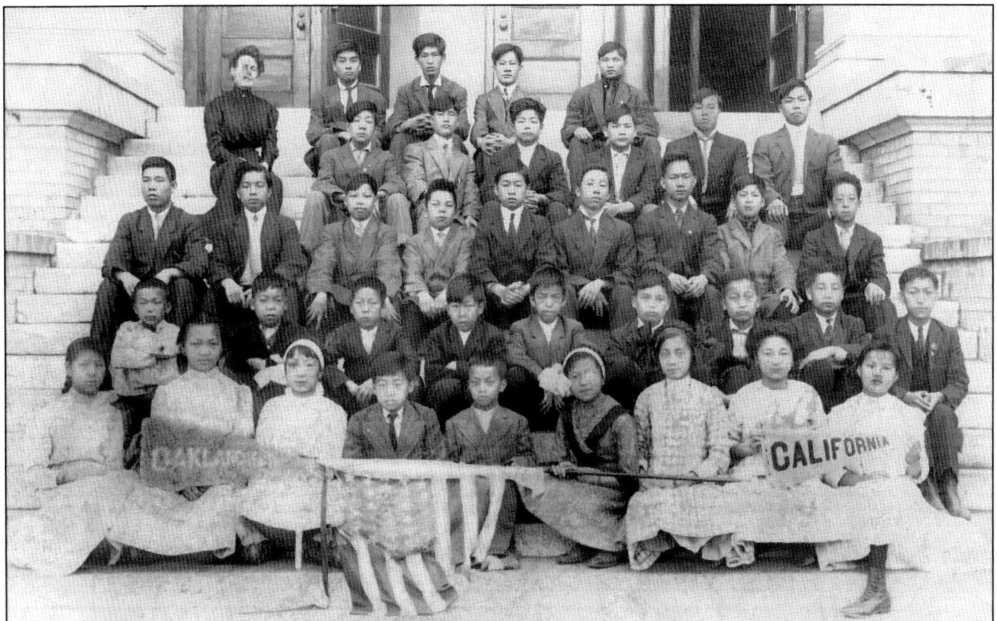

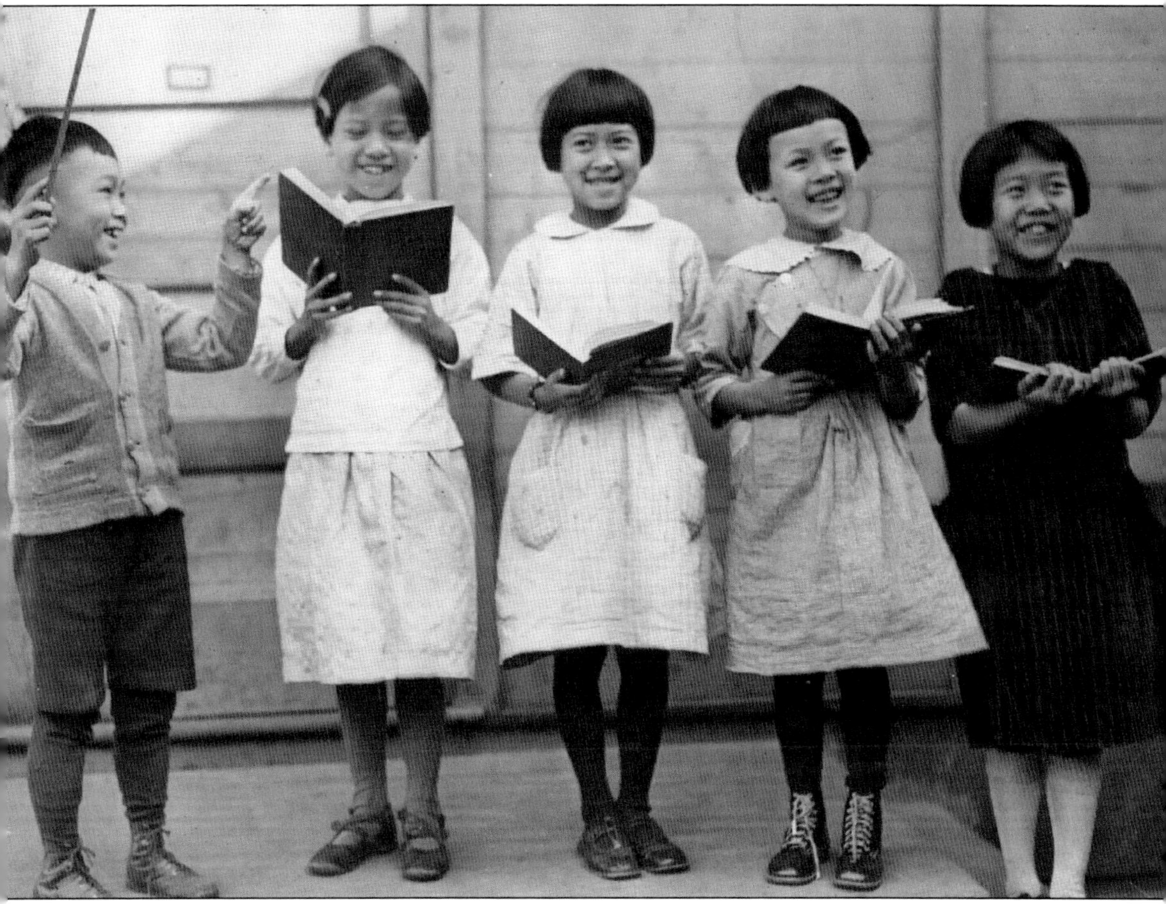

Clifton Fong, at left, orchestrates a musical number for (from left to right) Gon Huie, Mildred Quan, Low Wan Lee, and Margarette Lun, at Lincoln School in the 1920s. Effie Chew, daughter of the prominent Chinese American Ng Poon Chew, taught them. Effie was the first teacher of Chinese descent in the Oakland public schools. (Courtesy of Clifton Fong.)

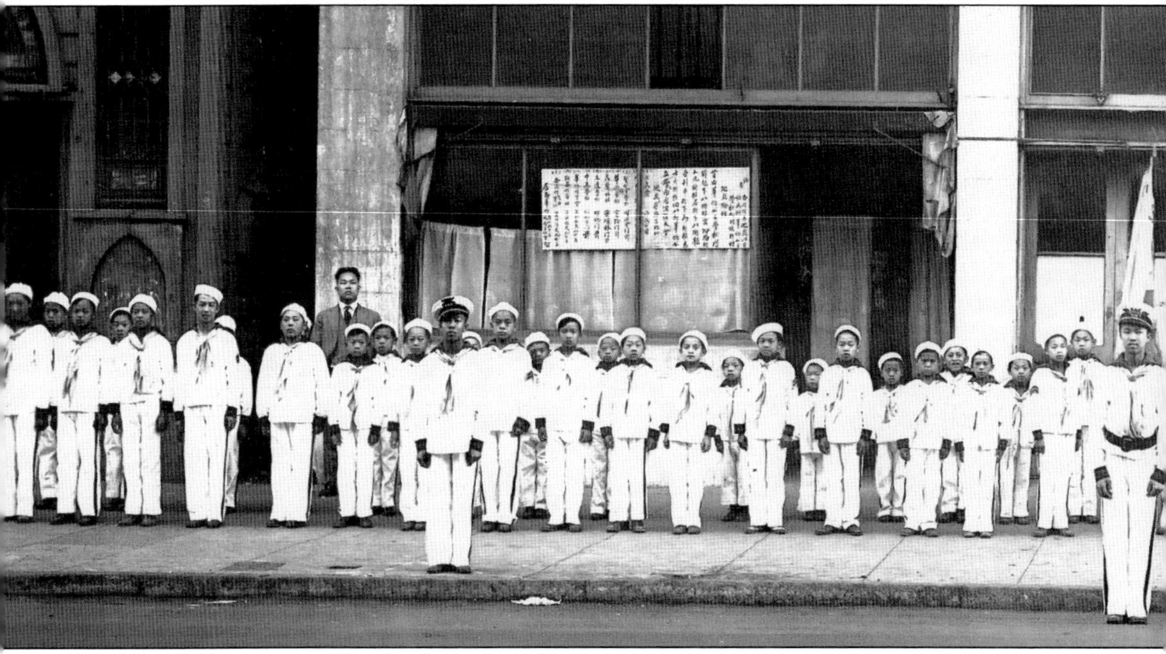

Students and teachers of the Wah Kue Chinese School line up in the 1920s in front of their building on Eighth Street between Webster and Harrison Streets. The school was known as the "Overseas Chinese Public School." Chinese-language schools are a regular feature of Chinatown. This building is currently the Joy Luck restaurant. The building to the left is the site of the Chinese Methodist Church. (Courtesy of Janet Lem.)

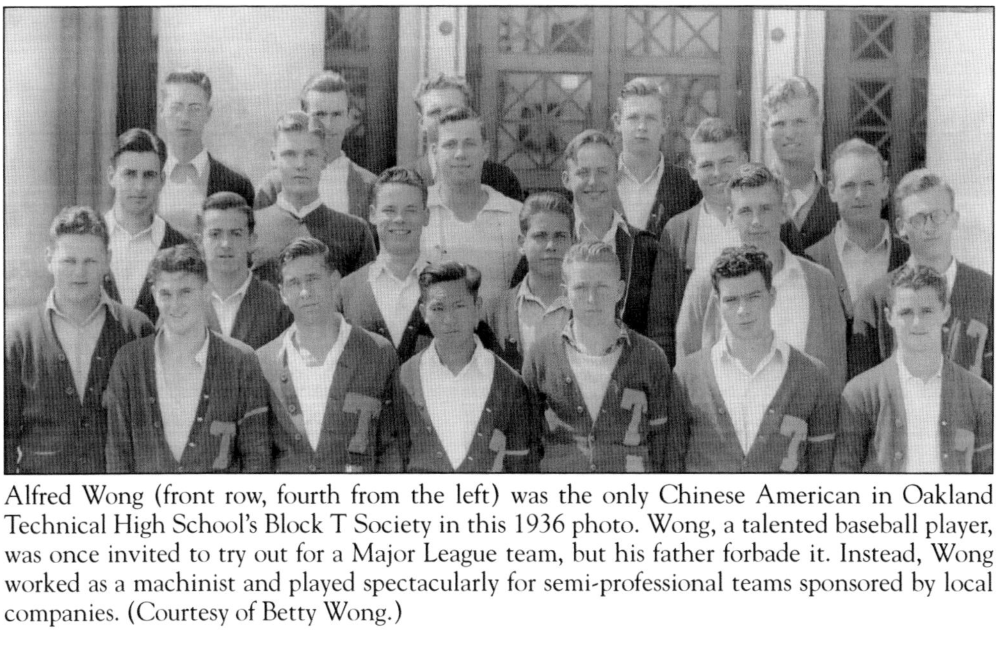

Alfred Wong (front row, fourth from the left) was the only Chinese American in Oakland Technical High School's Block T Society in this 1936 photo. Wong, a talented baseball player, was once invited to try out for a Major League team, but his father forbade it. Instead, Wong worked as a machinist and played spectacularly for semi-professional teams sponsored by local companies. (Courtesy of Betty Wong.)

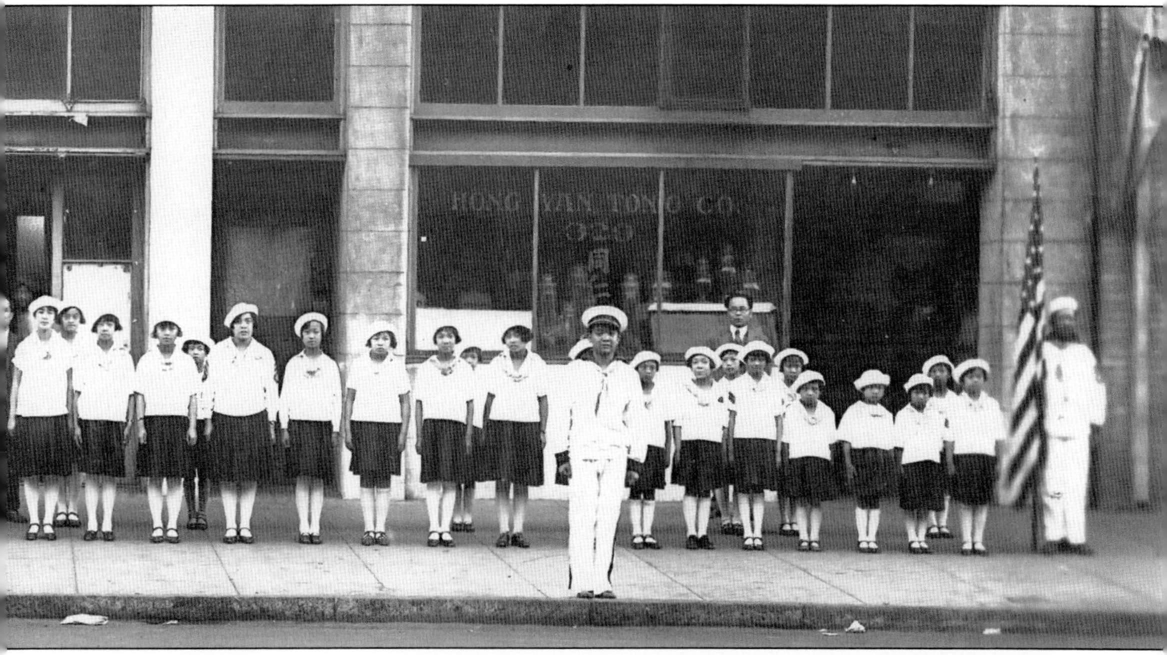

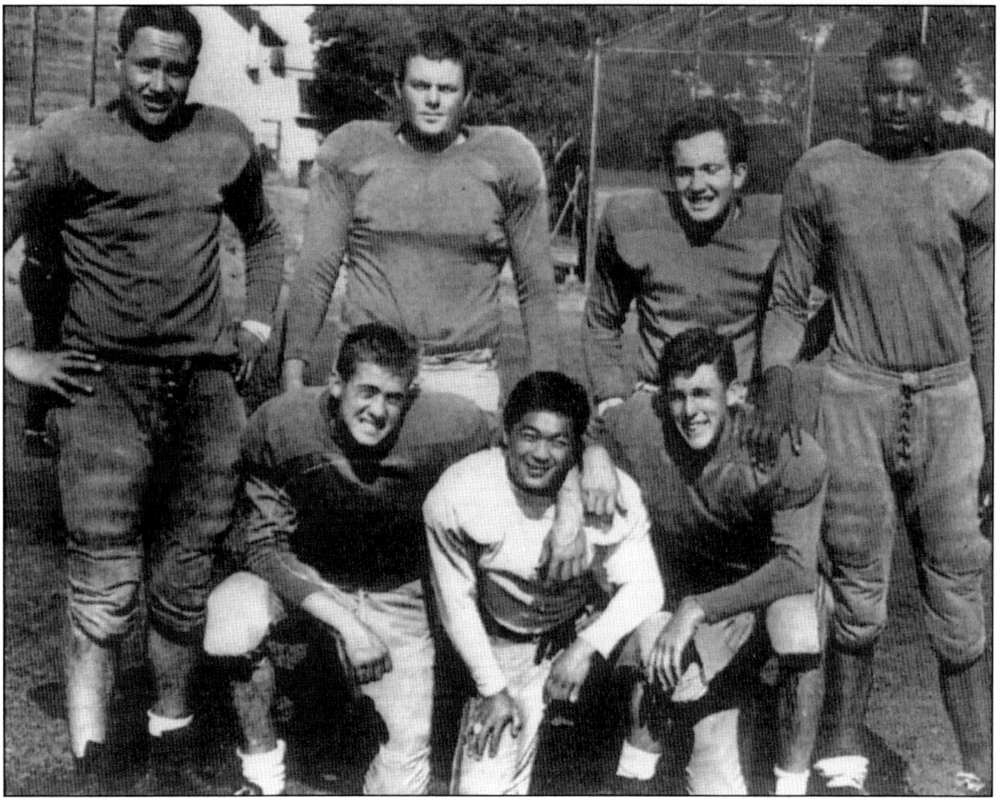

Jeff Chan (front row, center) played football for Oakland Technical High School, with John Brodie immediately to his left. Brodie went on to stardom at Stanford and the San Francisco 49ers. They were classmates in 1953. (Courtesy of Janet Lem.)

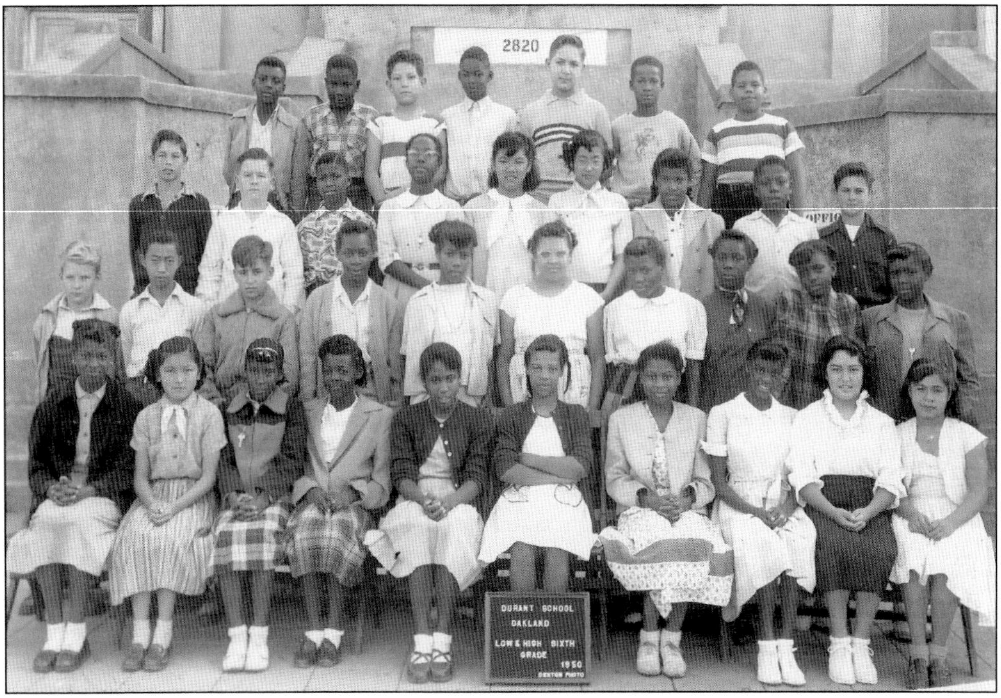

Most Oakland Chinese children before and even after World War II went to Lincoln School, but a few went to schools outside of Chinatown in that era. Here is May Lum (front row, second from left) attending Durant School in West Oakland in the 1940s. Her family owned the Star Market in that neighborhood. (Courtesy of May Young.)

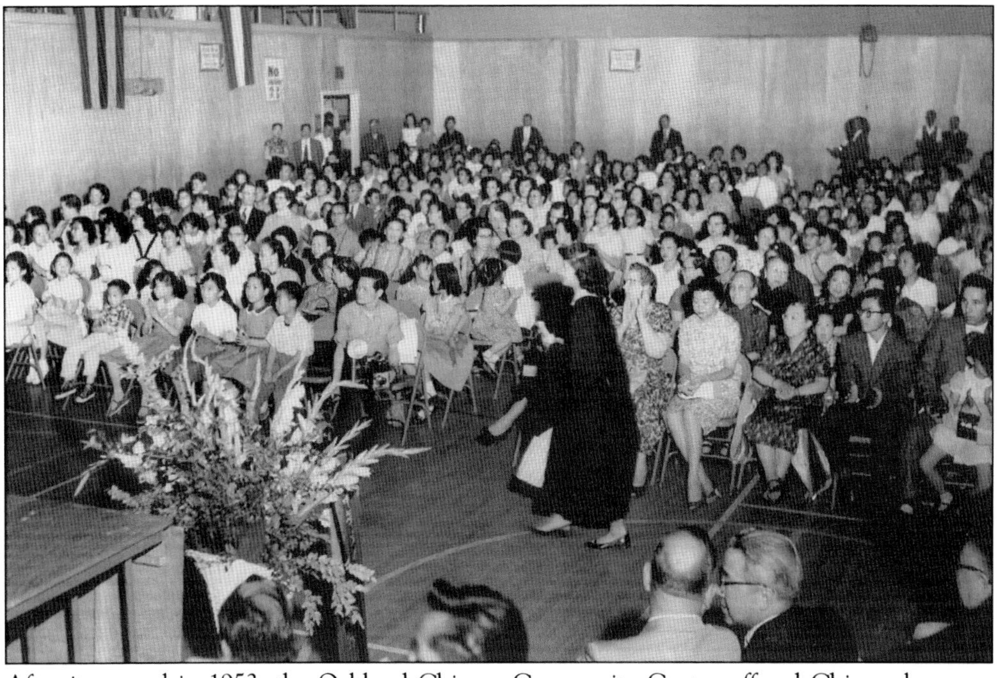

After it opened in 1953, the Oakland Chinese Community Center offered Chinese-language school. Here is a graduation ceremony from the 1950s. (Photo by and courtesy of Henry Woon.)

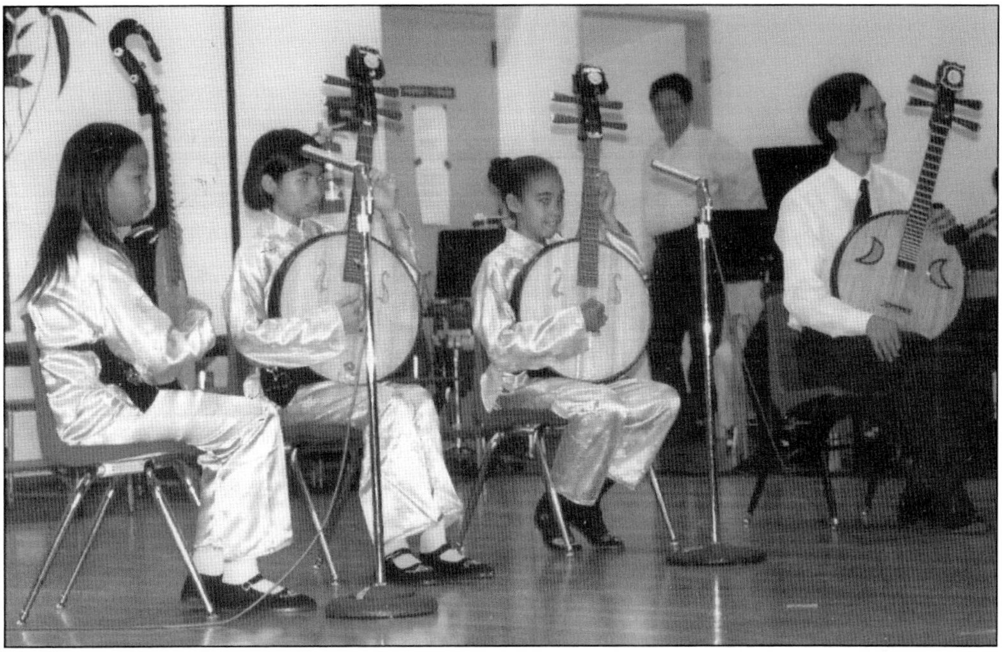

Lincoln School music teacher Sherlyn Chew started a Chinese orchestra at Lincoln School called the Purple Bamboo in 1995. Young bamboo is purple, and her goal is to teach young Lincoln students, whether Chinese or not, how to play Chinese instruments. Members of the 2001 Purple Bamboo orchestra are, from left to right, See's Lam, Victoria Chen, Jasmine Briggs, and Hai Yu Zhang. (Courtesy of Sherlyn Chew.)

Joseph Lee was an educational leader and community activist, and Dr. Janet Chan Lee a pioneering doctor. Beginning in 1938, Joseph rose through the ranks of the Oakland public schools and was principal at several schools before retiring 43 years later. Janet got her medical degree from the University of California at San Francisco in 1940, the first Chinese American woman from Oakland to do so. She began her practice as an obstetrician-gynecologist in 1943 and retired in 1985. (Courtesy of Dr. Janet Lee.)

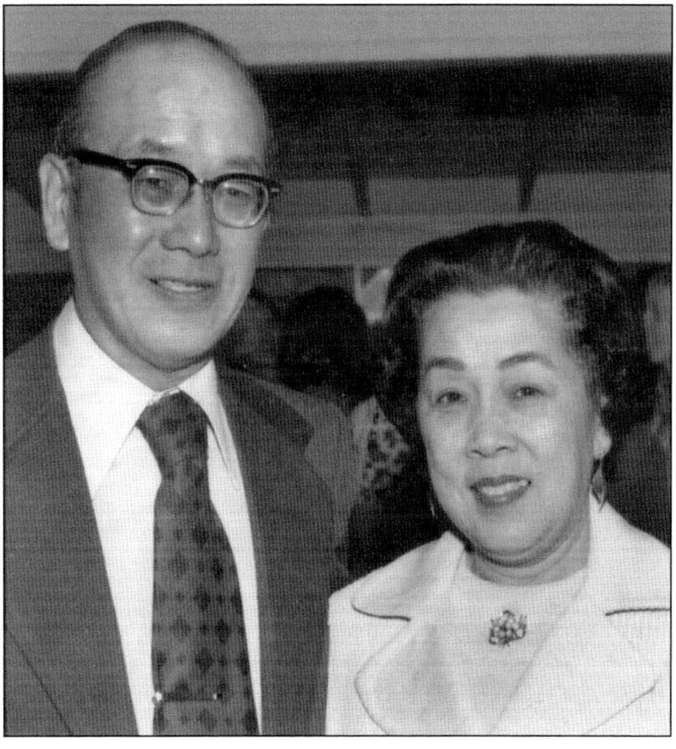

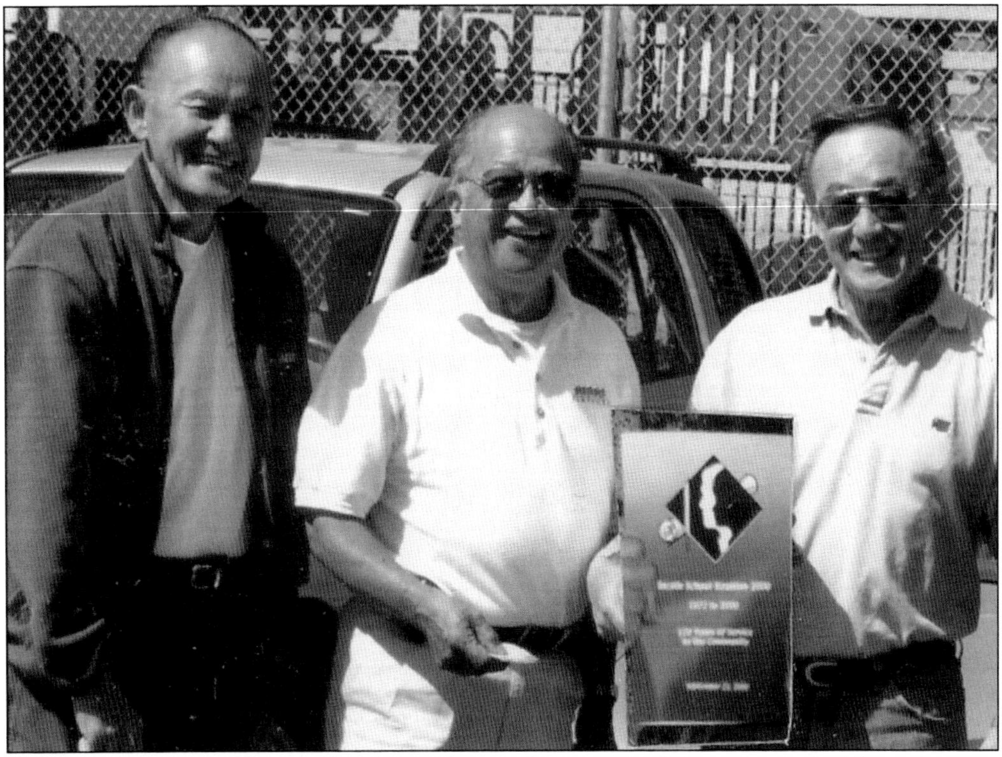

Pictured from left to right, Hawkins Lee, Wyman Chew, and Jeff Lee were part of the organizing committee for the Lincoln School reunion of the year 2000 that drew more than 1,000 alumni. (Courtesy of Janet Lem.)

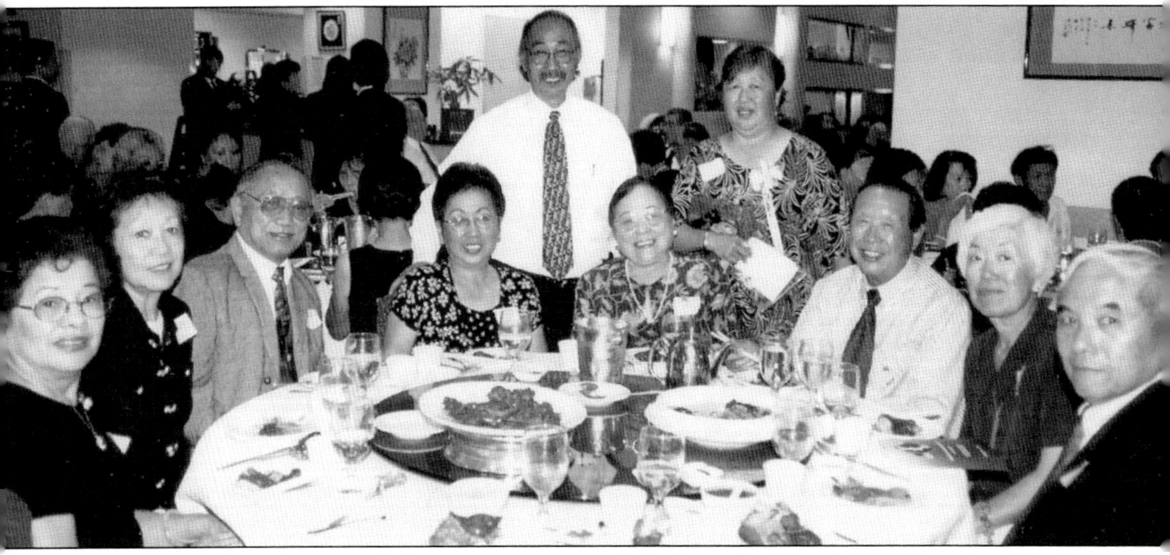

Janet Lem (standing at right) was an organizer of the Lincoln School 2000 Reunion. She has assembled class photos dating back many decades. Also attending the 2000 Lincoln reunion were her husband, John (standing at left), and seated, from left to right, are Susan (Fong) Wong, Helen Chew Lee, Harvey Soo Hoo, Mary Soo Hoo, Doris Quon, Paul Quon, Jessie S. Yee, and Thomas Yee. (Courtesy of Janet Lem.)

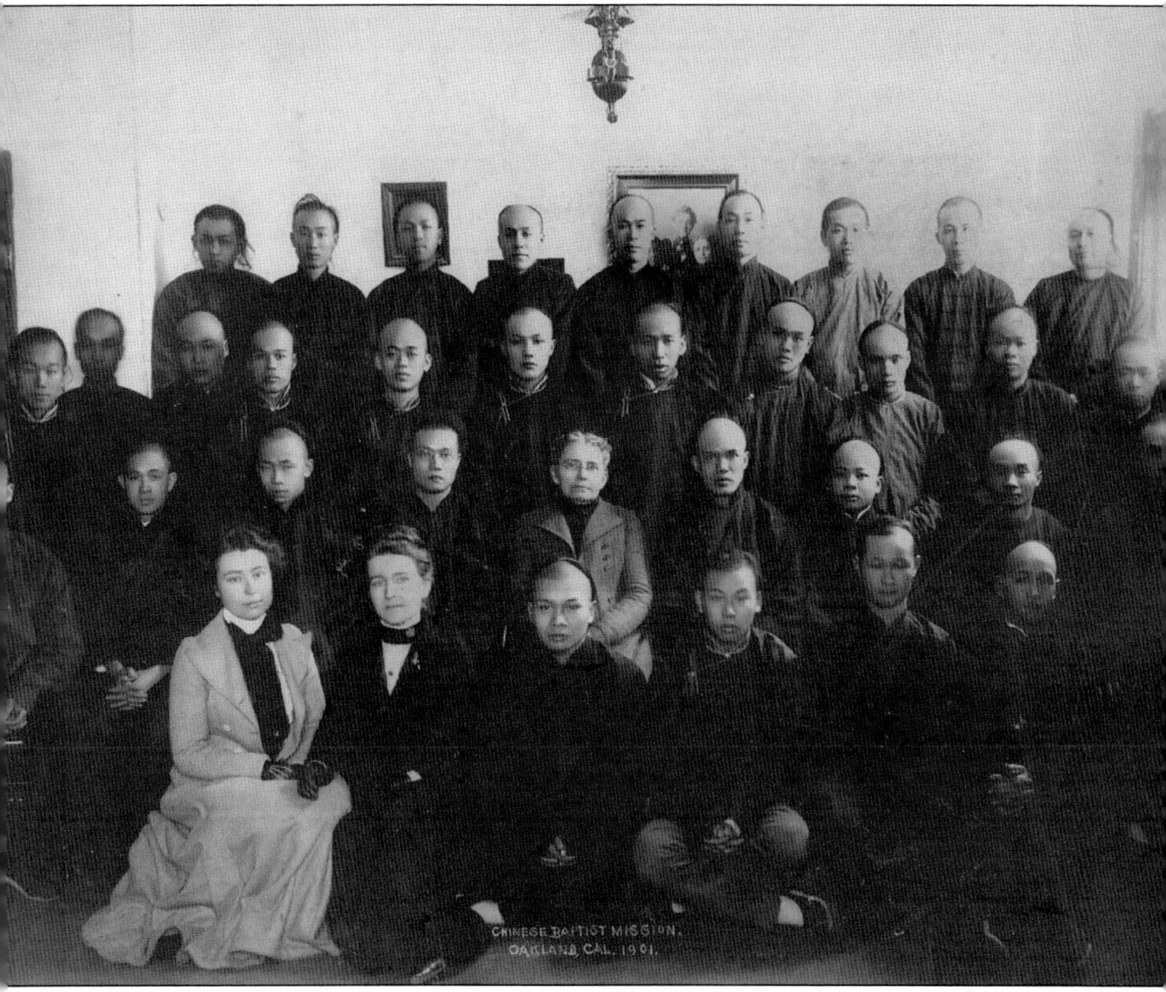

This 1901 photo shows three Baptist missionaries with Chinese men congregants with shaved foreheads and wearing traditional tunics. The Baptist Church has been active in recruiting Oakland Chinese converts since the late 1800s. The church bought a house at 823 Webster Street, between Eighth and Ninth Streets, which became the Chinese Independent Baptist Church until it moved to 280 Eighth Street. (Courtesy of Chinese Independent Baptist Church, Oakland.)

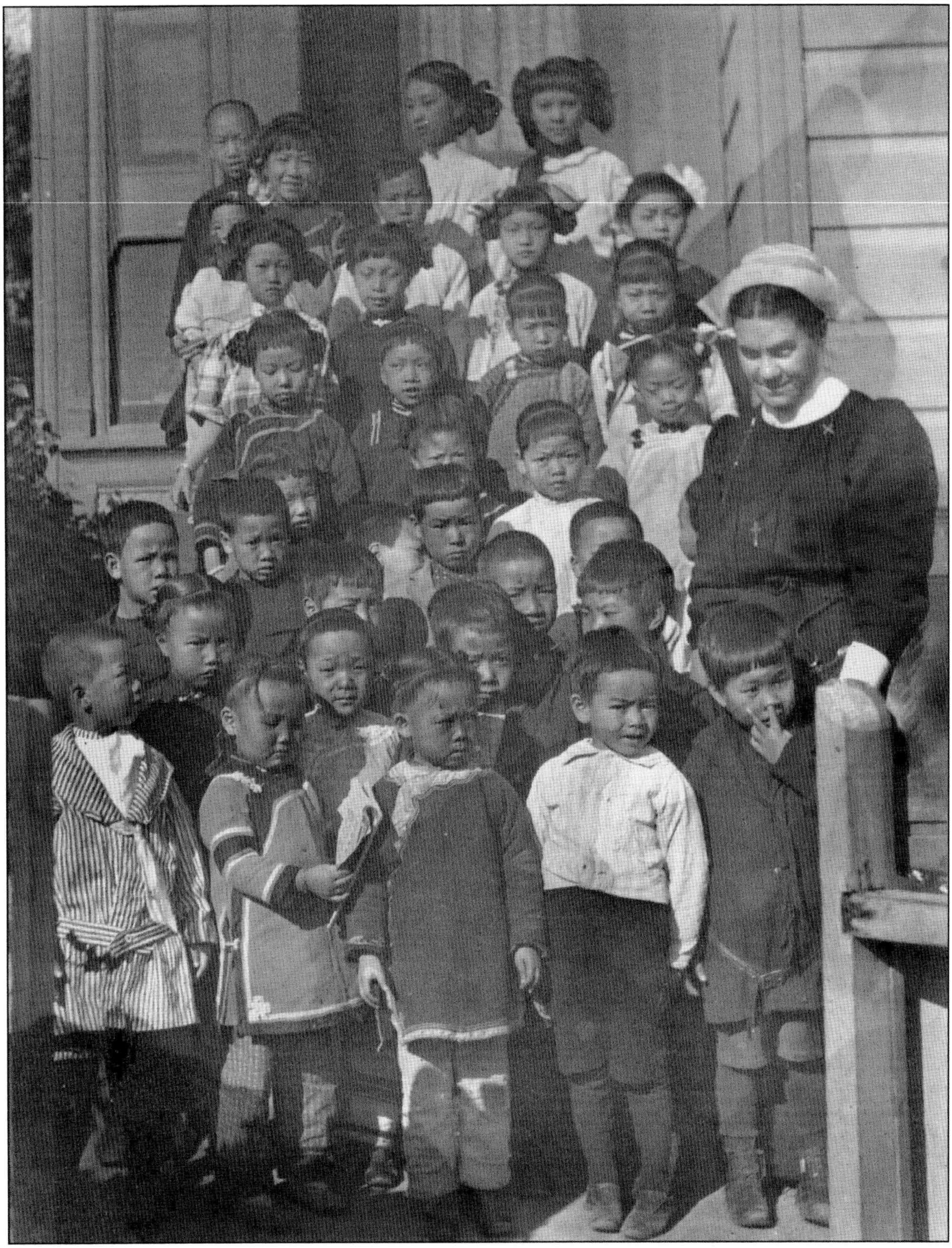

Episcopal Deaconess Emma Drant watches over Chinatown children in the early 1900s, at the True Sunshine Mission, 320 Sixth Street. The mission eventually became the Episcopal Church of Our Saviour on Harrison Street between Tenth and Eleventh Streets. When the Bay Area Rapid Transit was built in the 1960s, it consumed the block where the mission was. That block became a park. BART's headquarters took over what was then Madison Square Park. (Courtesy of Rev. Dr. Fran Toy.)

Ng Poon Chew, seen here in 1925, was born in China in 1866, came to California in 1880, and was ordained a Presbyterian minister in 1892. He was one of the founders of the first Chinese daily newspaper in the United States, *Chung Sai Yat Po*, using it and other public forums to speak out for Chinese Americans. A frequent national speaker in eloquent English, he was called the "Chinese Mark Twain," for his quick-witted humor. He moved to Oakland in 1906 and lived here until his death in 1931. (Courtesy of the Oakland Tribune Collection, the Oakland Museum of California, Gift of Alameda Newspaper Group.)

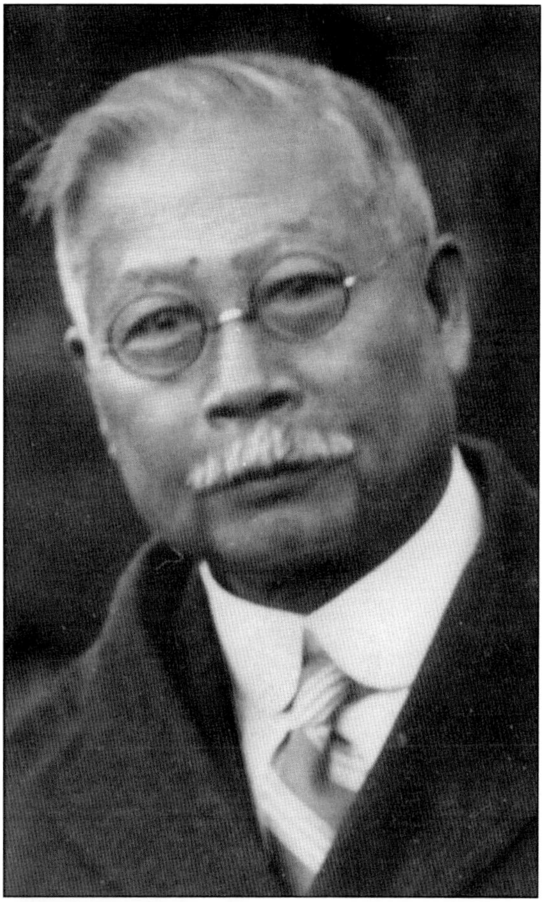

The Reverend Frank Mar gave his final sermon at the Chinese Presbyterian Church in July 1984, retiring after 20 years of service. Born in China in 1922 and emigrating in 1932, Reverend Mar advocated on behalf of Chinese immigrants and young people. He led Chinatown campaigns for a culture center and affordable housing. A major affordable housing project near Chinatown is named after him. (Photo by Eugene Go, courtesy of Mary Mar.)

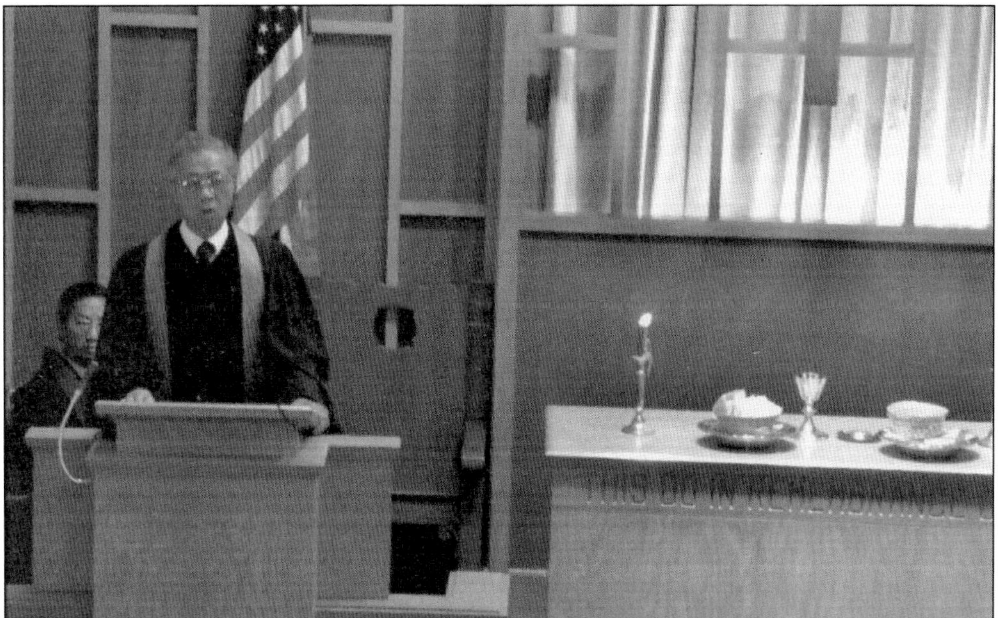

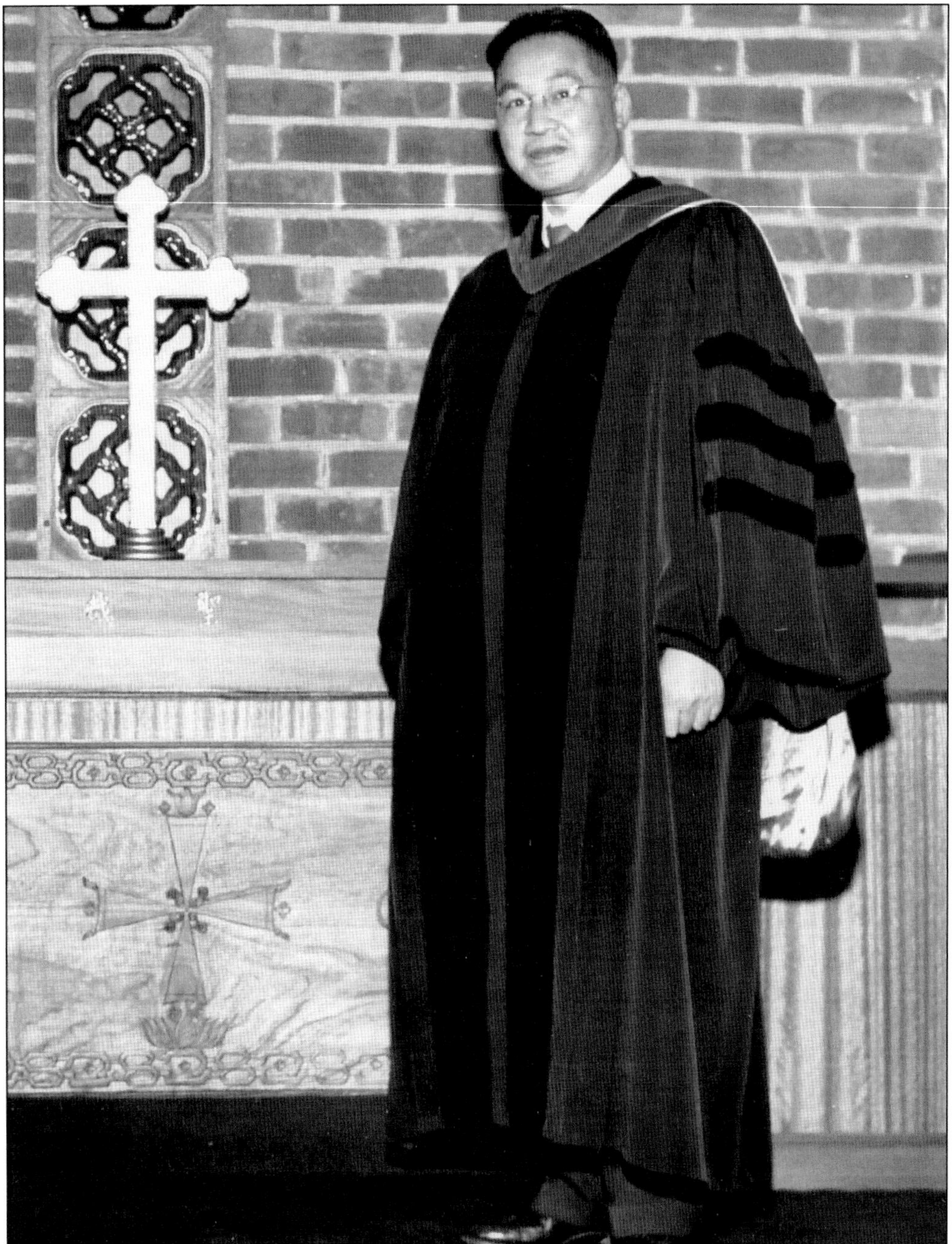

The Reverend Edwar Lee was born in San Francisco in 1902 of Chinese immigrants. He was the first American-born Chinese to become a Methodist minister. He served pastorates in San Jose, Watsonville, Stockton, Oakland, Sacramento, and Vallejo. He was with the Oakland Chinese Methodist Church, which began in 1887, from 1935 to 1970. Among the Oakland Chinatown organizations in which he was active were the Wa Sung Service Club and the Chinese American Citizens Alliance. From 1927 to 1939, Reverend Lee was an interpreter at the Angel Island Immigration Station. (Courtesy of Chinese Community United Methodist Church.)

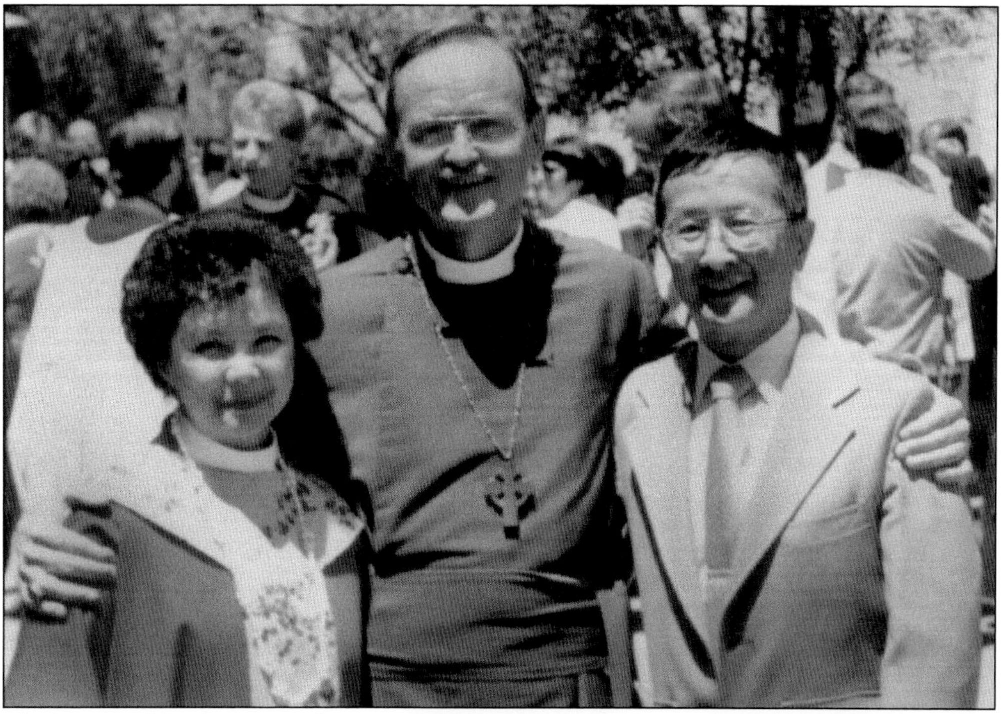

The Reverend Dr. Fran Toy of Oakland was ordained on June 8, 1985, as the first Asian American woman Episcopal priest in the United States. She is with the bishop, Rt. Rev. William E. Swing, and her husband, Arthur C. Toy. She is affiliated with the Episcopal Church of Our Saviour on Harrison Street, between Tenth and Eleventh Streets. (Courtesy of Rev. Dr. Fran Toy.)

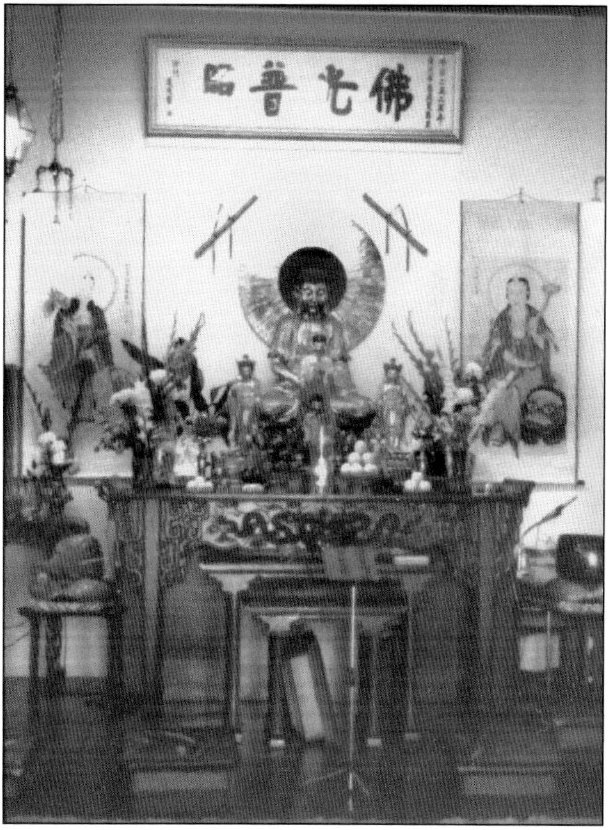

Oakland Chinese Buddhists also have a house of worship, a temple at Seventh and Oak Streets. This 1987 photo shows the temple's interior. (Courtesy of the Oakland Public Library.)

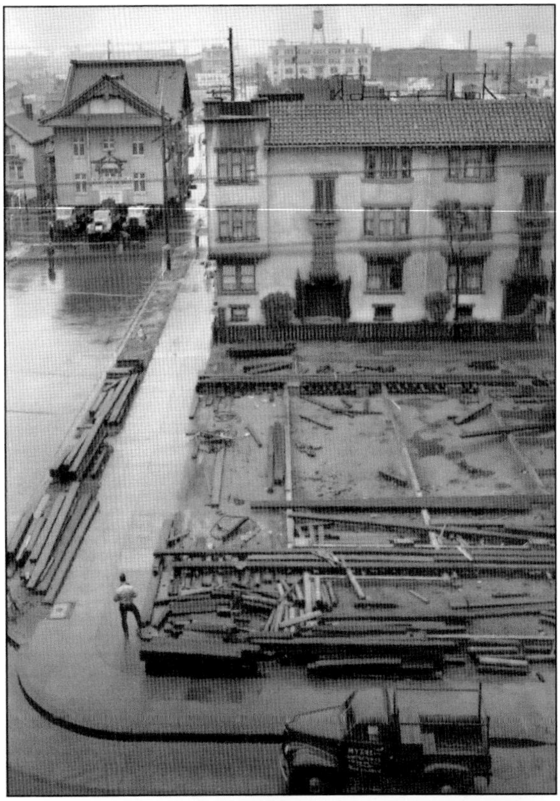

The Buddhist Church of Oakland, a Japanese American institution, had to be physically moved in 1950 because the Nimitz Freeway was being built near the church's Sixth Street site. Church leaders found an empty space at Ninth and Jackson Streets in Chinatown. The church began in 1901 and had several locations in Chinatown in its early years, on Sixth and Seventh Streets. (Photo by Tom Okada, courtesy of Buddhist Church of Oakland.)

The Buddhist Church of Oakland was at Sixth and Jackson Streets in 1916, when this photo of the congregation was taken. (Courtesy of Buddhist Church of Oakland.)

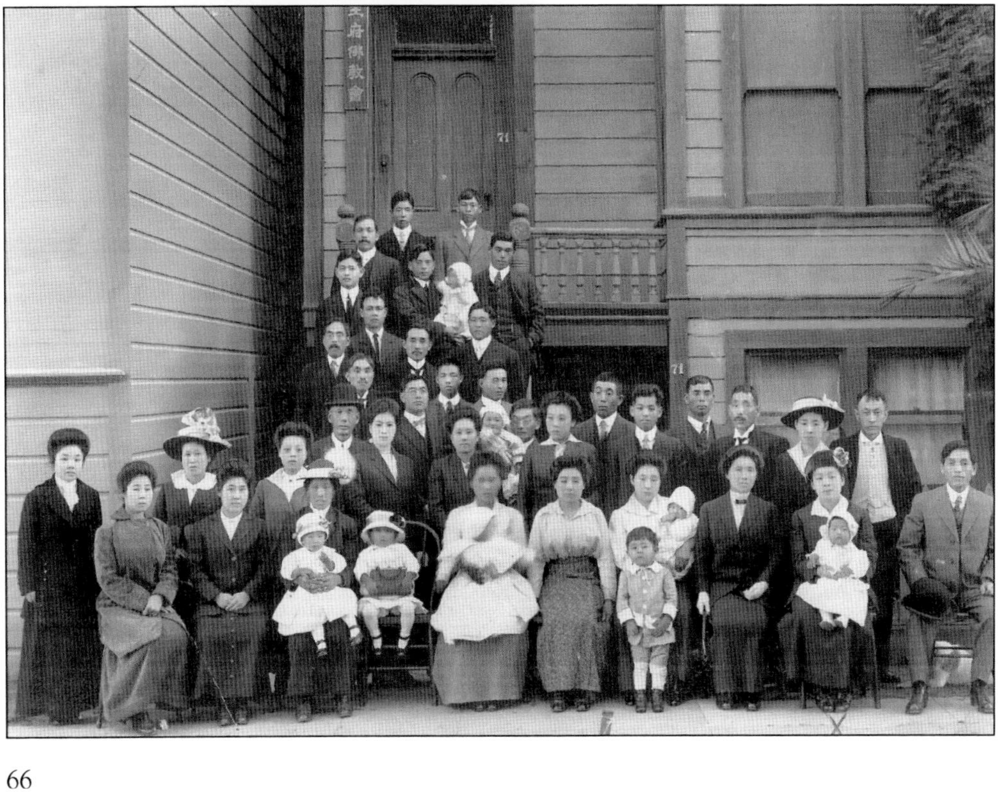

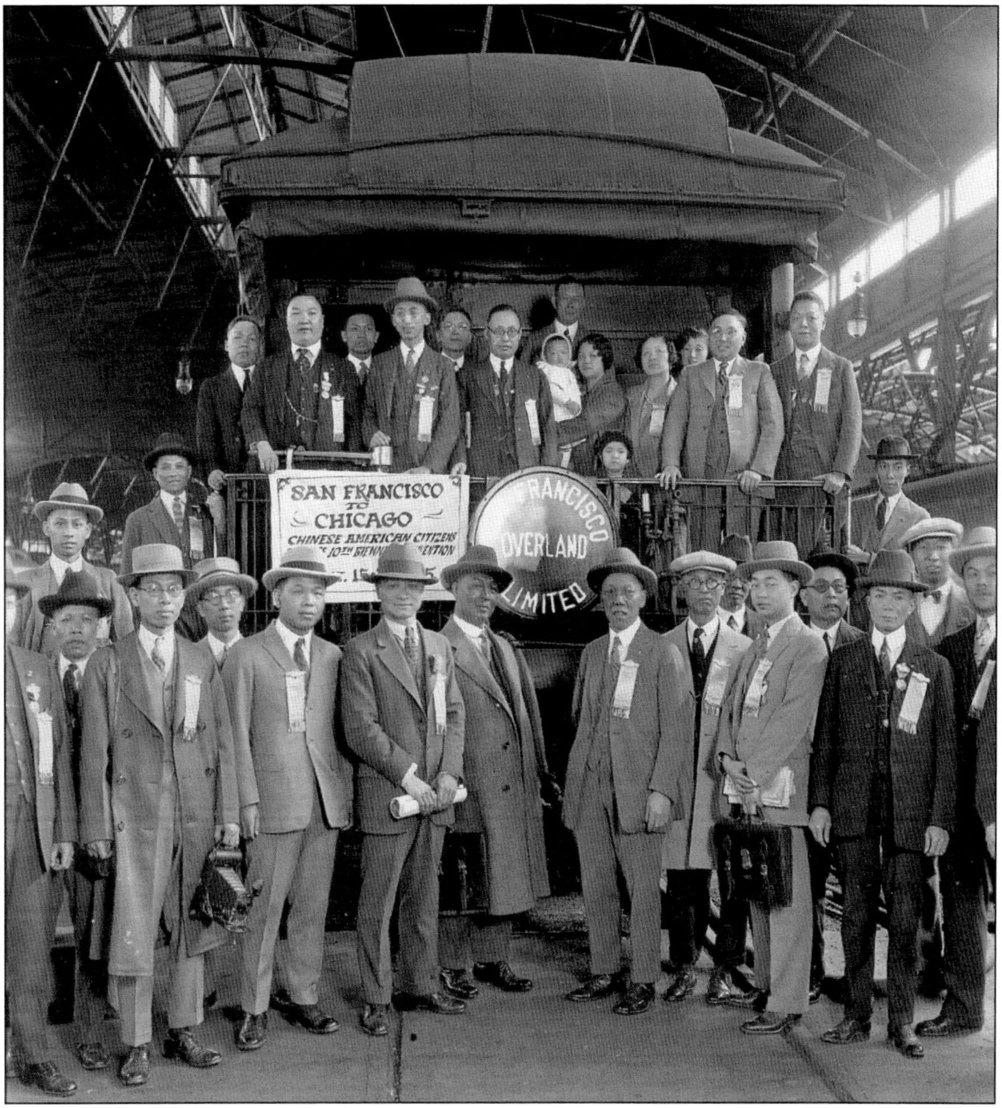

Oakland members of the Chinese American Citizens Alliance (CACA) get ready to board a train at Sixteenth and Wood Streets in West Oakland, bound for a national convention in Chicago in 1925. Changing its name to CACA in 1915, it began in 1895 in San Francisco as the Native Sons of the Golden State, a group of American born Chinese. It was formed to combat anti-Chinese sentiments and accelerate the assimilation of Chinese. (Courtesy of Art Tom.)

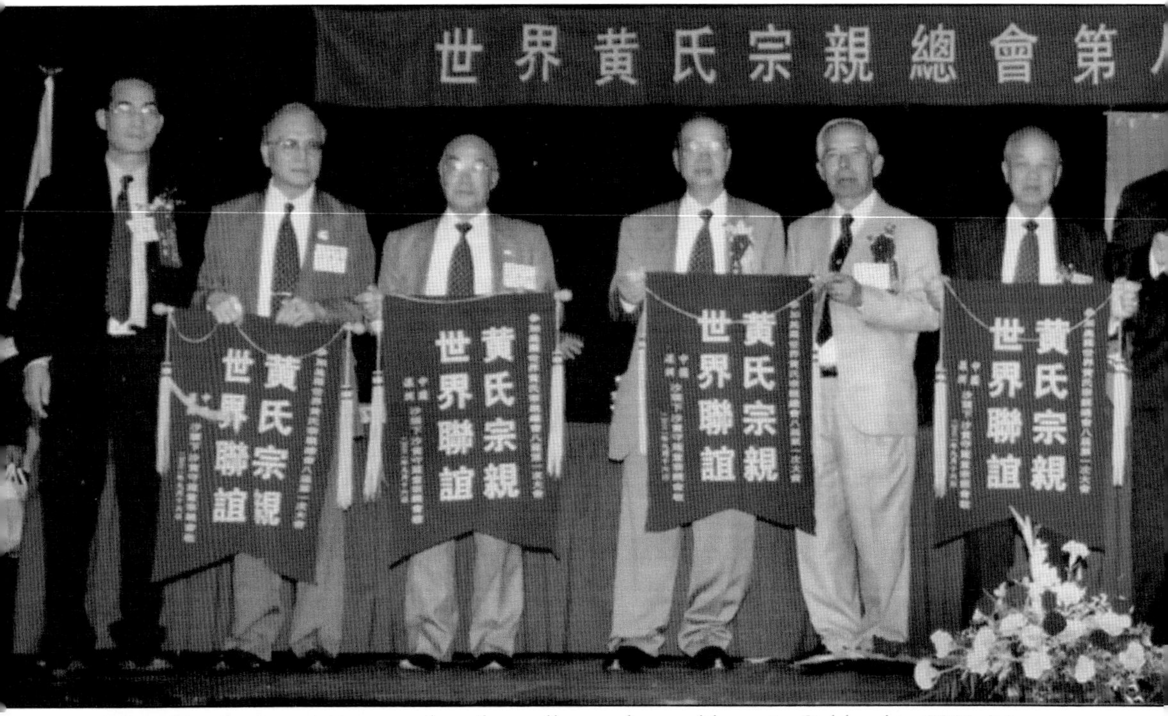

Wong Family Association members from all over the world met in Oakland in 2002. Most were from Malaysia, China, Singapore, Laos, Thailand, Mexico, Hong Kong, Korea, Canada, and U.S. cities like New York, Chicago, Boston, Arizona, Los Angeles, Portland, and Seattle. The

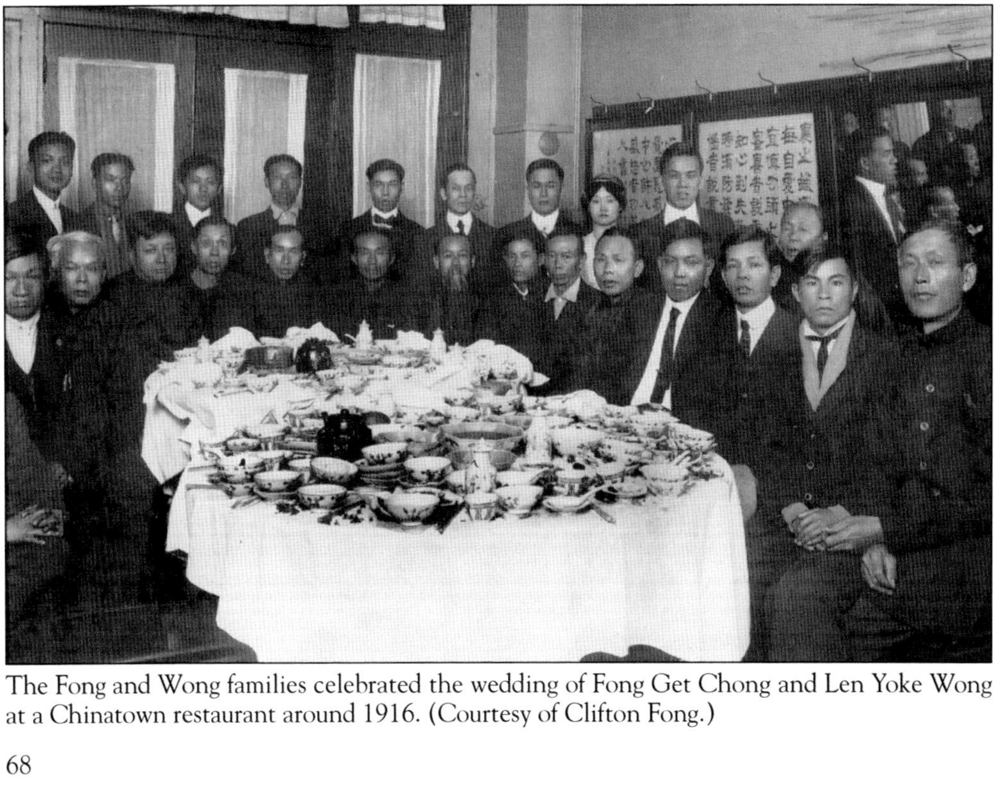

The Fong and Wong families celebrated the wedding of Fong Get Chong and Len Yoke Wong at a Chinatown restaurant around 1916. (Courtesy of Clifton Fong.)

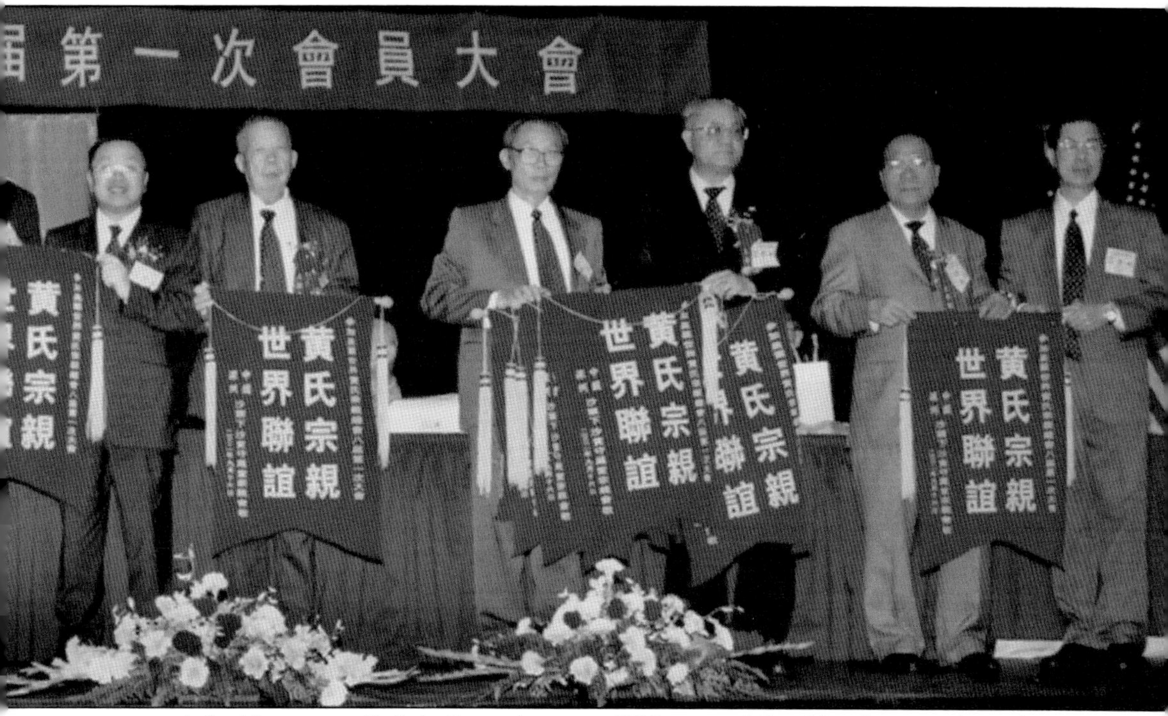

association's building is on Eighth Street between Webster and Franklin Streets, above busy retail shops. (Courtesy of Wong Family Association of Oakland.)

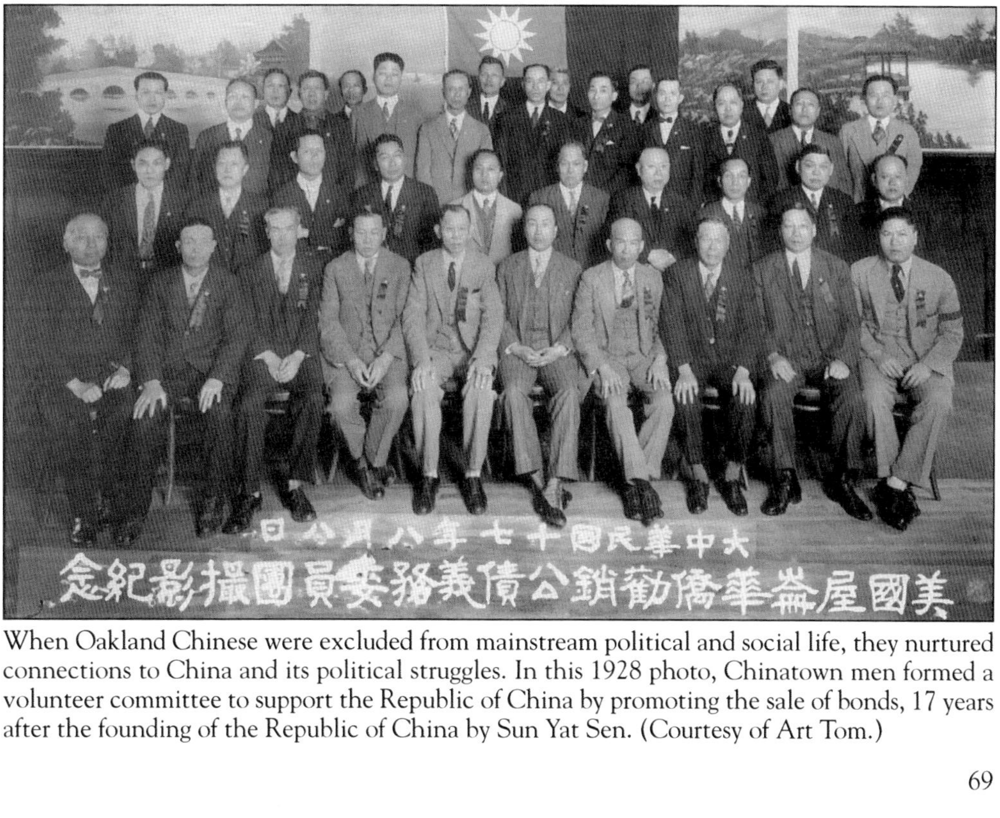

When Oakland Chinese were excluded from mainstream political and social life, they nurtured connections to China and its political struggles. In this 1928 photo, Chinatown men formed a volunteer committee to support the Republic of China by promoting the sale of bonds, 17 years after the founding of the Republic of China by Sun Yat Sen. (Courtesy of Art Tom.)

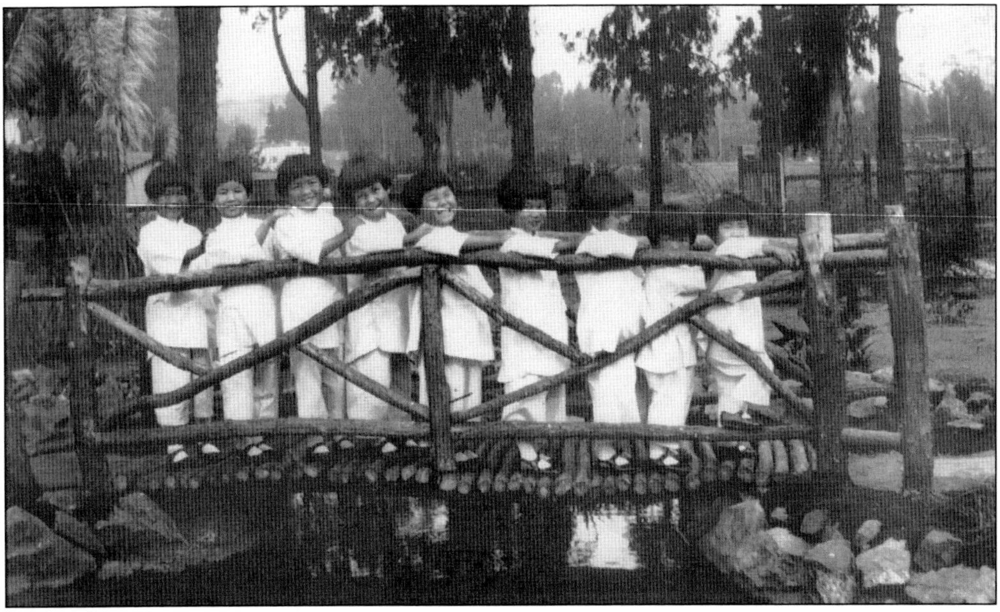

The Ming Quong Home occupied two Oakland sites. The one in Chinatown housed Oakland Chinese girls who were orphaned or motherless. This late 1920s photo was taken at the home's Mills College site. The girls are, from left to right, Betty Low, Eva Lum, Monica Wong, Eva Chin, Ellen Wu, Genevieve Ko, Mary Fong, Connie Lee, and Dorothy Quan. (Courtesy of Emily Chow.)

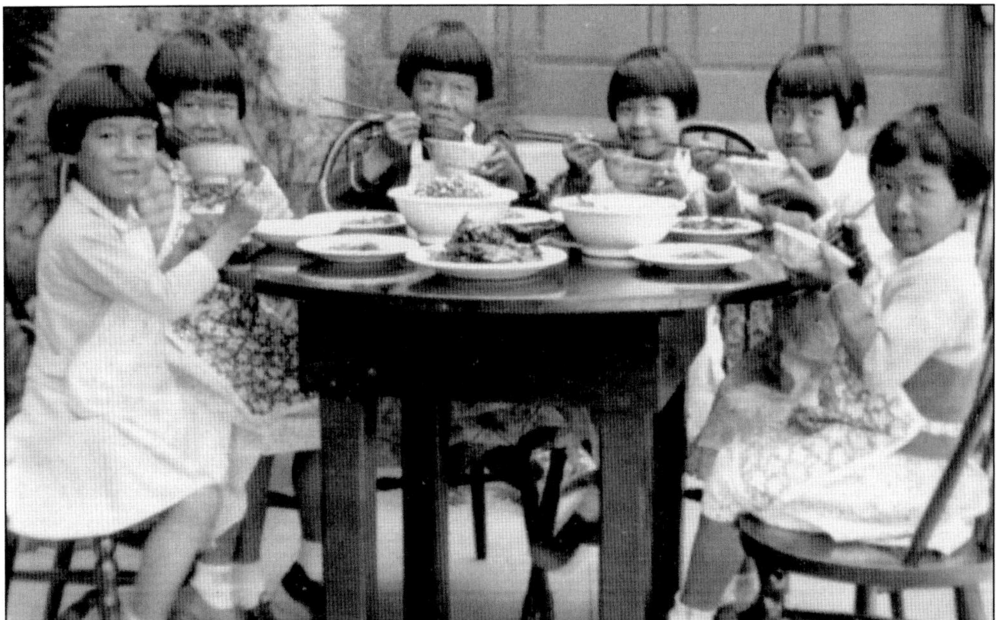

These Ming Quong girls share a meal at the Mills College site in East Oakland in the early 1930s. They are, from left to right, Mary Wong, Luella Wong, Louise Wong, Fanny Wong, Dorothy Quan and Maribel Wong. Mary and Louise are sisters as are Luella and Maribel. (Courtesy of Emily Chow.)

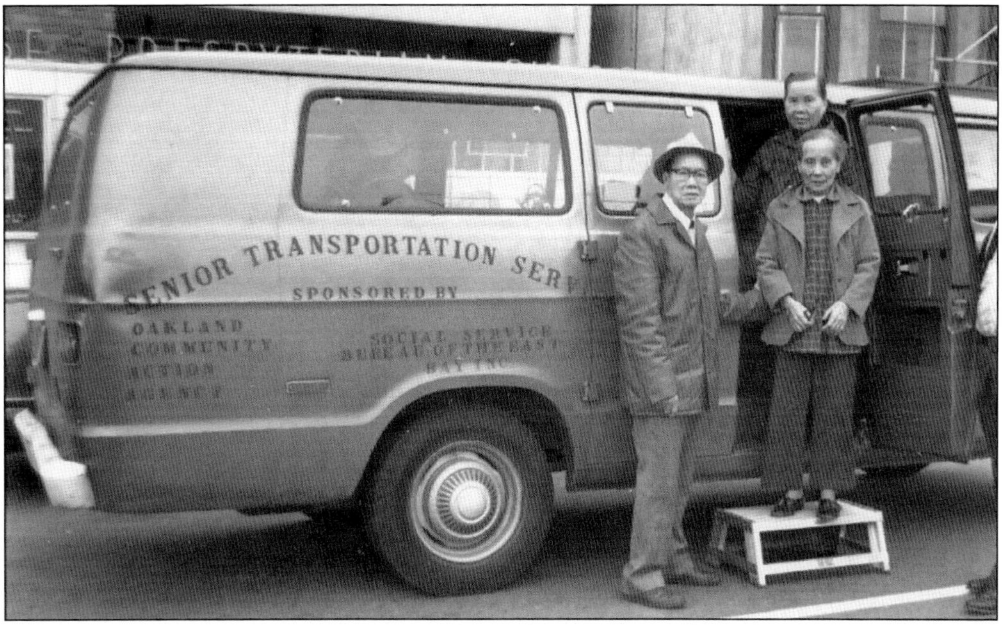

The Oakland Chinese Community Council, now known as Family Bridges Inc., began in 1969 to serve poor and low-income Chinese immigrants, especially the elderly. This 1978 photo shows the council's van in front of its old office on Eighth Street between Harrison and Alice. Family Bridges has expanded its services to needy immigrants of many different ethnic backgrounds. (Courtesy of Family Bridges Inc.)

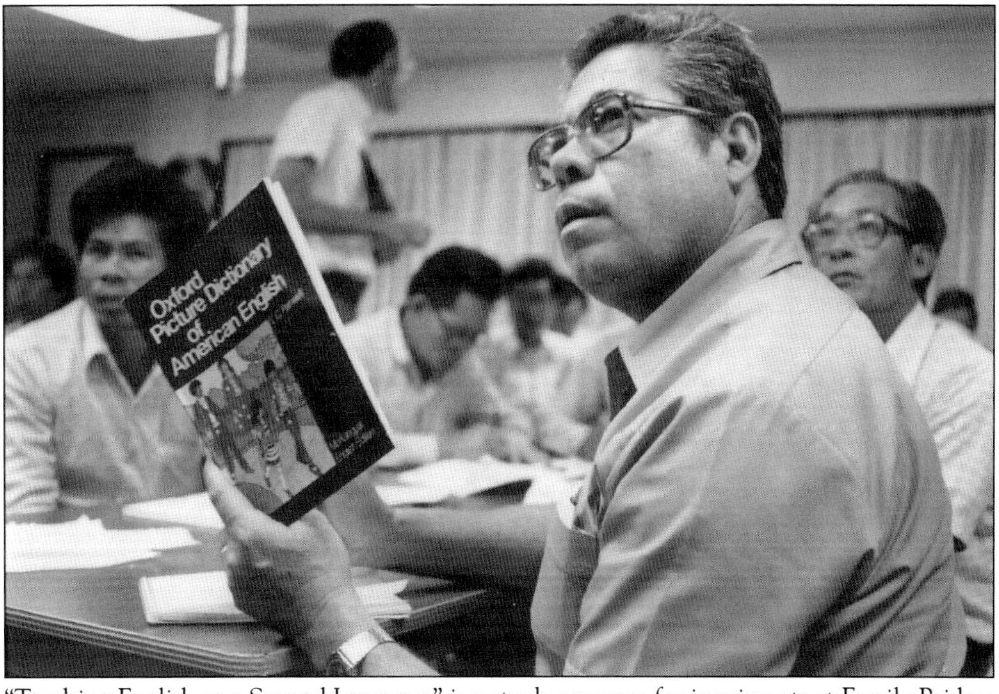

"Teaching English as a Second Language" is a staple program for immigrants at Family Bridges Inc. Most, but not all, of these immigrants are Chinese. Those pictured are unidentified. (Courtesy of Family Bridges Inc.)

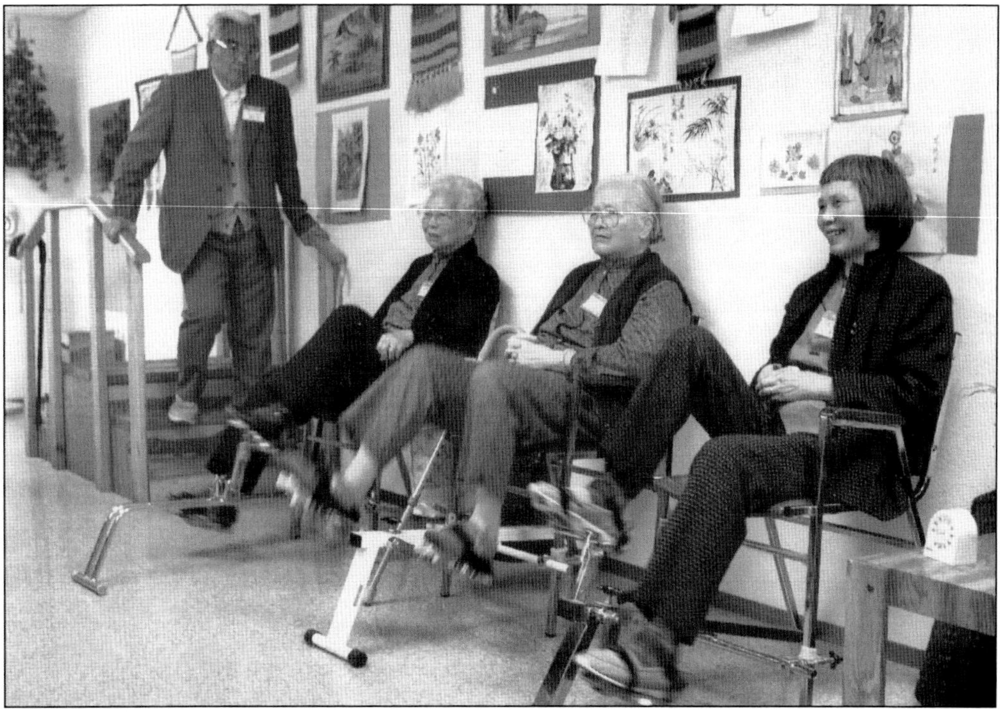

Regular exercise is important for the elderly, and here several unidentified clients of the Oakland Chinese Community Council, now called Family Bridges Inc., peddle on stationary devices while a man climbs steps. (Courtesy of Family Bridges Inc.)

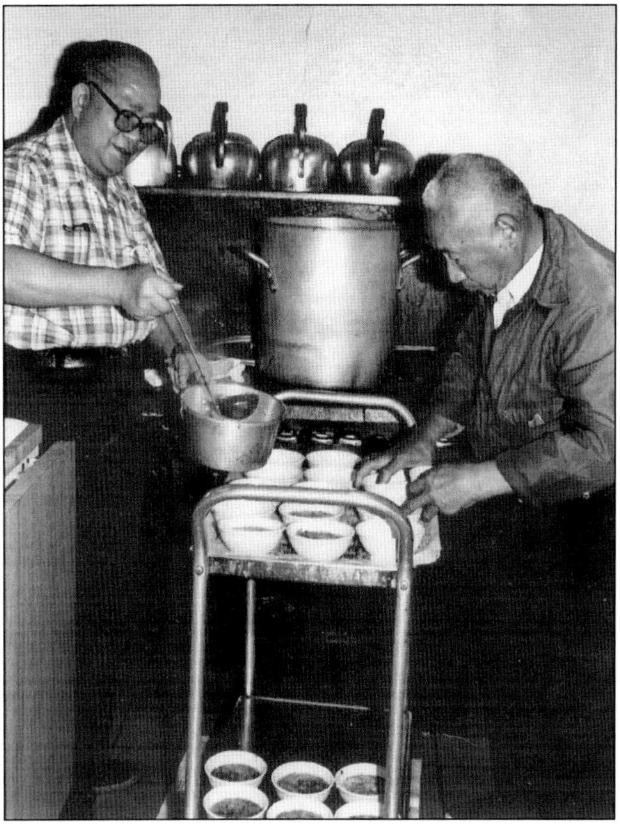

Meals are cooked and served to the needy elderly of Chinatown in this undated photo by the Oakland Chinese Community Council. (Courtesy of Family Bridges Inc.)

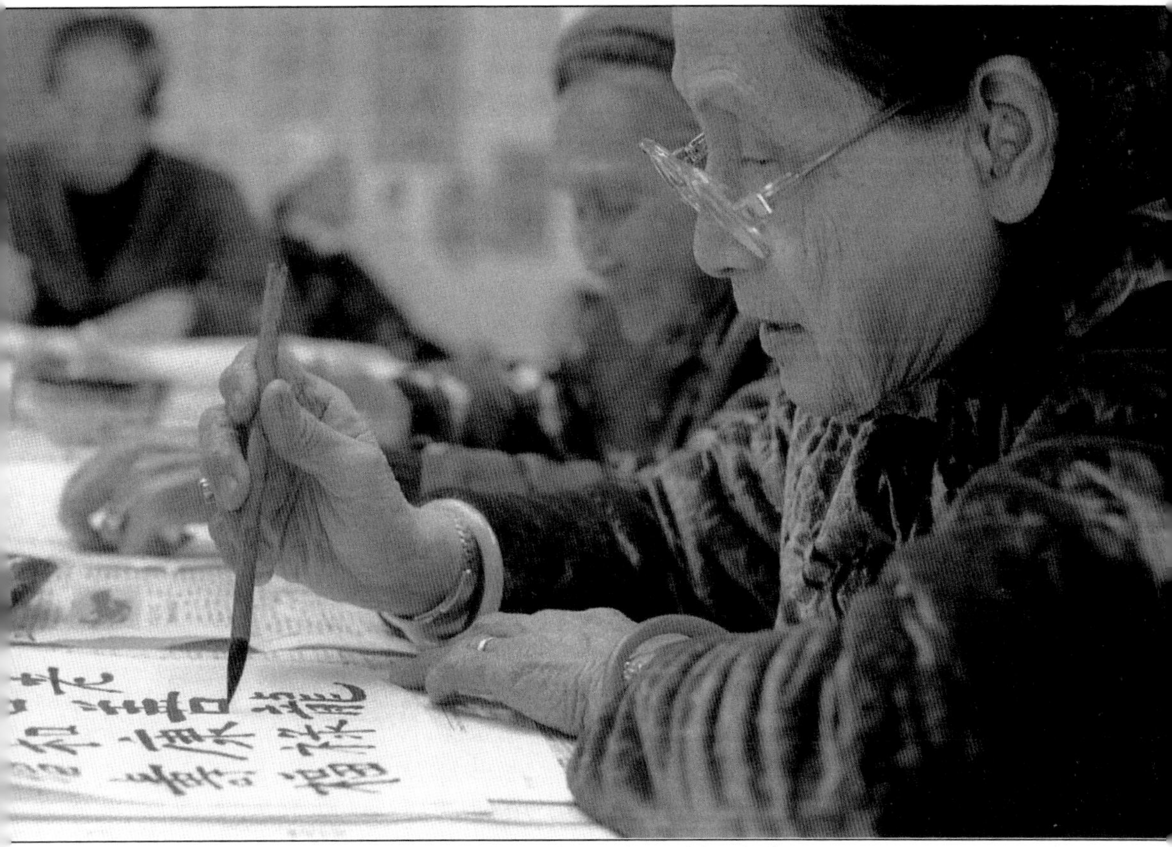

An unidentified woman practices her calligraphy at the Oakland Chinese Community Council, now known as Family Bridges Inc. (Courtesy of Family Bridges Inc.)

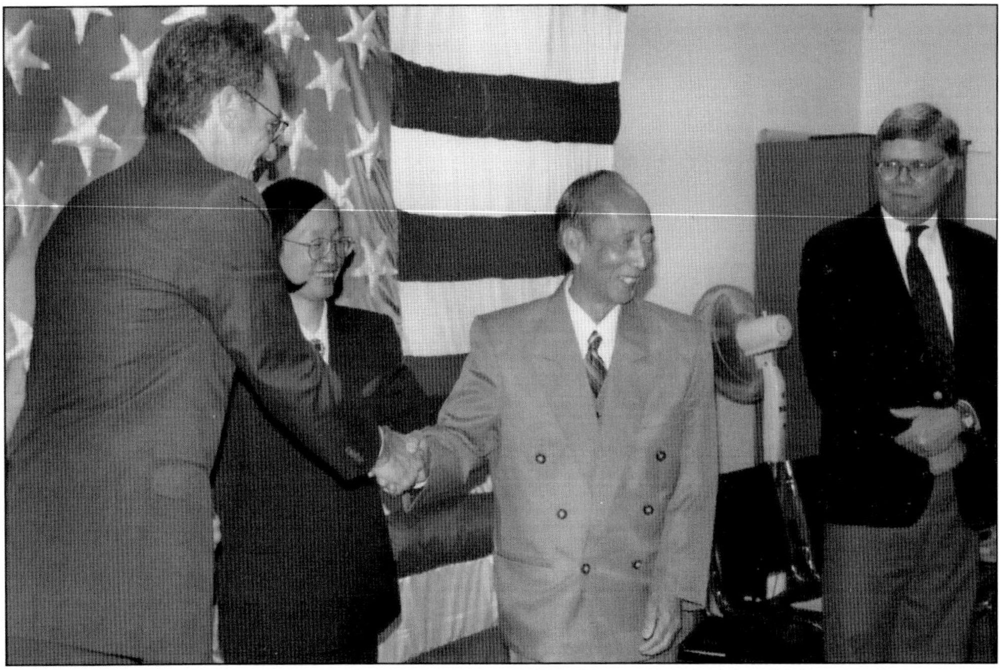

Two U.S. Immigration and Naturalization Service officials visit the Oakland Chinese Community Council in 1996 to encourage citizenship naturalization for non-citizen Chinatown residents. One official congratulates an OCCC client on gaining his U.S. citizenship, as an OCCC staff member looks on. Federal welfare reform legislation that year had a negative impact on non-citizens and the agency and INS encouraged non-citizens to go through the naturalization process. (Courtesy of Family Bridges Inc.)

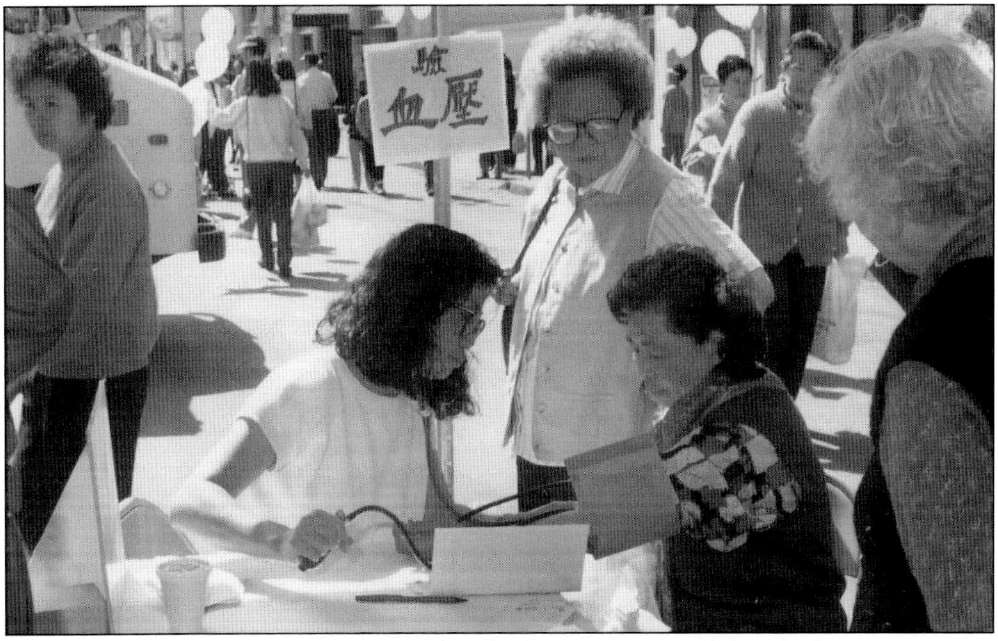

This 1991 health fair, sponsored by the Oakland Chinatown Lions Club and other organizations, offered free basic health services to Chinatown residents. (Photo by and courtesy of Henry Woon.)

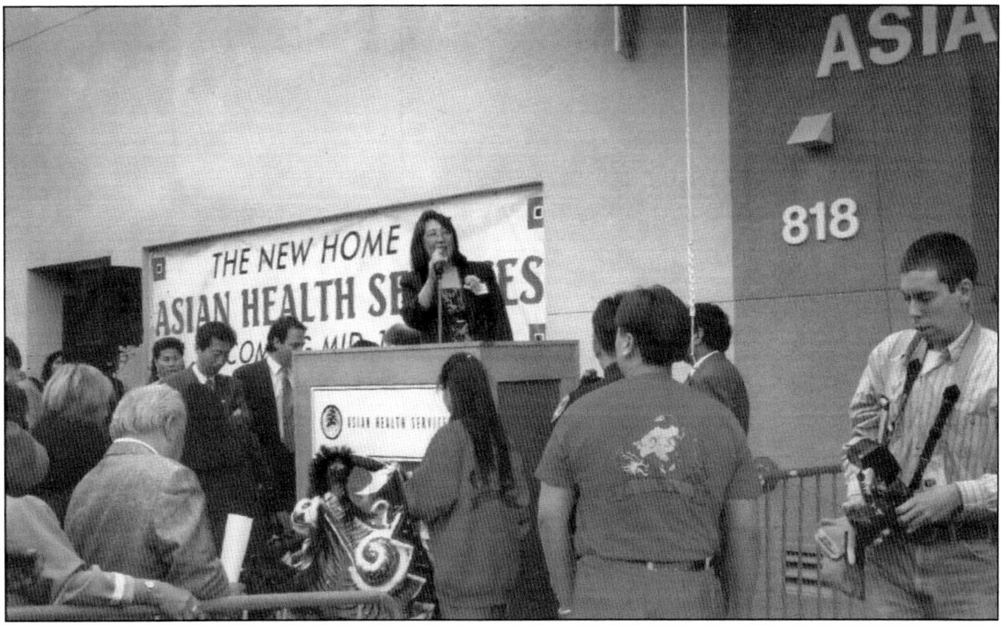

Since 1974, the Asian Health Services has offered low-cost health services in different Asian languages to Chinatown residents. It moved from the Asian Resource Center on Eighth and Harrison Streets to its own building at Eighth and Webster Streets. The grand opening occurred in 1996. The Lantern Restaurant occupied that building previously. At the microphone is Sherry Hirota, the agency's long-time executive director. (Courtesy of Asian Health Services.)

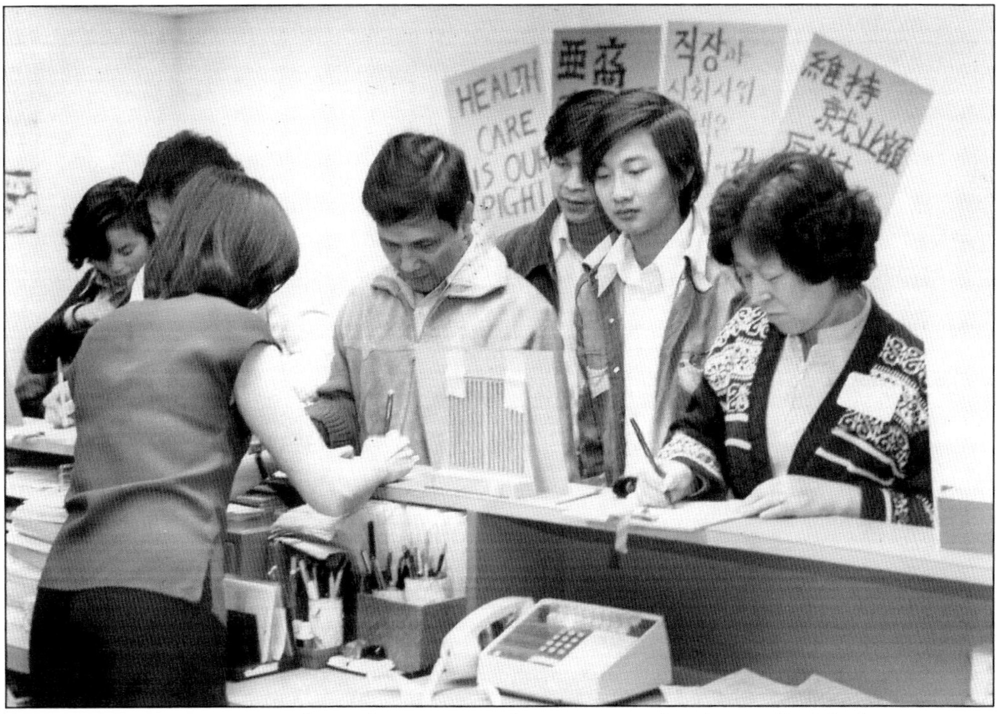

Clients line up to register for information and services at the Asian Health Services new building at Eighth and Webster Streets. (Courtesy of Asian Health Services.)

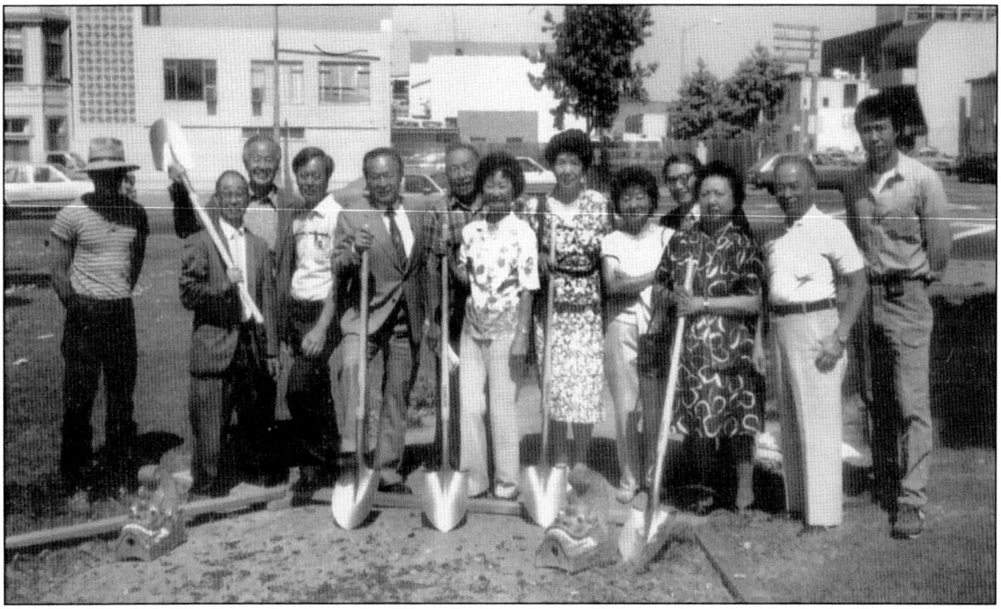

Homer Lee (second from left) led the Chinese Garden project at Harrison Railroad Park at Seventh and Harrison Streets. Others participating in the 1986 project ground-breaking are (from left to right) unidentified, Woon Lam (third from left), Bo Gin, Elwood OwYang, unidentified, Mabel Lee, Mrs. Elwood OwYang, Marion Fong, Dr. Clifton Fong, Helen OwYang, Calvin OwYang, and unidentified. (Courtesy of Homer Lee.)

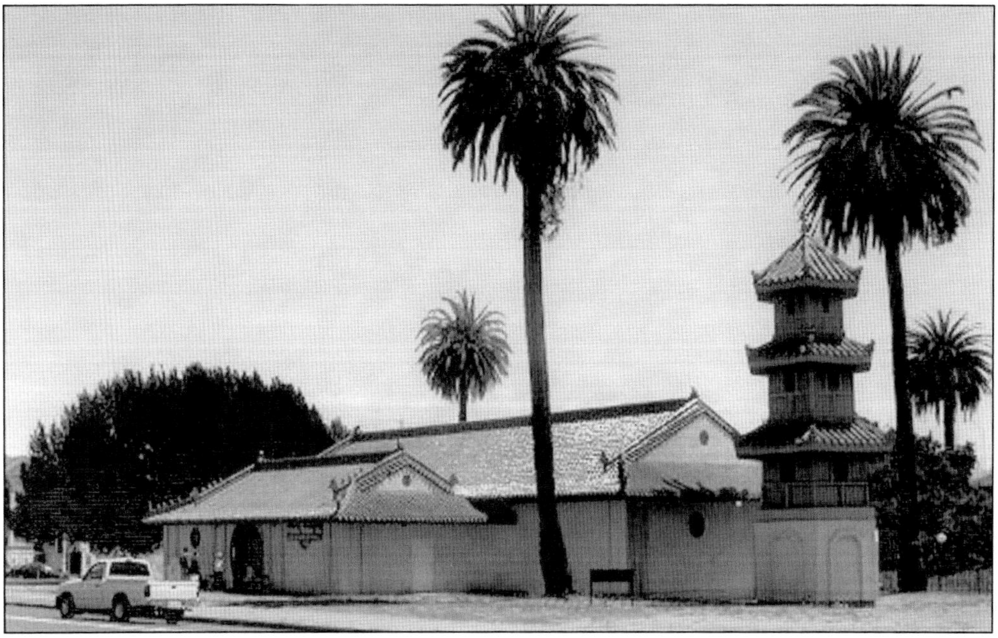

The Chinese Garden project, designed by Henry Chang, features a Hall of Pioneers and Sun Yat Sen Memorial Hall, along with a pagoda, on the right, at Seventh and Harrison Streets in what was once called Harrison Railroad Park. The hall serves as a senior care facility, but is also a general-purpose social hall. The Oakland Chinese Consolidated Association and the Oakland Chinatown Lion's Club sponsored the project. (Courtesy of Henry Chang.)

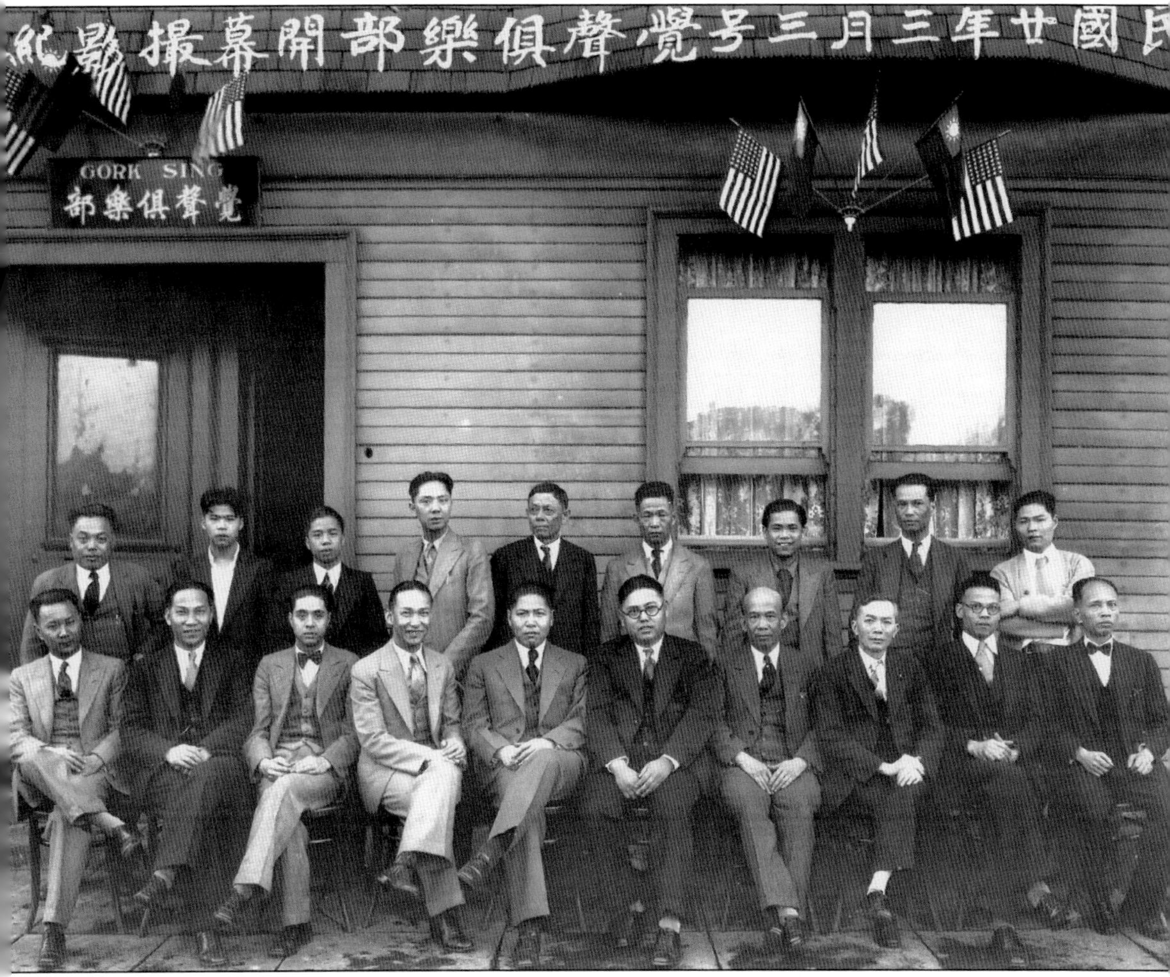

The Gork Sing Musical Social Club had its grand opening meeting on Harrison Street, around the corner from Eighth Street, in this 1931 photo. Art Tom's father, Tom Lung, is in the front row, third from the right. Art Wong, a prominent Chinatown businessman, is seated in the front row, fifth from the left. The other men are unidentified. (Courtesy of Art Tom.)

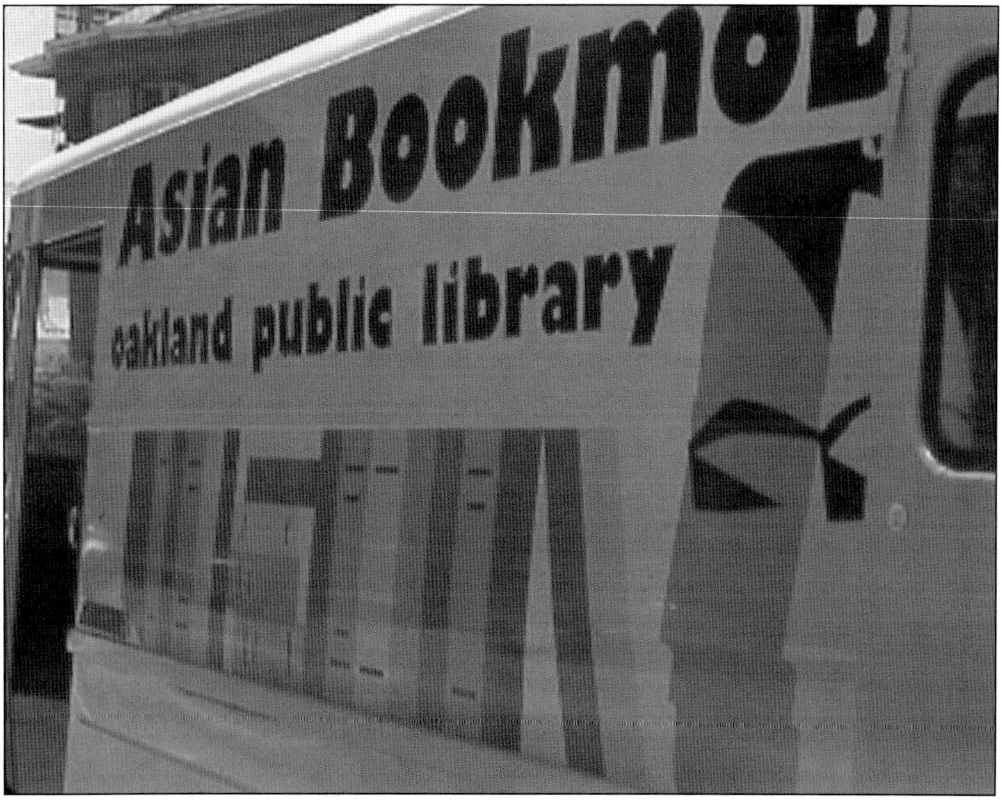

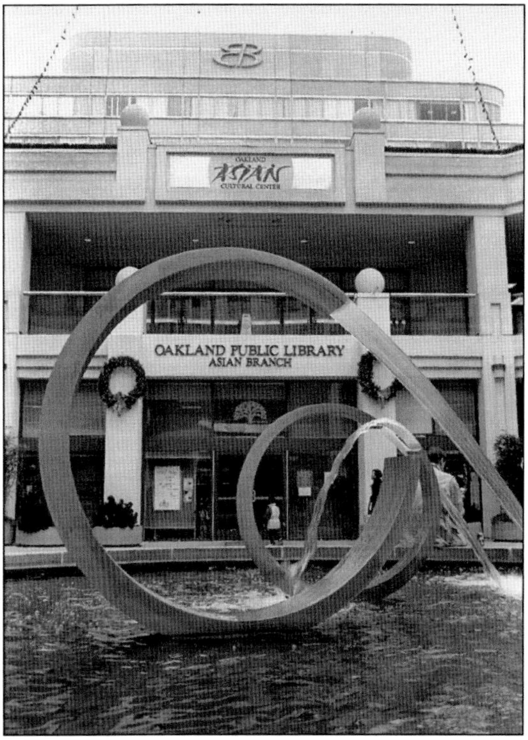

The Asian Branch of the Oakland Public Library began as a bookmobile in 1975. It then moved into the Park Boulevard branch. In 1981, it moved to Chinatown and finally into its ground-floor space in the Pacific Renaissance Plaza in 1995. It is the busiest branch in the city's library system with its collection of works in many different Asian languages. (Photo by and courtesy of Russell Lowe.)

Inside the Pacific Renaissance Plaza are two cultural pillars of contemporary Chinatown, the Oakland Asian Cultural Center (second floor) and the Asian Branch of the Oakland Public Library. (Photo by and courtesy of Kathy Sloane.)

An unidentified woman studies a book of Chinese jade sculptures in the Asian Branch Library. (Photo by and courtesy of Kathy Sloane.)

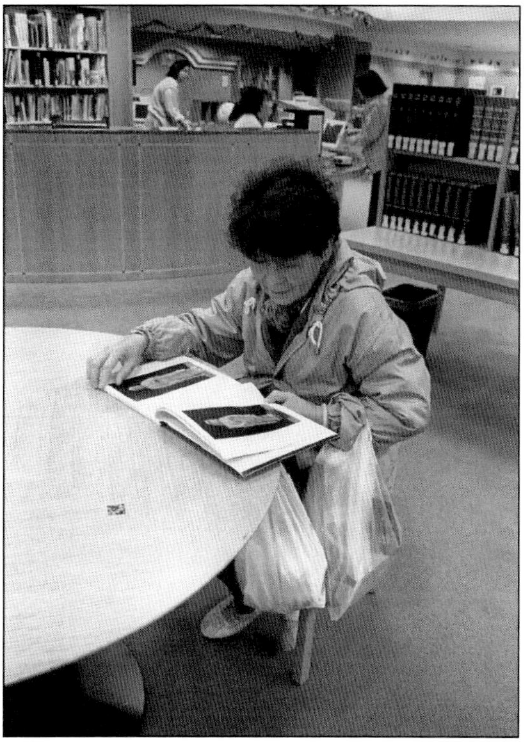

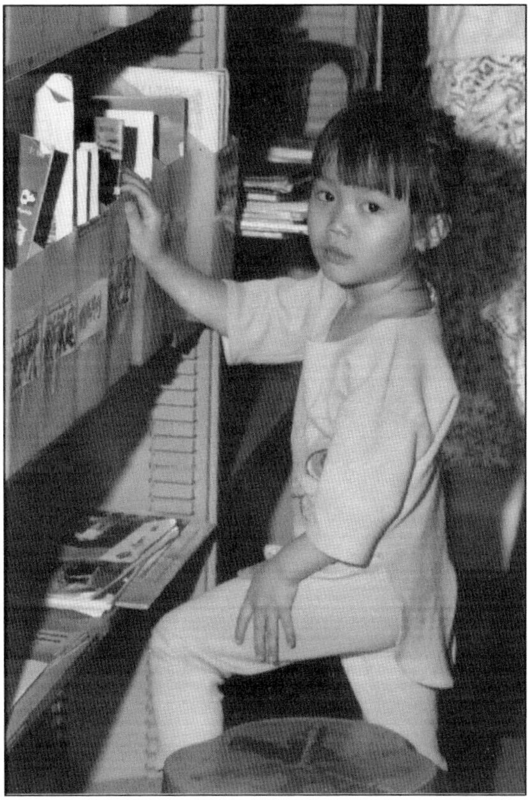

An unidentified girl looks for a book at the Asian Branch Library. (Photo by and courtesy of Henry Woon.)

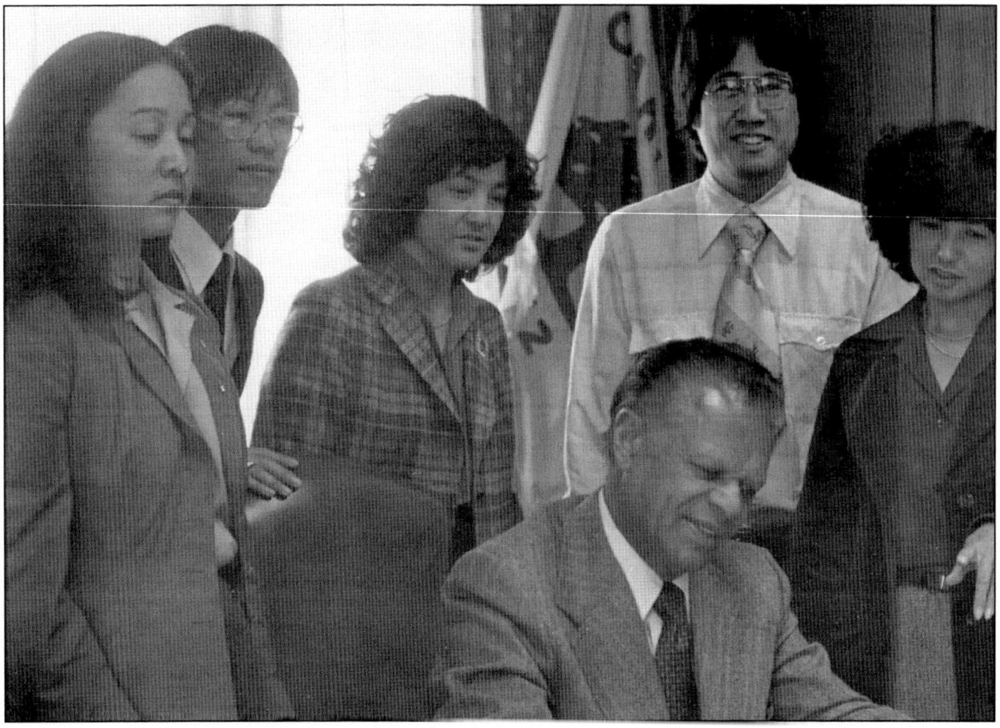

Oakland Mayor Lionel Wilson signs a local declaration of Asian Pacific Heritage Week in the late 1970s or early 1980s, celebrated at the Oakland Museum of California. Community members included, from left to right, unidentified, Greg Chew, Nellie Wong, unidentified, and Leslie Yee. (Courtesy of William Wong.)

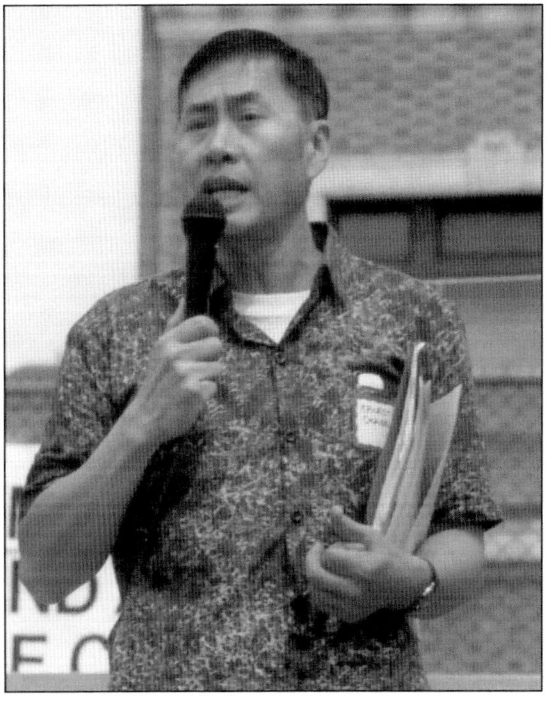

Ernest Chann, a community historian and volunteer, speaks at the 1988 Mid-Autumn Festival in Lincoln Square, under the auspices of the yet-to-be-built Oakland Asian Cultural Center. Chann has long been active as a volunteer at the Oakland Museum of California and the Asian Branch library. (Courtesy of East Bay Asian Local Development Corporation.)

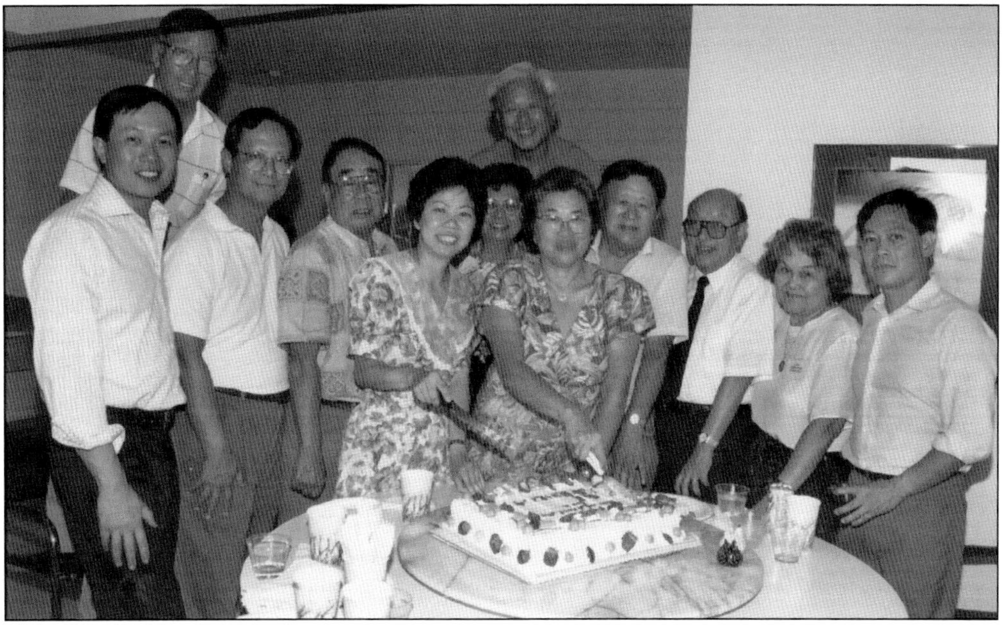

Leaders and volunteers celebrate at the Oakland Asian Cultural Center in the early 1990s. From left to right, they are (front row) Alan Yee, Yui Hay Lee, Frank Ogawa, Josephine Hui, Beatrice Wong, Mary Mar, Howard Ah-Tye, Peter Chan, Ivy Down, and unidentified; (back row), Dick Young and John Sue. (Photo by and courtesy of Henry Woon.)

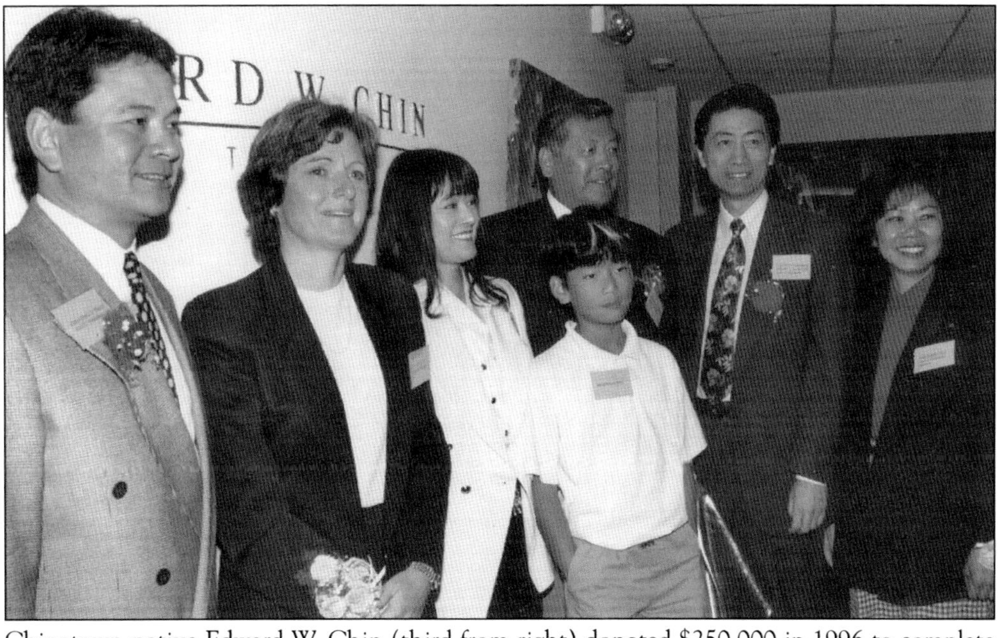

Chinatown native Edward W. Chin (third from right) donated $250,000 in 1996 to complete the multipurpose room of the Oakland Asian Cultural Center. Chin has been a successful businessman and philanthropist. Also pictured in this dedication of the Edward W. Chin multipurpose room are, from left to right, Chuong Tran, unidentified, Yuri Chin, Chin, and their son Bradley, Oakland City Councilman Henry Chang, and Josephine Hui, executive director of the center. (Courtesy of Oakland Asian Cultural Center.)

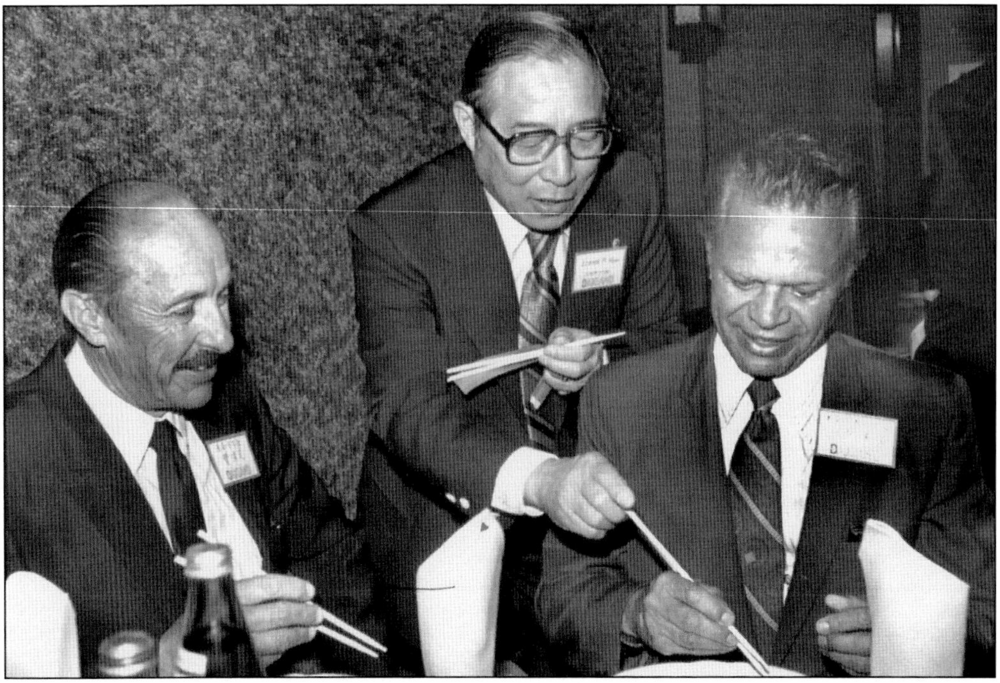

Edward B. Wong shows Oakland Mayor John Reading and Mayor-elect Lionel Wilson how to use chopsticks in 1977. Wong led efforts to redevelop the Chinatown core after World War II. He ran a small business services company, was the first Chinese American city planning commissioner, and was active in numerous Chinatown organizations. (Courtesy of the Oakland Tribune Collection, the Oakland Museum of California, Gift of Alameda Newspaper Group.)

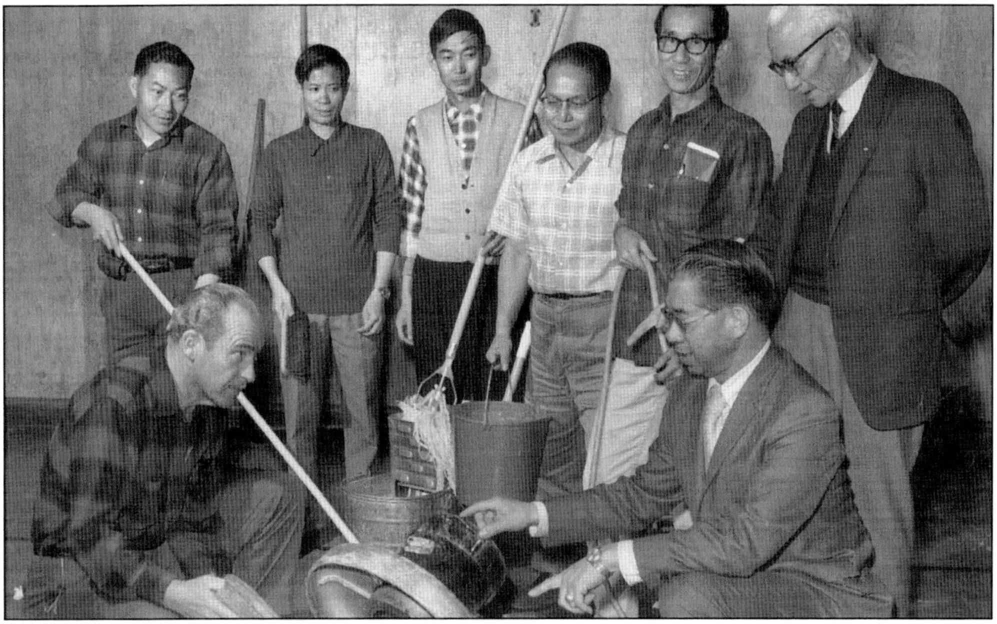

Community leader Dr. Raymond Eng (kneeling at right), who became the first Chinese American to serve on the Oakland City Council, started a job-training program for Chinese immigrants in the 1960s. (Courtesy of Weylin Eng.)

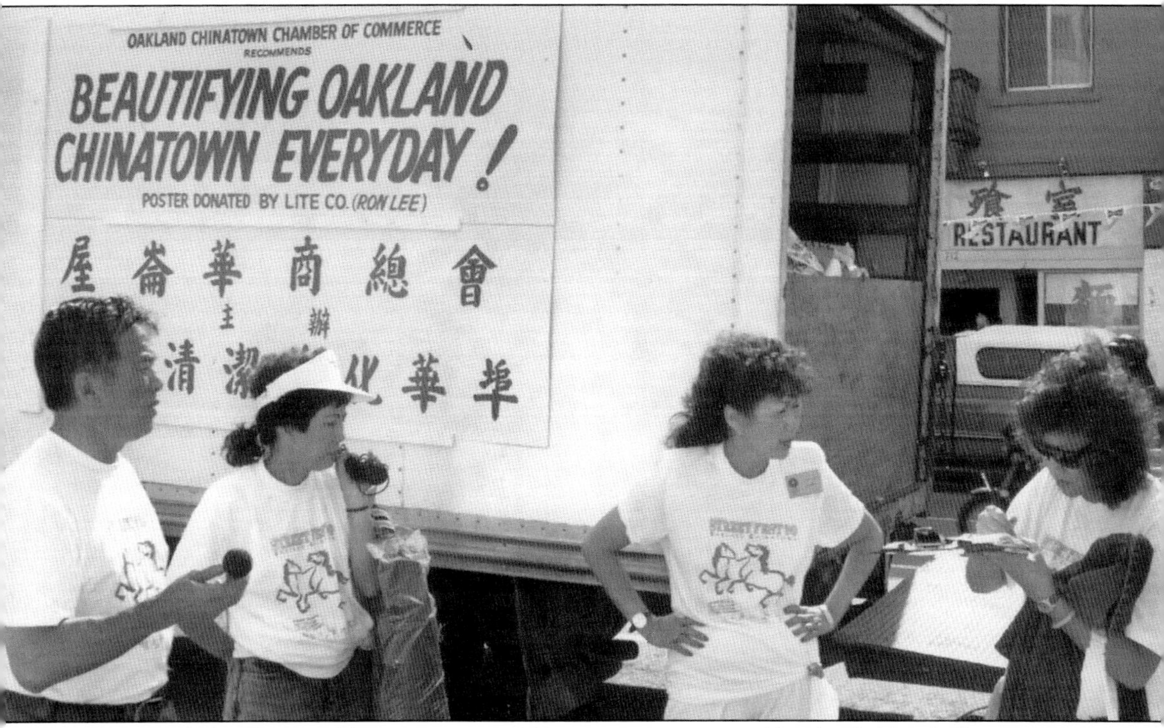

Volunteers help clean up Chinatown in a 1990 campaign sponsored by the Oakland Chinatown Chamber of Commerce. They are, from left to right, Bill Louie, Jane Wong, Tere Lee, and Venetia Young. (Photo by and courtesy of Henry Woon.)

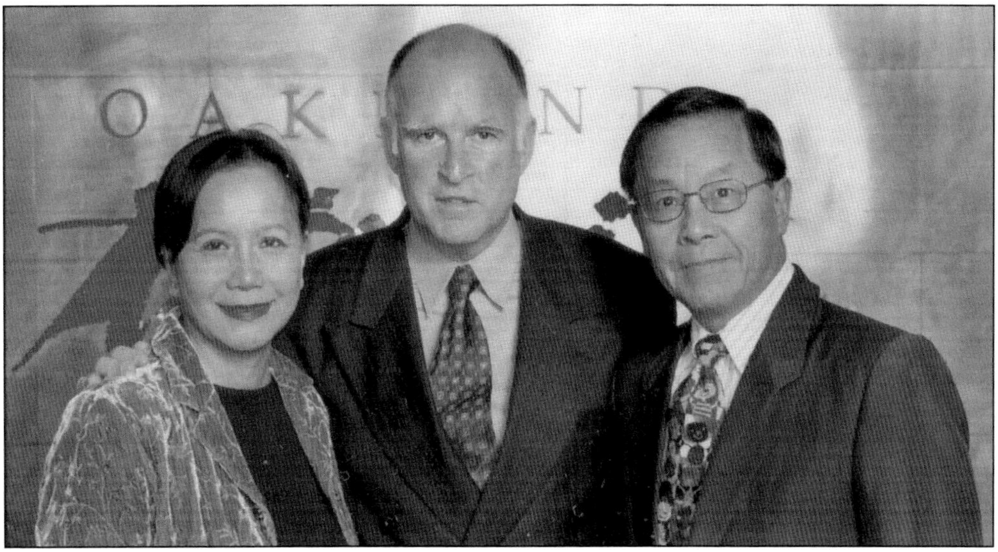

Jennie and George Ong, with Mayor Jerry Brown in this 2001 photo, have long been Chinatown business and community leaders. She is executive director of the Oakland Chinatown Chamber of Commerce and he is an attorney, businessman, volunteer, and activist with the chamber and other organizations. The chamber started the StreetFest, which began in 1988 and draws thousands of visitors to Chinatown on the last weekend of August. (Courtesy of George Ong.)

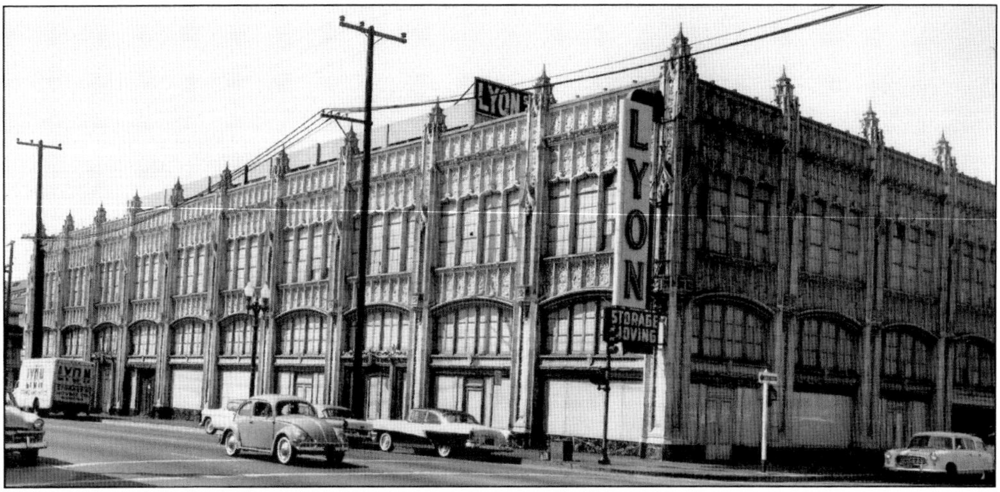

The East Bay Asian Local Development Corporation (EBALDC) began to renovate the old Lyons Storage Building at Harrison and Ninth Street, shown in this 1958 photo, into the Asian Resource Center for nonprofit social service agencies in the late 1970s. It was the first of many projects of EBALDC, a nationally recognized organization. (Photo by the Downtown Property Owners Association, courtesy of the Oakland Public Library.)

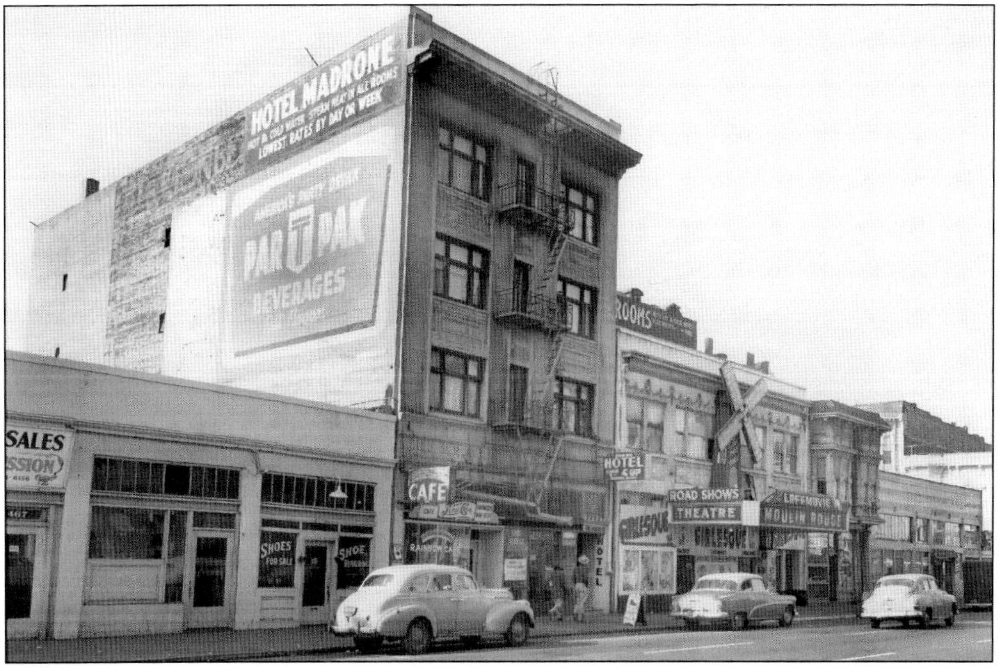

The tall building on the south side of Eighth Street between Washington Street and Broadway, shown in this 1958 photo, is the Madrone Hotel. It adjoined the notorious Moulin Rouge, a former strip joint. EBALDC renovated the Madrone into a single-room-occupancy residence for low-income people. The Moulin Rouge no longer exists. (Photo by the Downtown Property Owners Association, courtesy of the Oakland Public Library.)

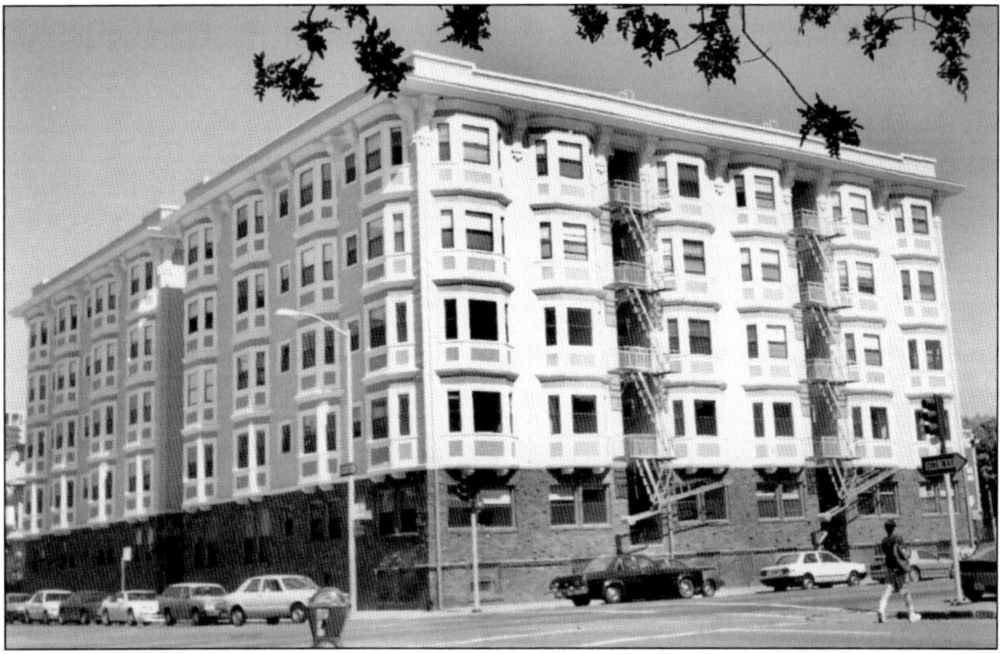

The Madison Square Apartments at Madison and Ninth Streets was also rehabilitated by EBALDC into affordable housing units. (Courtesy of EBALDC.)

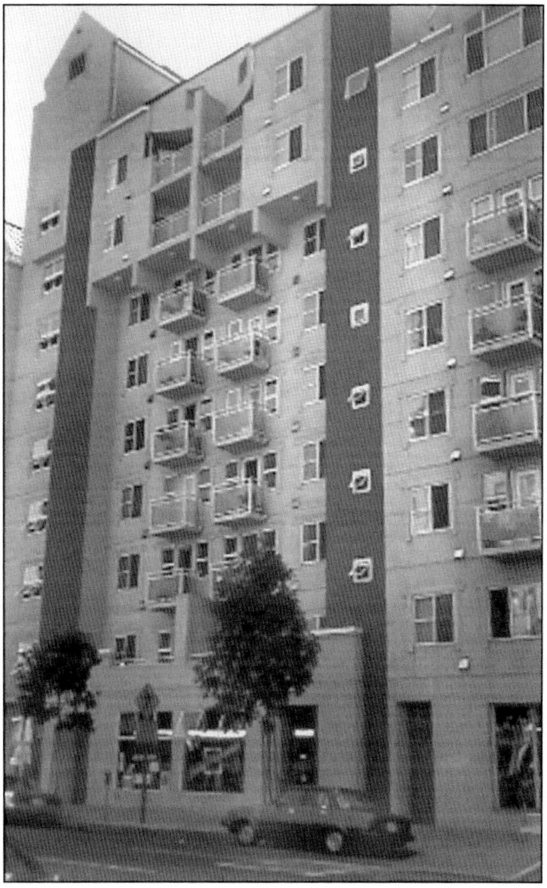

The Frank Mar Community Housing Project at Thirteenth and Harrison Streets, named after the late Presbyterian minister and community activist, is also an EBALDC project. (Photo by and courtesy of Ernest Chann.)

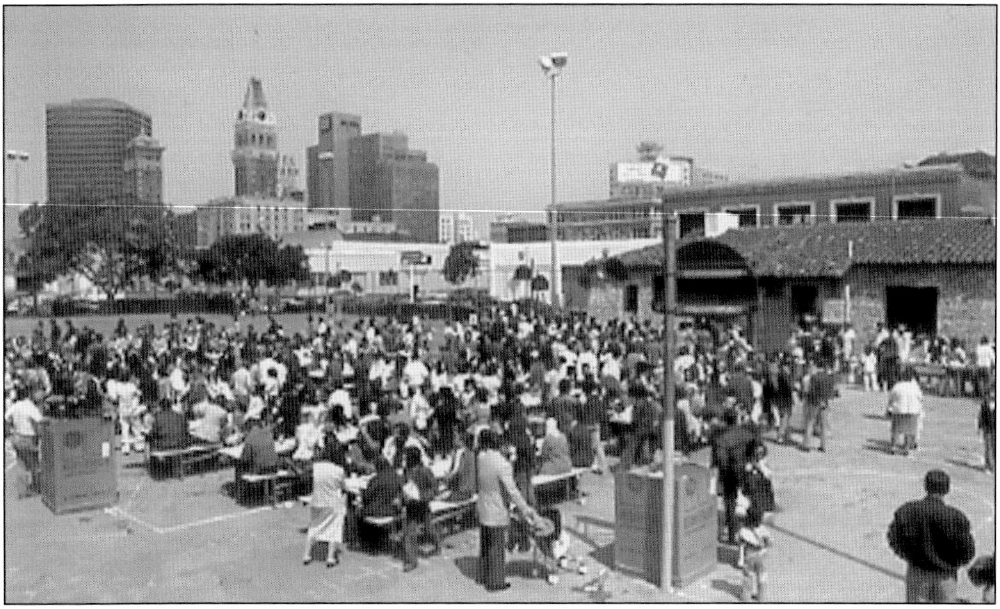

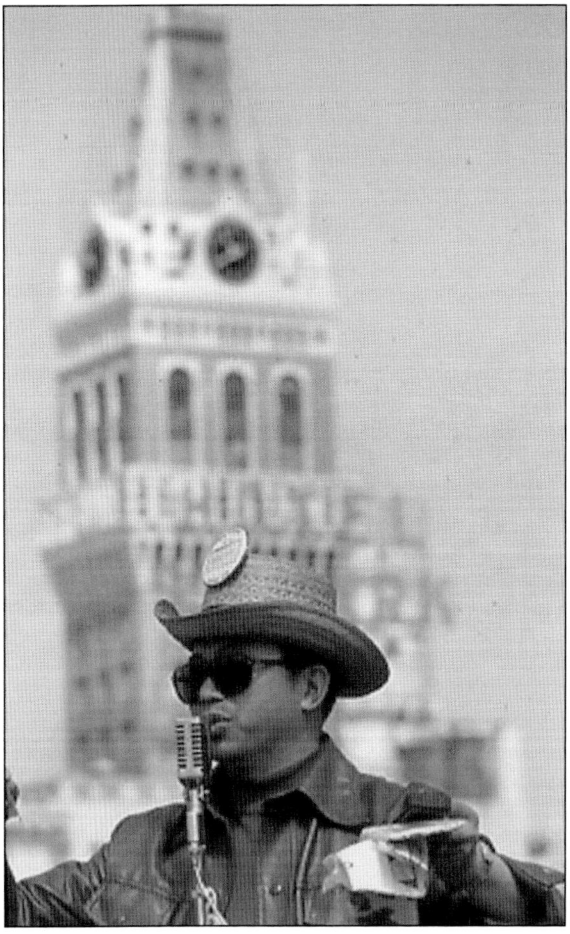

Since 1956, the Wa Sung Community Service Club has sponsored the popular Easter Pancake Breakfast in Lincoln Square. Hundreds of Oakland Chinese and their relatives and friends gather every Easter Sunday morning for this special Chinatown event. Here is an overview of the pancake breakfast in the late 1970s. (Photo by and courtesy of Russell Lowe.)

Dr. Kenneth Hoh was an optometrist and community leader with Wa Sung Community Service Club and other organizations in the late 1970s. (Photo by and courtesy of Russell Lowe.)

The Wa Sung Community Service Club raised funds to construct the Oakland Chinatown Playground Project in Lincoln Square in 1969. The main feature is a replica of a Chinese junk boat that generations of young children have enjoyed. (Courtesy of Wa Sung Community Service Club.)

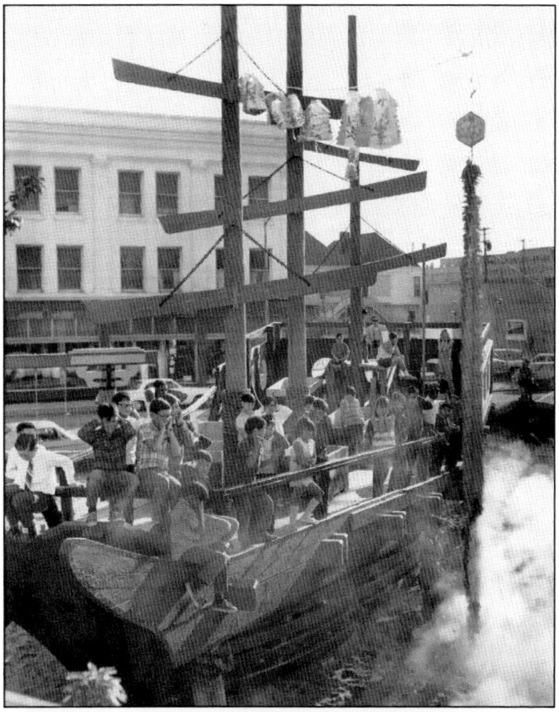

Howard Ah-Tye was a community historian and volunteer with organizations like Wa Sung Community Service Club. He served on an Oakland Chinatown history committee headed by Rev. Frank Mar in the 1970s. Ah-Tye, who grew up in Stockton but lived in Oakland for more than 60 years, wrote prolifically about Chinese Americans and Oakland Chinatown. The Chinese Presbyterian Church published his articles under the title, *Resourceful Chinese*. (Courtesy of Valerie Fintel.)

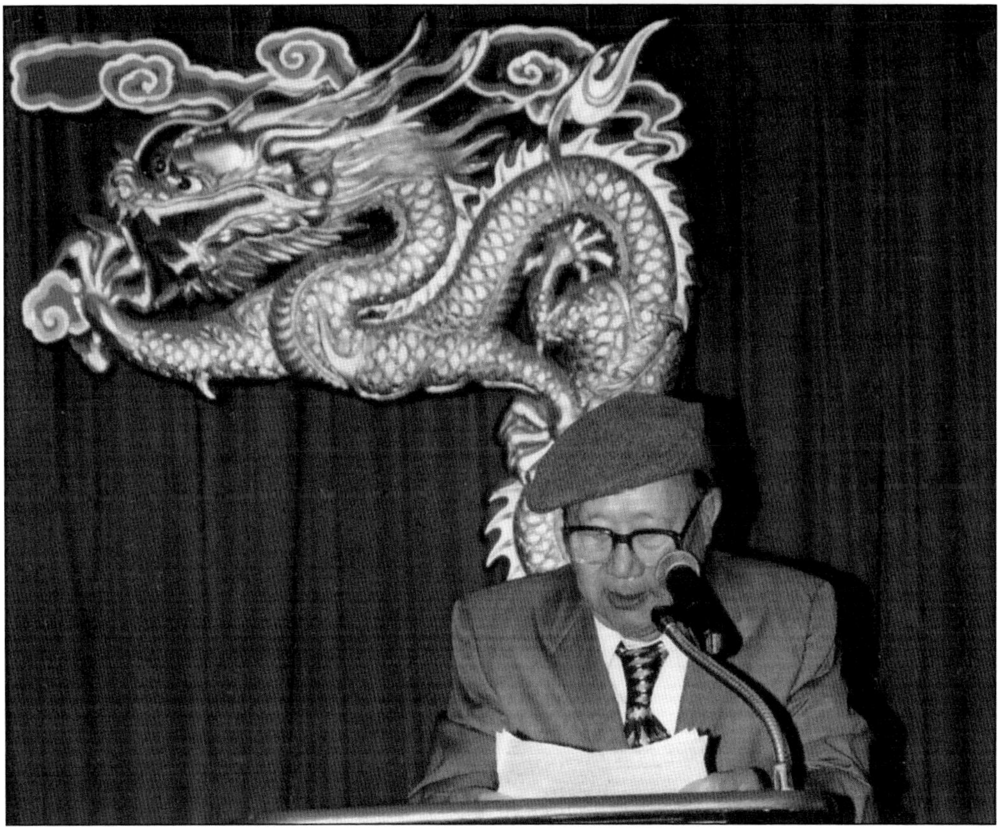

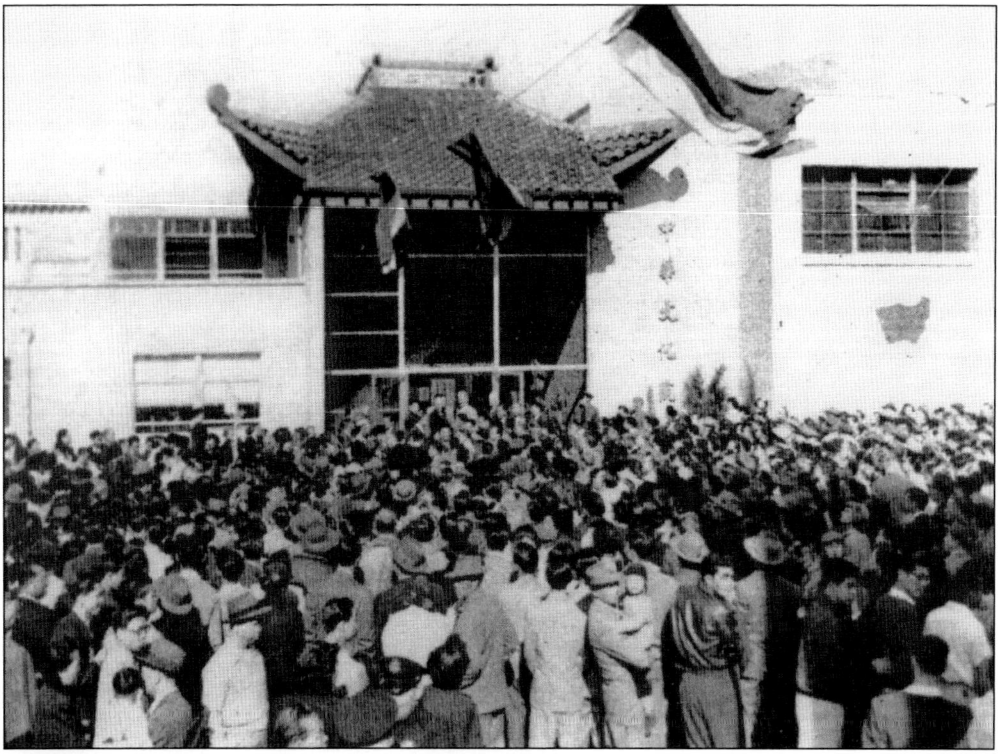

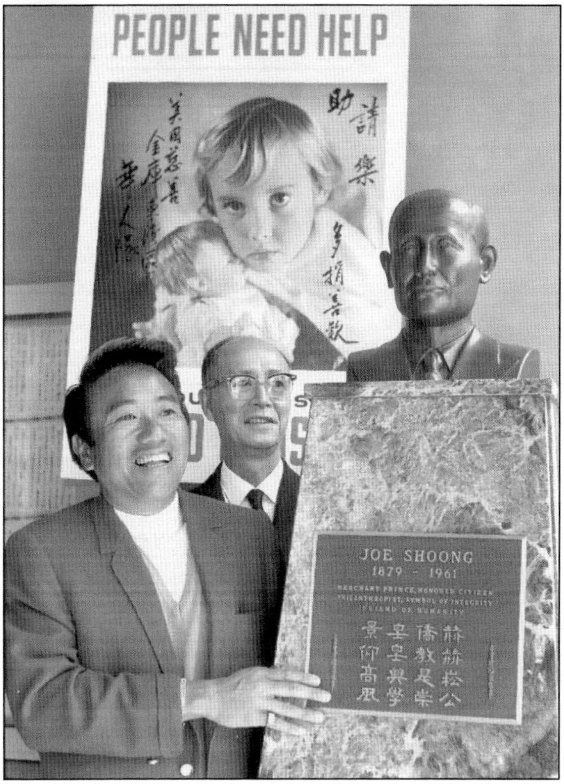

A huge crowd gathered for the grand opening of the Oakland Chinese Community Center at Ninth and Harrison Streets in 1953. Joe Shoong, founder of the National Dollar Stores, supported the center's construction, along with many Chinatown groups and individuals. The center holds Chinese school classes, among other activities. (Courtesy of the Oakland Public Library.)

Milton Shoong contributed $1,000 in his father Joe Shoong's name to the United Bay Area Crusade in 1967. Andrew Lowe (behind Shoong) accepted the donation as chairman of the United Bay Area Crusade for the Oakland Chinese community. (Courtesy of the Oakland Tribune Collection, the Oakland Museum of California, Gift of Alameda Newspaper Group.)

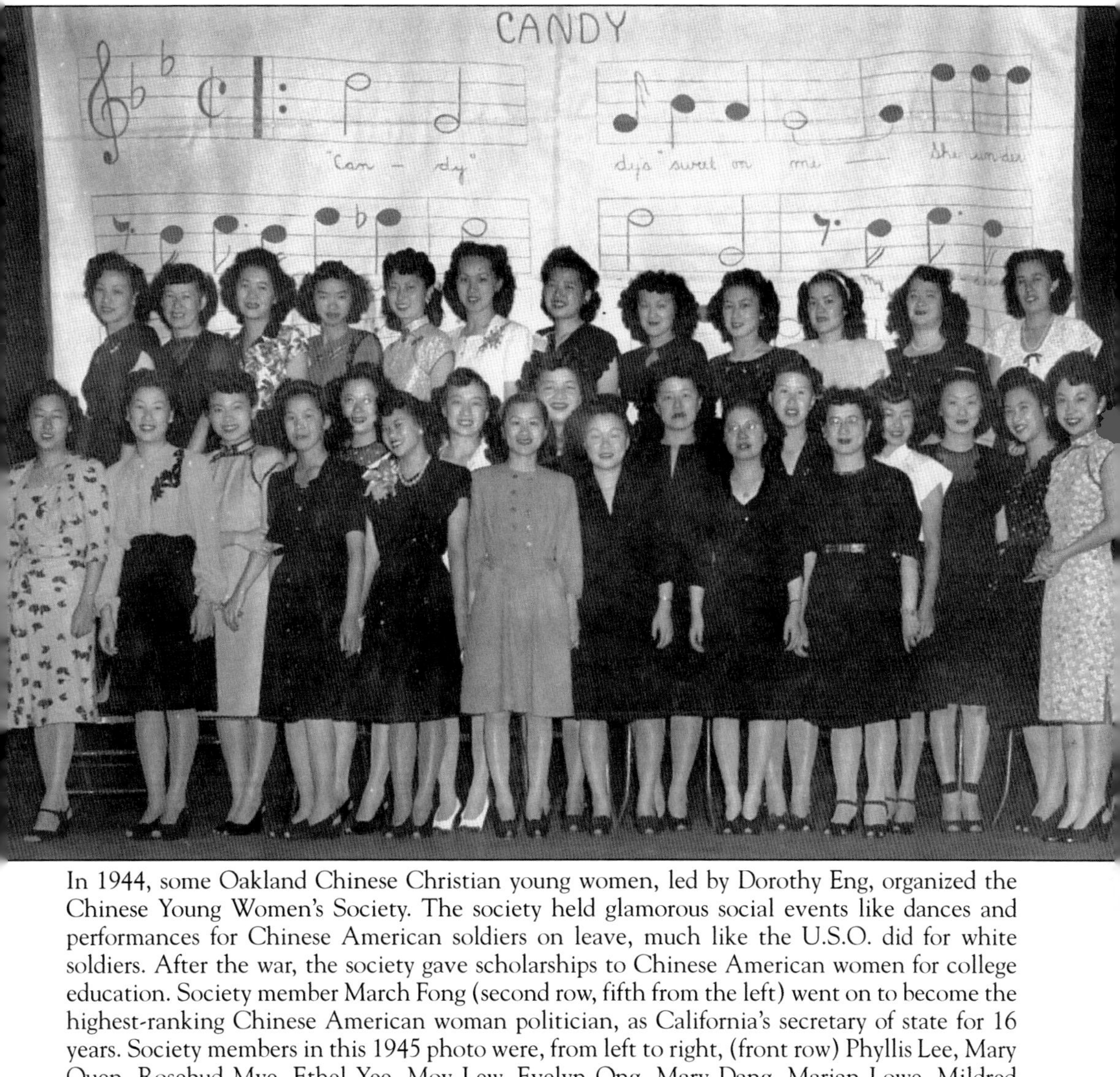

In 1944, some Oakland Chinese Christian young women, led by Dorothy Eng, organized the Chinese Young Women's Society. The society held glamorous social events like dances and performances for Chinese American soldiers on leave, much like the U.S.O. did for white soldiers. After the war, the society gave scholarships to Chinese American women for college education. Society member March Fong (second row, fifth from the left) went on to become the highest-ranking Chinese American woman politician, as California's secretary of state for 16 years. Society members in this 1945 photo were, from left to right, (front row) Phyllis Lee, Mary Quen, Rosebud Mye, Ethel Yee, Moy Lew, Evelyn Ong, Mary Dang, Marian Lowe, Mildred Chang, Elizabeth Tom, Agnes Chang, Lillian Tom, Ruth Lew, Emma Wong, Daisy Fong, Sue Chuck, Patricia Lee, and Eugenia Mye; (back row) Inez Wong, Evelyn Lee, Anna Lee, Frances Chop, March Fong, Rosalie Wong, unidentified, Captoria Lee, Helen Yuen, Amy Chew, Rhoda Quan, and unidentified. (Courtesy of Dorothy Eng.)

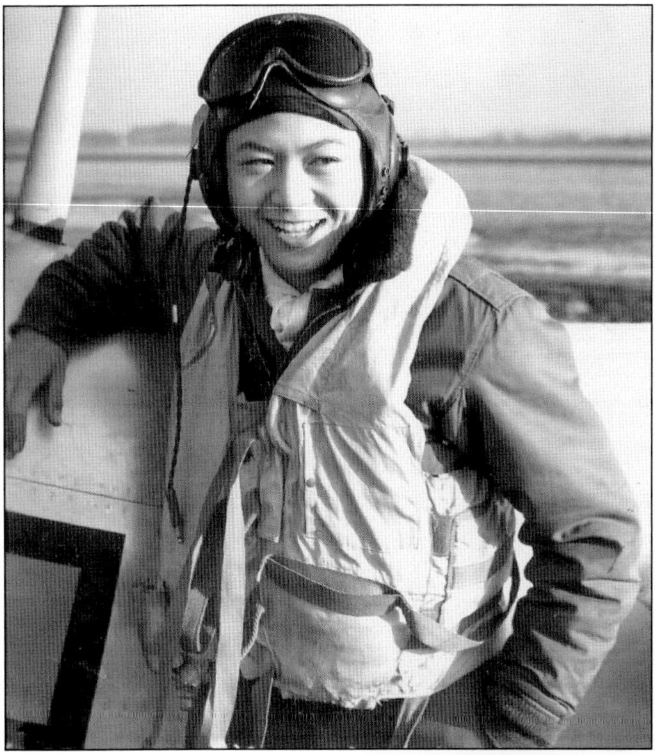

Arthur Wong Jr. of Oakland served during World War II. (Courtesy of the Oakland Tribune Collection, the Oakland Museum of California, Gift of Alameda Newspaper Group.)

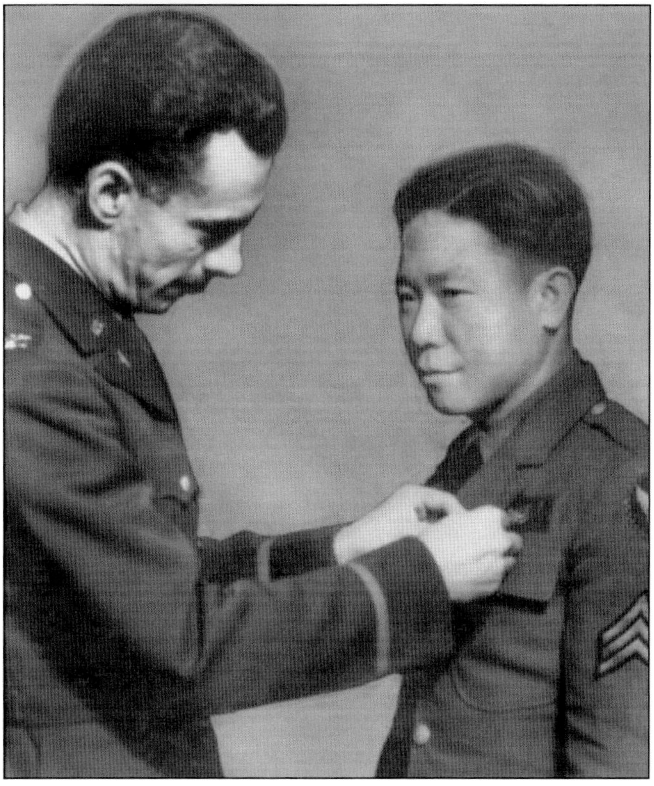

Sgt. Thomas Fong of Oakland received the Air Medal in 1944 for his service in bombing missions over Europe during World War II. (Courtesy of the Oakland Tribune Collection, the Oakland Museum of California, Gift of Alameda Newspaper Group.)

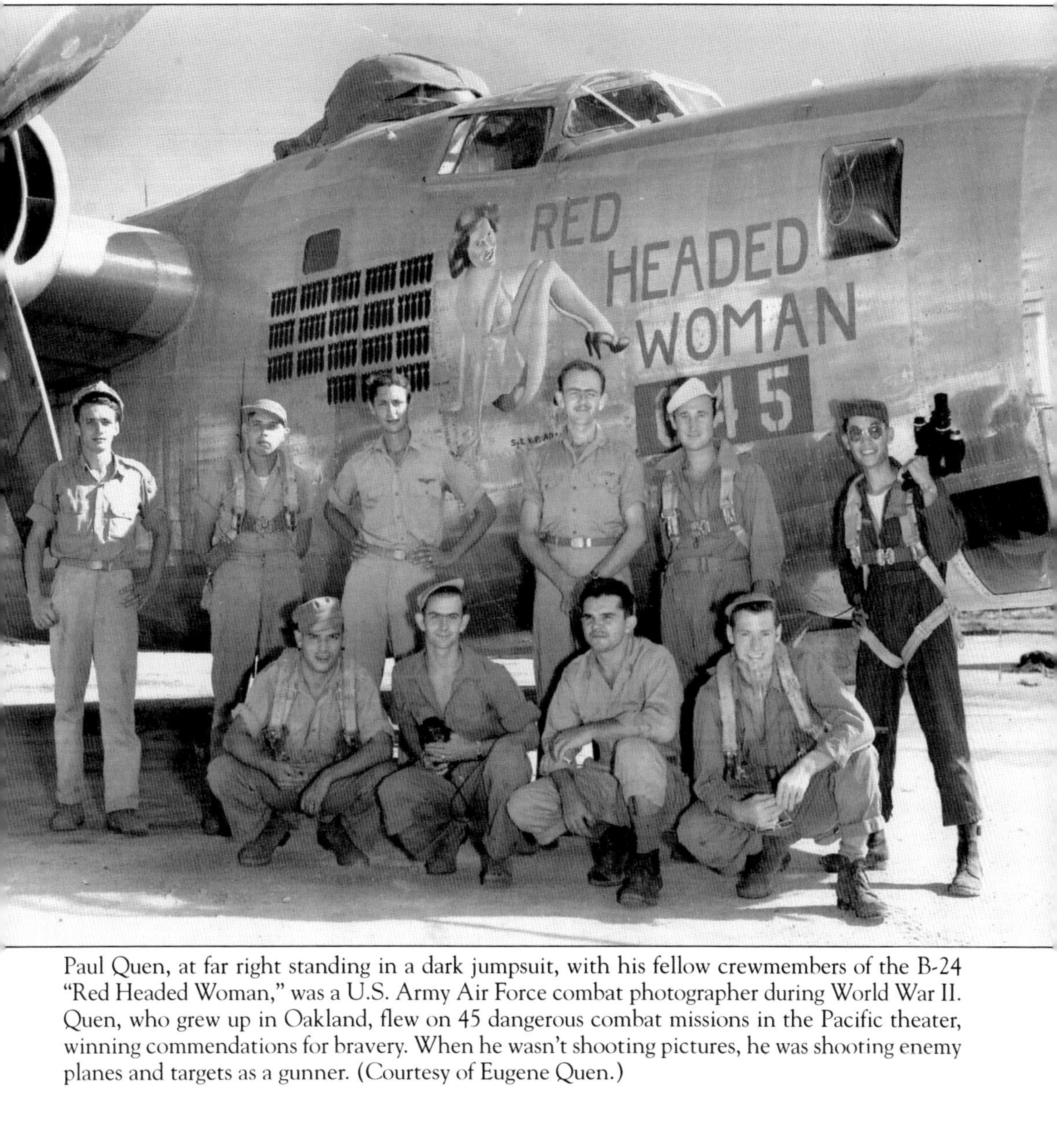

Paul Quen, at far right standing in a dark jumpsuit, with his fellow crewmembers of the B-24 "Red Headed Woman," was a U.S. Army Air Force combat photographer during World War II. Quen, who grew up in Oakland, flew on 45 dangerous combat missions in the Pacific theater, winning commendations for bravery. When he wasn't shooting pictures, he was shooting enemy planes and targets as a gunner. (Courtesy of Eugene Quen.)

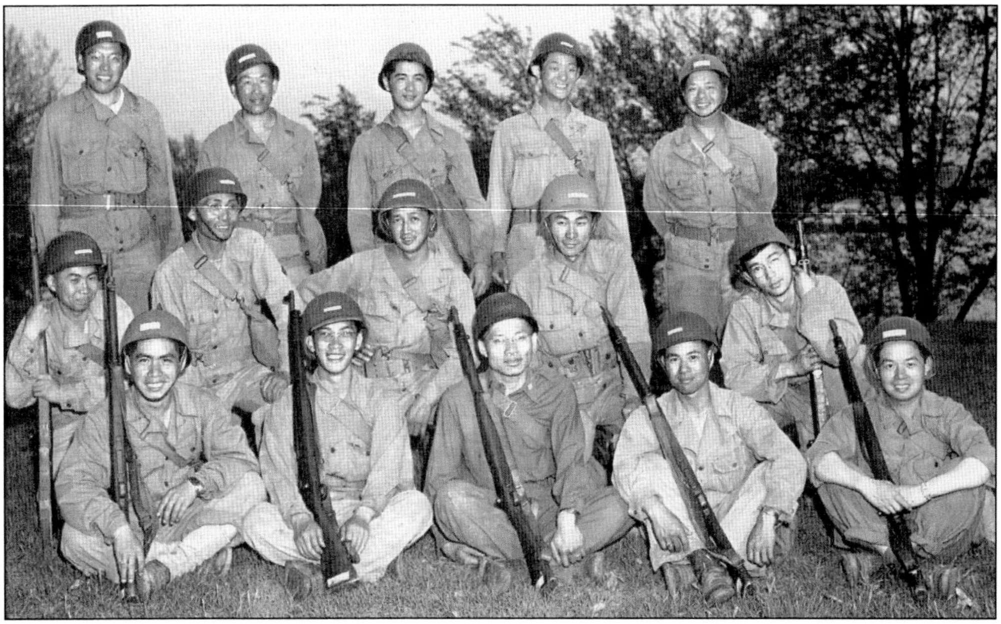

Richard Lee of Oakland is in the front row, far right, of this group of otherwise unidentified Bay Area Chinese American soldiers on an Army base during World War II. All cooked or cleaned latrines and lived in isolated barracks. Lee complained to his son that he and other Chinese American soldiers weren't allowed in combat. The weapons were for show only. (Courtesy of Lee Mun Wah.)

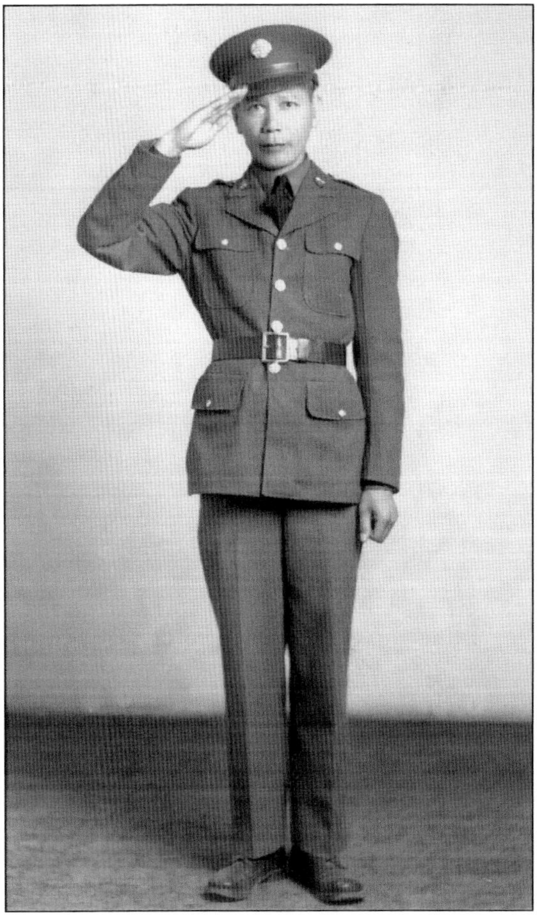

Jimmy Yuen of Oakland served in World War II. (Courtesy of May Young.)

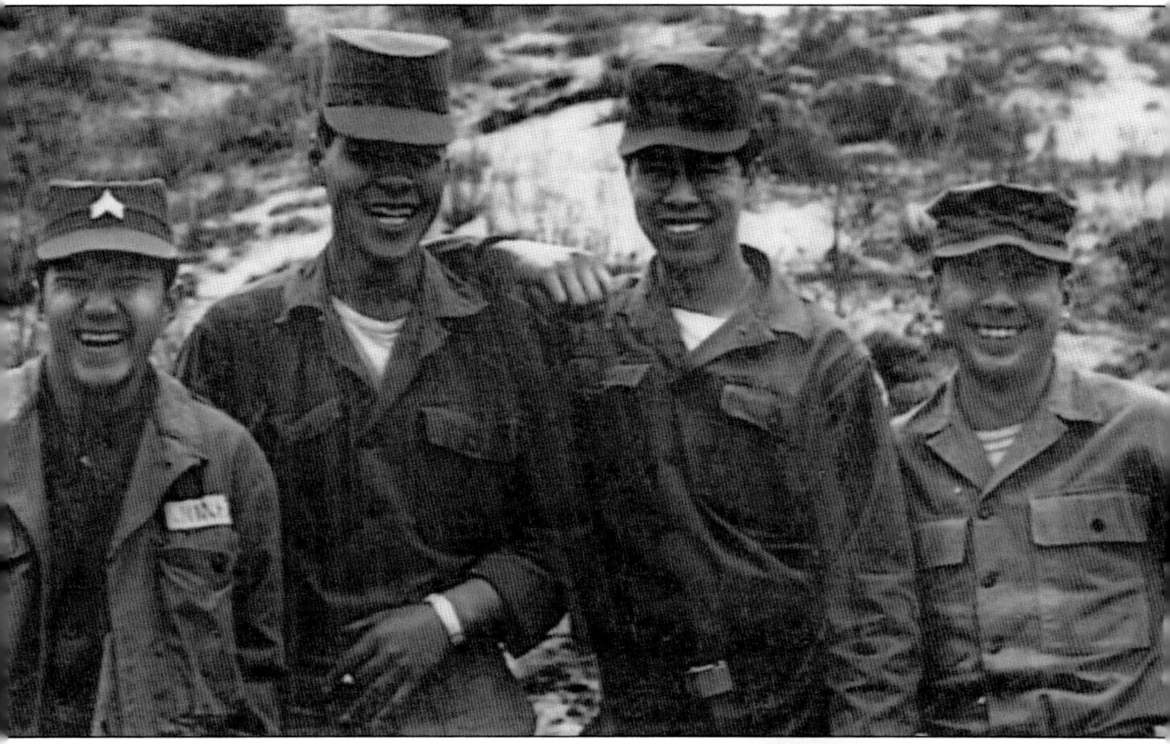

Four Oakland Chinatown men met in 1954 in the Chor Wan Valley of South Korea. From left to right, they are Gilbert Jone, Bob Lee, Al Look, and Art Fong. They served in different units but met after the conflict ended. The photographer was their Chinatown buddy, Jason Chan. (Courtesy of Art Fong.)

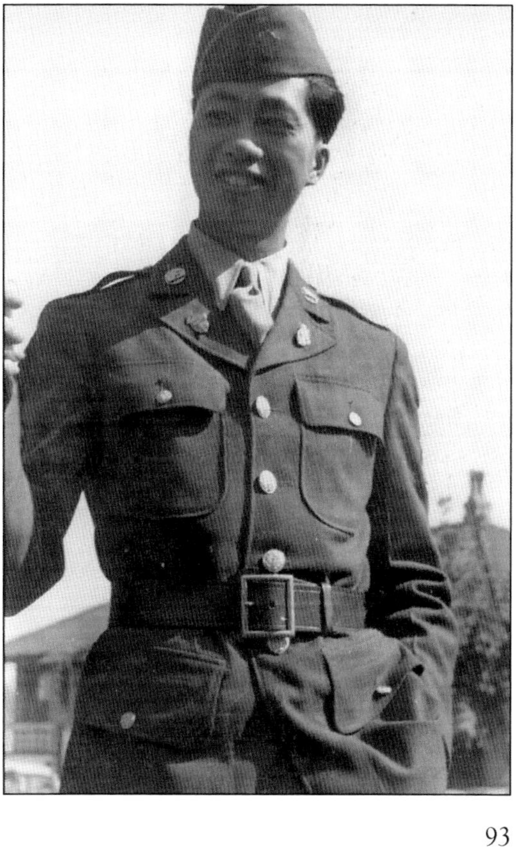

Corp. Frank Mar, who later became an activist Presbyterian minister and community leader in Chinatown, served in the U.S. Army during World War II. His military service came about 10 years after he emigrated from China. (Courtesy of Mary Mar.)

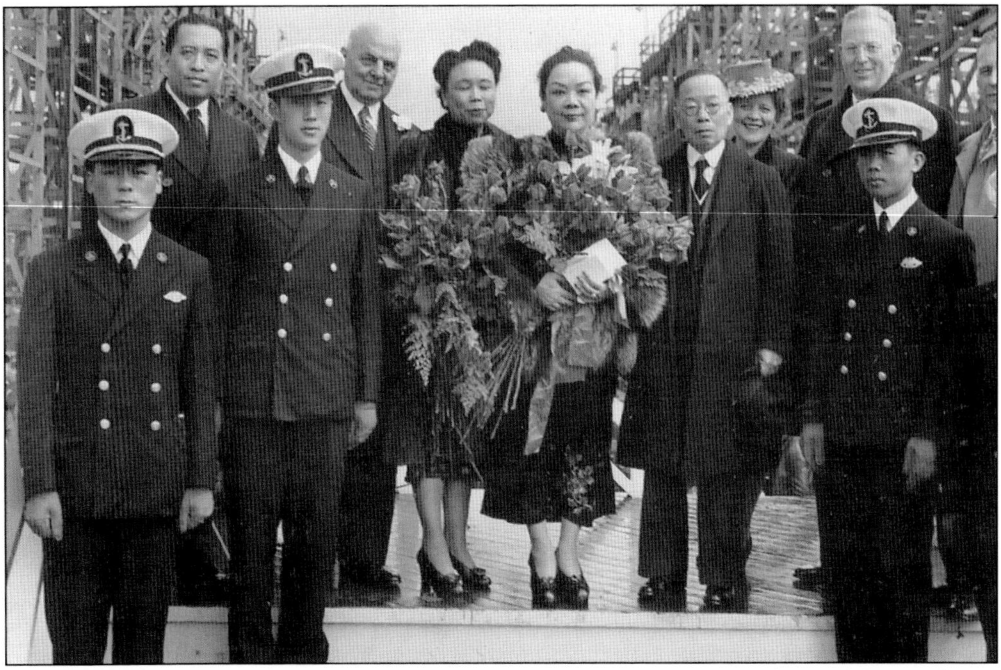

Merchant Marine Albert R. Wong (front row at left) and Dewey F. Wong (second from right, in uniform), both from Oakland, pose with dignitaries at the christening of the *Sun Yat Sen*, a new Liberty ship, in the 1940s. Also in the picture are California Governor Earl Warren (back row, second from right) and Mrs. Warren, to his right, and Madame Chiang Kai-shek, holding the bouquet. The others are unidentified. (Courtesy of Luella Mak.)

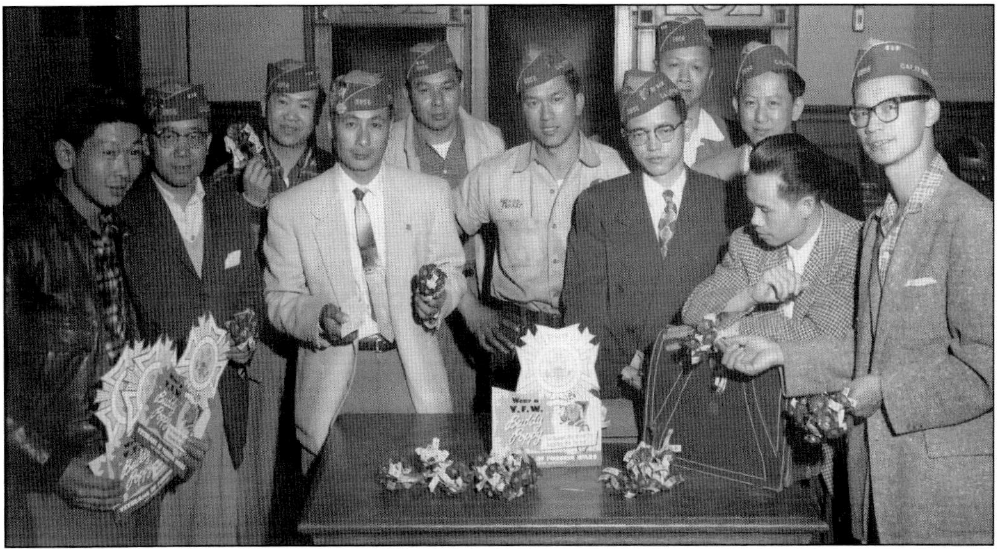

These members of Veterans of Foreign Wars, East Bay Chinatown Post 3956, were all Oakland Chinatown men, who served in World War II. In this May 22, 1959 photo they are, from left to right, Kenneth Chin, Richard Moy, Harry Soo Hoo, Lloyd Jang, Henry Ow Yang, Bill Louie, Richard Wong, Harry Wong, Alfred Chan, Charles Chinn, and John Gee Wong. They were raising funds to help families of needy veterans by selling golden poppies. Photo by and courtesy of Henry Woon.)

Four

POLITICS AND ACTIVISM

Chinese Americans are often thought to be politically apathetic. That has not been the case with some Oakland Chinese. Political activism of one sort or another, from speaking out publicly against injustice to winning elected office, has been a hallmark for Oakland Chinese.

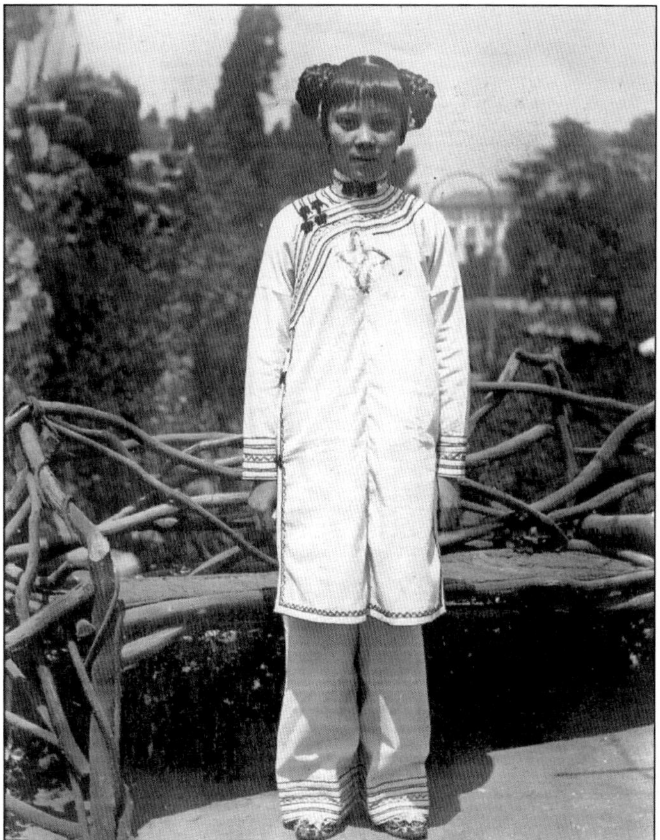

Emma Hoo Tom was one of two Oakland Chinese American women to be the first of their race and gender to register to vote in the United States. She achieved that in 1911, when she was 22 years old. The other woman was Clara Chan Lee, wife of pioneering Oakland dentist Dr. Charles Lee. Their history-making activism came at a time when American women had just won voting rights. Their husbands, who were active in the Native Sons of the Golden State (later called the Chinese American Citizens Alliance), were said to have encouraged the two women to break new ground. They could register to vote because they were born in the United States and thus were citizens. (Courtesy of Art Tom.)

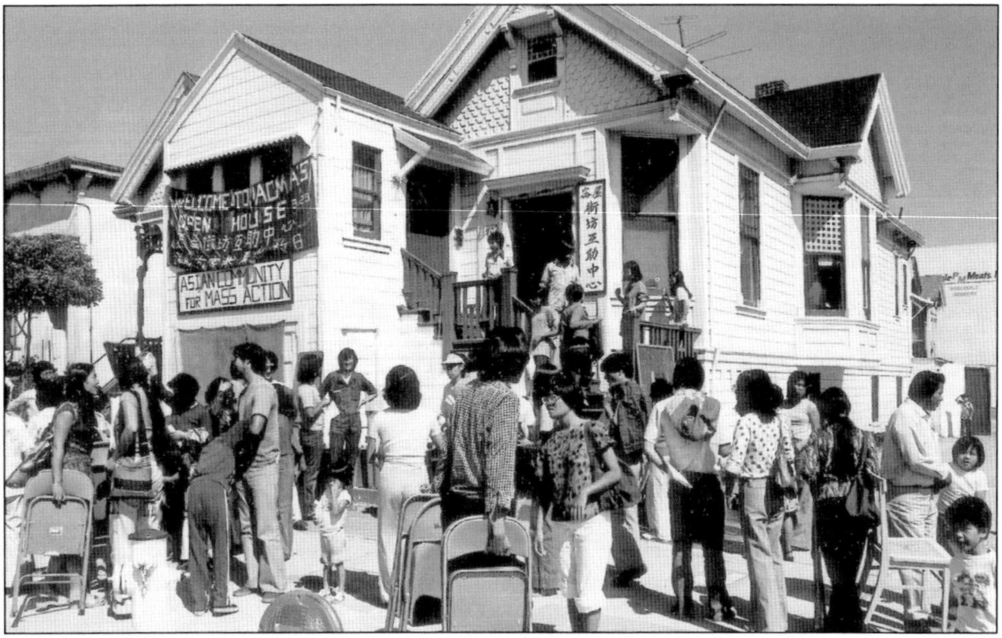

Asian Community for Mass Action, shown organizing in front of house on Alice Street between Seventh and Eighth Streets in the mid-1970s, was one of several progressive organizations that formed in the late 1960s and 1970s. They addressed emerging Chinatown issues such as gangs, youth employment, citizenship for immigrants, and bilingual services. Some organizers later went on to social-service work in the community, others became academics and professionals. (Photo by and courtesy of Russell Lowe.)

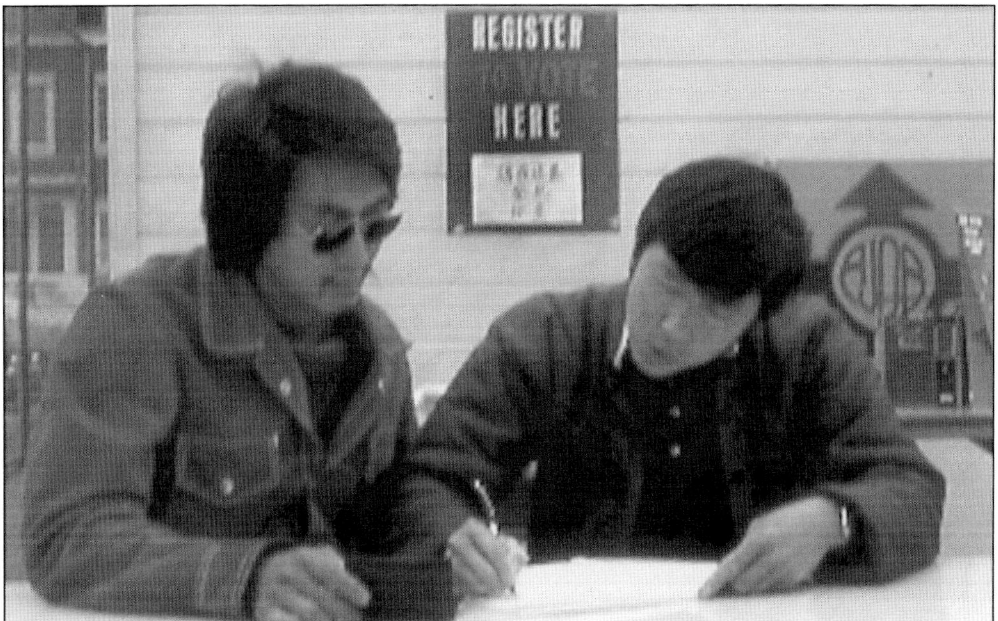

Russell Lowe (right) helps an unidentified man register to vote in the late 1970s in Lincoln Square. Today, Lowe is a San Francisco-based assistant to U.S. Senator Dianne Feinstein. (Courtesy of Russell Lowe.)

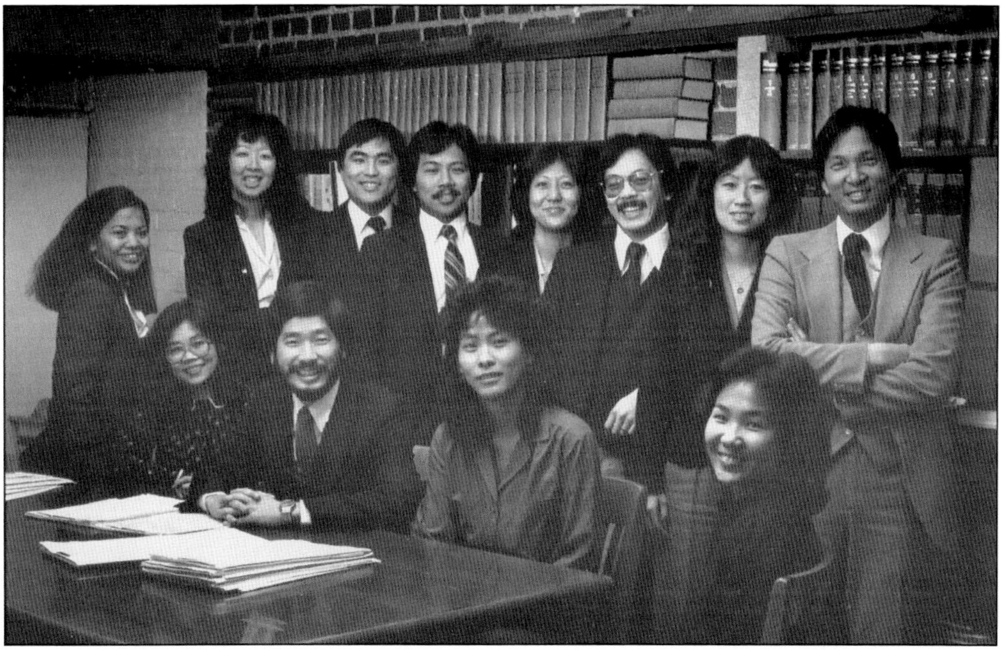

The Asian Law Caucus began in Oakland in the mid-1970s, providing legal services to low-income Asian immigrants. It later moved to San Francisco. Shown in this 1980s photo in Oakland are, from left to right, (front row) Madge Bello, Don Tamaki, Nancy Wong, and unidentified; (back row) Bobbie Camacho, Debbie Lim, Dennis Hayashi, Bill Tamayo, Joyce Matsumori, Ed Lee, Vicky Chin, and Gene Lam. (Courtesy of Asian Law Caucus.)

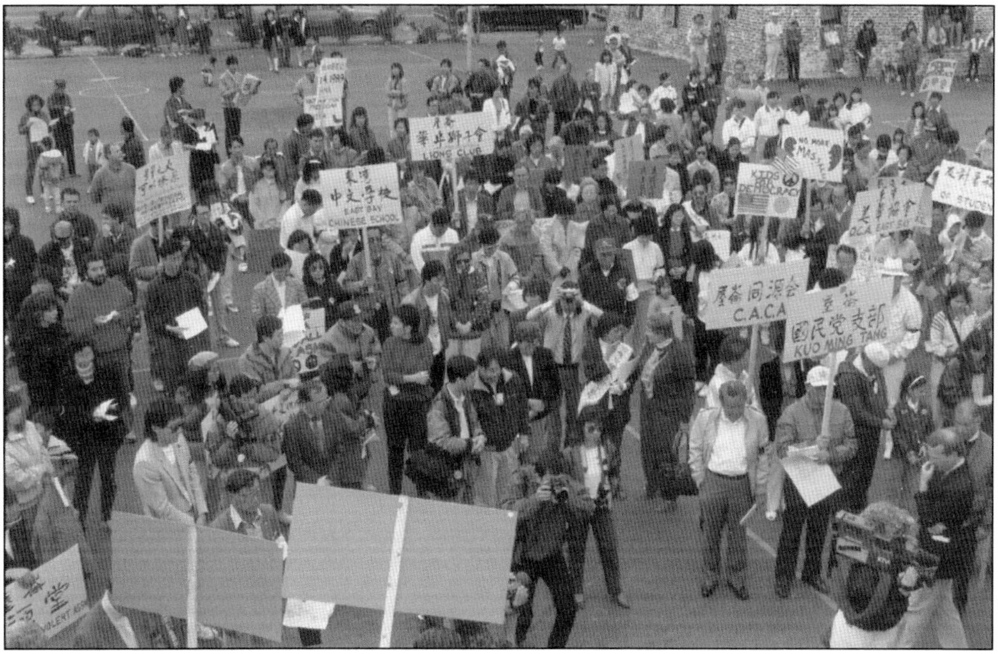

The Tiananmen Square massacre in China on June 4, 1989 drew protests around the world among ethnic Chinese. On June 11, 1989, Oakland Chinese Americans made their voices heard in Lincoln Square. (Photo by and courtesy of Henry Woon.)

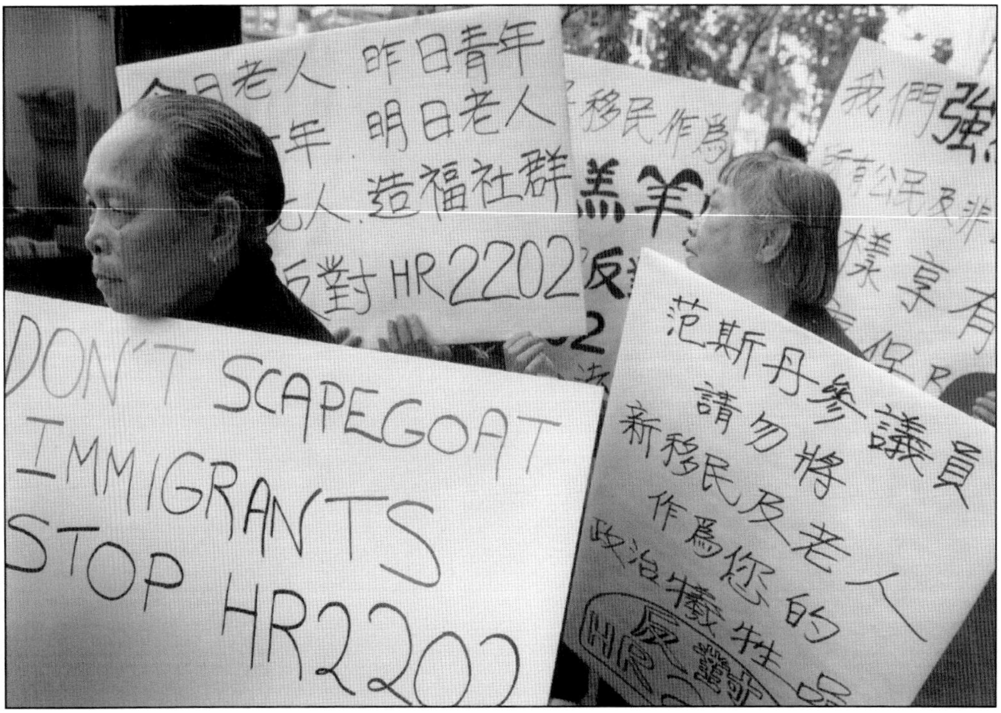

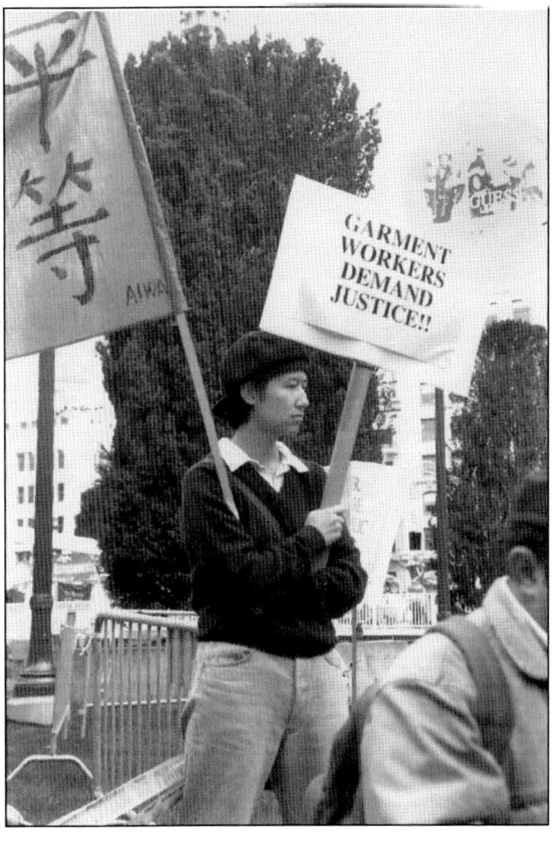

Elderly Chinatown residents demonstrate against HR2202, which was a 1996 Congressional proposal to limit immigration to the United States. (Courtesy of Family Bridges Inc.)

A member of Oakland Chinatown-based Asian Immigrant Women Advocates (AIWA) demonstrates in San Francisco on behalf of garment workers, most of whom are either Chinese or Asian immigrant women. Founded in 1983, AIWA works on behalf of limited English-speaking Asian immigrant women, youths, and their families for better working conditions. It has won notable victories including its case against Jessica McClintock, a major fashion label. (Courtesy of Asian Immigrant Women Advocates.)

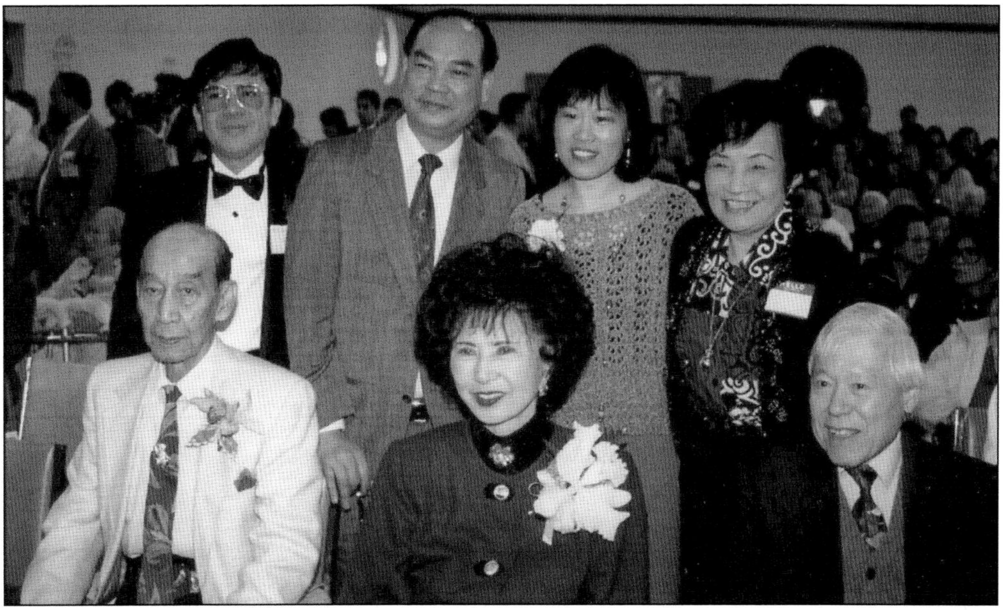

March Fong Eu (front row, in center) is honored on her birthday at the Chinese Garden Project at Seventh and Harrison Streets in 1994. Eu began her political career in Oakland, and in 1974 became the highest-ranking Chinese American politician when she won statewide office as secretary of state, serving for 16 years. She was also a U.S. ambassador in the 1990s. Others pictured are, from left to right, (front row) legendary Hong Kong martial-arts movie star Guan Duk Hing, Fong Eu and her husband, Henry Eu, and (second row) Andre Leung, Milton Fong, Joyce Cheng, and unidentified. (Photo by and courtesy of Henry Woon.)

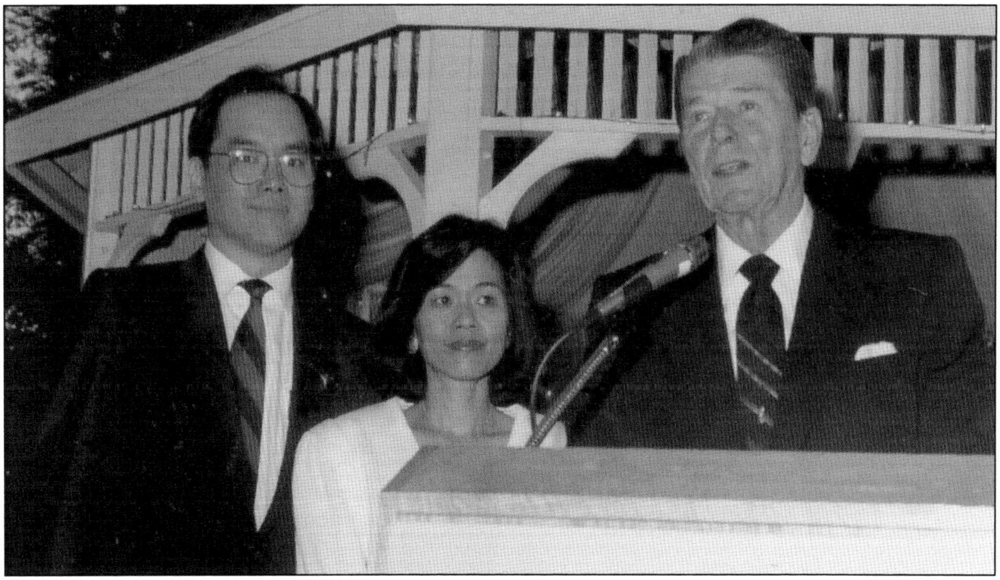

Matt Fong (left) and his wife Paula listen to President Ronald Reagan at a 1990 fundraiser for Fong's California controller campaign. Fong was elected state treasurer in 1995 after serving on the state board of equalization. Fong was born and attended school in Oakland, the son of March Fong Eu, who also held statewide office as a Democrat. A Republican, Fong ran unsuccessfully for the U.S. Senate in 1998. (Courtesy of Matt Fong.)

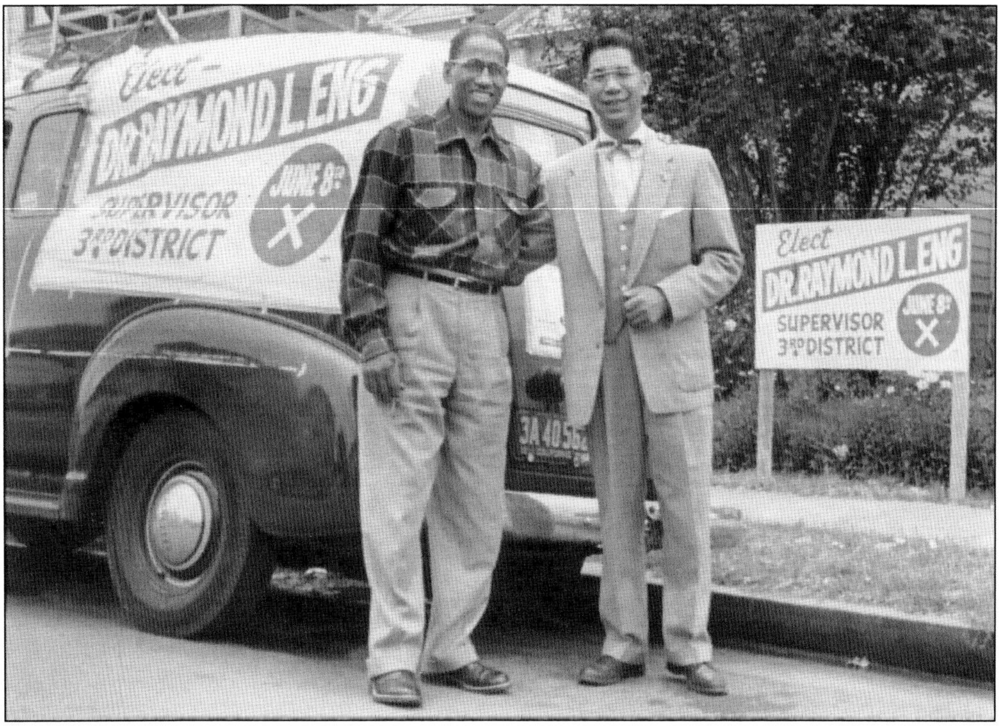

Dr. Raymond Eng campaigned with a supporter for an Alameda County Board of Supervisors seat in the 1960s. He lost that race and several others before being elected in 1967 to the Oakland City Council, where he served for 16 years. He was the first Chinese American on the city council. (Courtesy of Weylin Eng.)

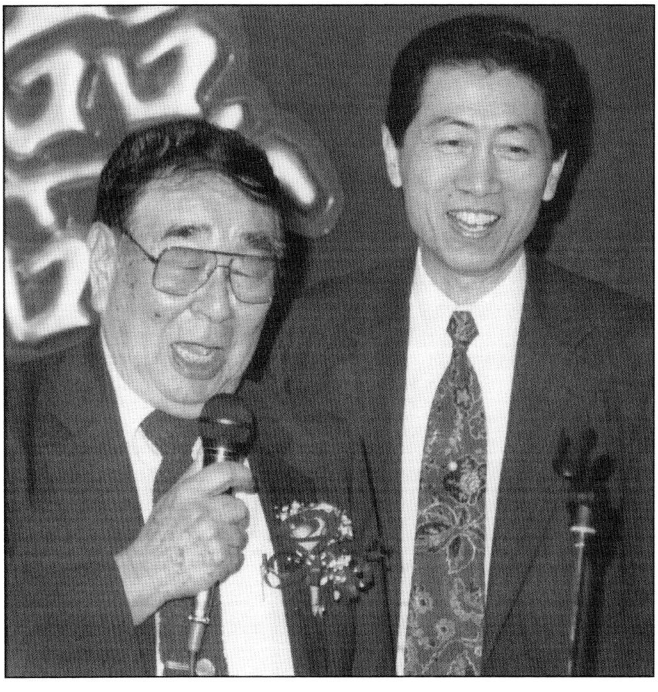

In this 1992 photo, Frank Ogawa, at left, shares a podium with Henry Chang. At the time, Ogawa was a long-serving Oakland City Councilman. Chang was a Chinatown community leader and businessman later appointed to fill Ogawa's seat when he died in 1995. Chang has since been re-elected twice in his own right. (Photo by and courtesy of Henry Woon.)

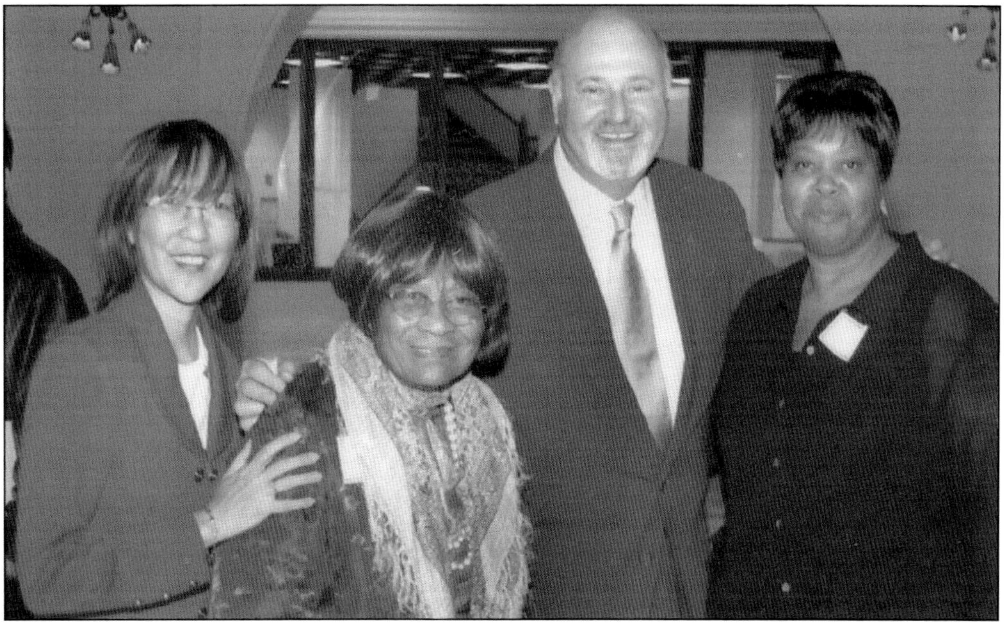

Wilma Chan, shown here at left, made history when she and Jean Quan were the first Asian American women elected to the Oakland School Board in 1990. Chan then served on the Alameda County Board of Supervisors and is now in the state assembly. Others in this 2004 photo are, from left to right, Gracie Johnson, Rob Reiner, and Marva Lyons. The women are family day-care providers. Reiner is the well-known actor, director, and early-childhood advocate. (Courtesy of Wilma Chan.)

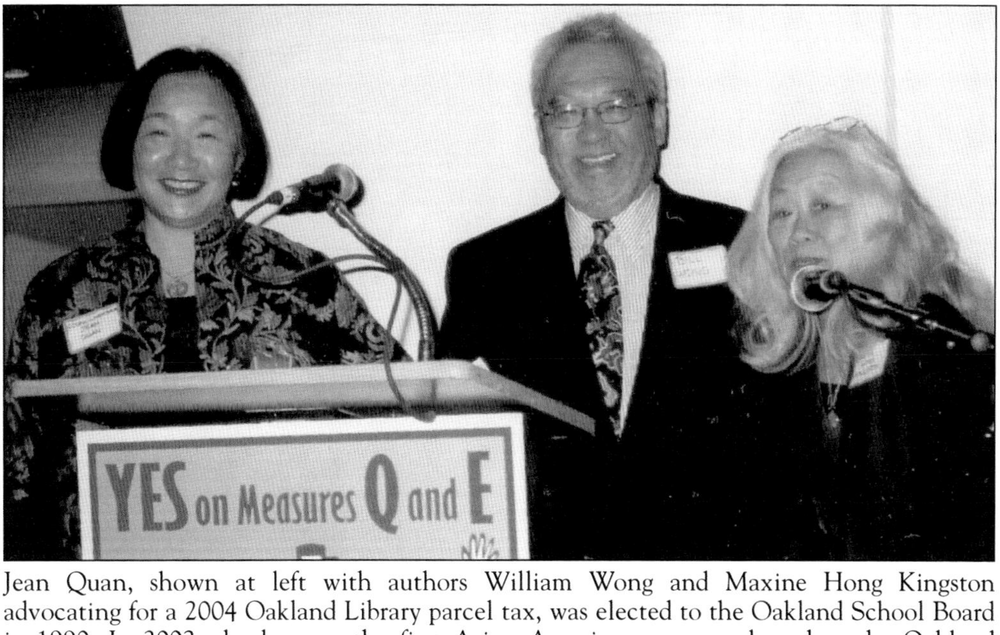

Jean Quan, shown at left with authors William Wong and Maxine Hong Kingston advocating for a 2004 Oakland Library parcel tax, was elected to the Oakland School Board in 1990. In 2002, she became the first Asian American woman elected to the Oakland City Council. Quan's Oakland roots go back to the 1906 San Francisco earthquake, when her great-grandfather and his three sons moved to Oakland. (Photo by and courtesy of Joyce Mende Wong.)

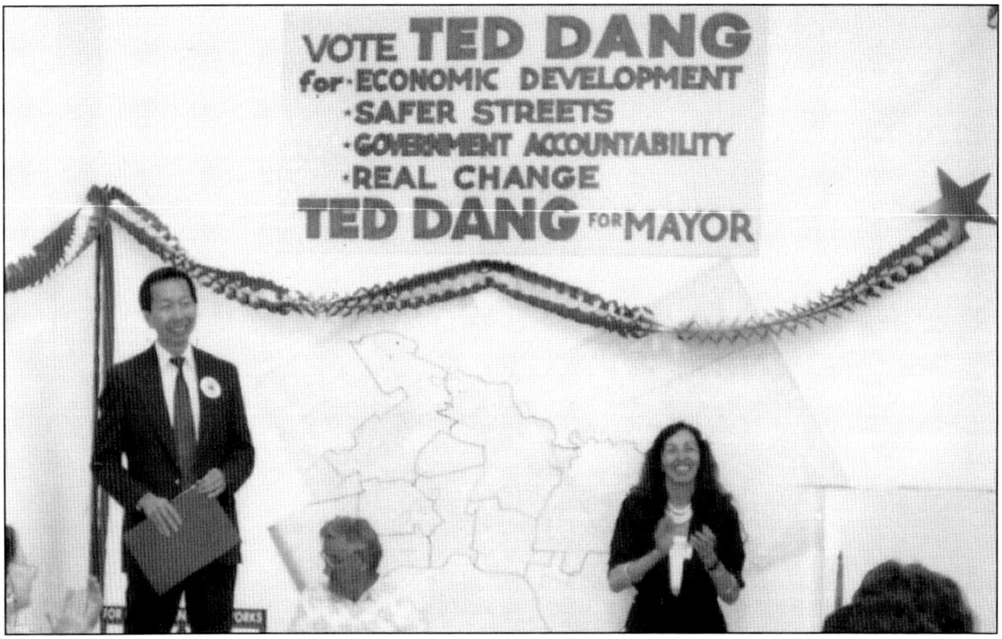

Ted Dang talks to his campaign staff during his 1994 bid to become Oakland mayor. He lost to incumbent Elihu Harris after his surprise second-place finish in the primary election. An Oakland native, Dang has long been active in Chinatown and civic affairs. He is a successful real estate developer. (Courtesy of Ted Dang.)

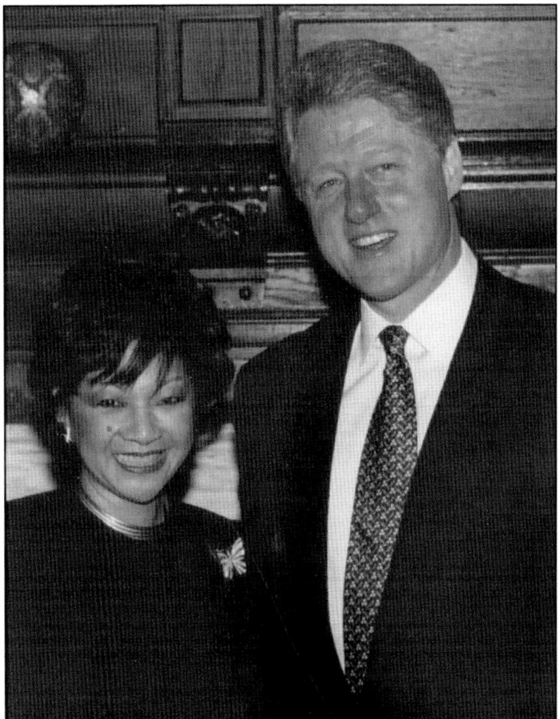

Maeley Tom, seen here with President Bill Clinton, attended Lincoln School in the 1950s, when she was Maeley Lock. She was a key assistant in the State Legislature to Democratic leaders Willie Brown and David Roberti and has been a leader among national Asian American Democrats. She helped establish the Office of Asian Pacific Affairs in the legislature and has advised many young political activists. (Photo by Larry S. Glenn, courtesy of Maeley Tom.)

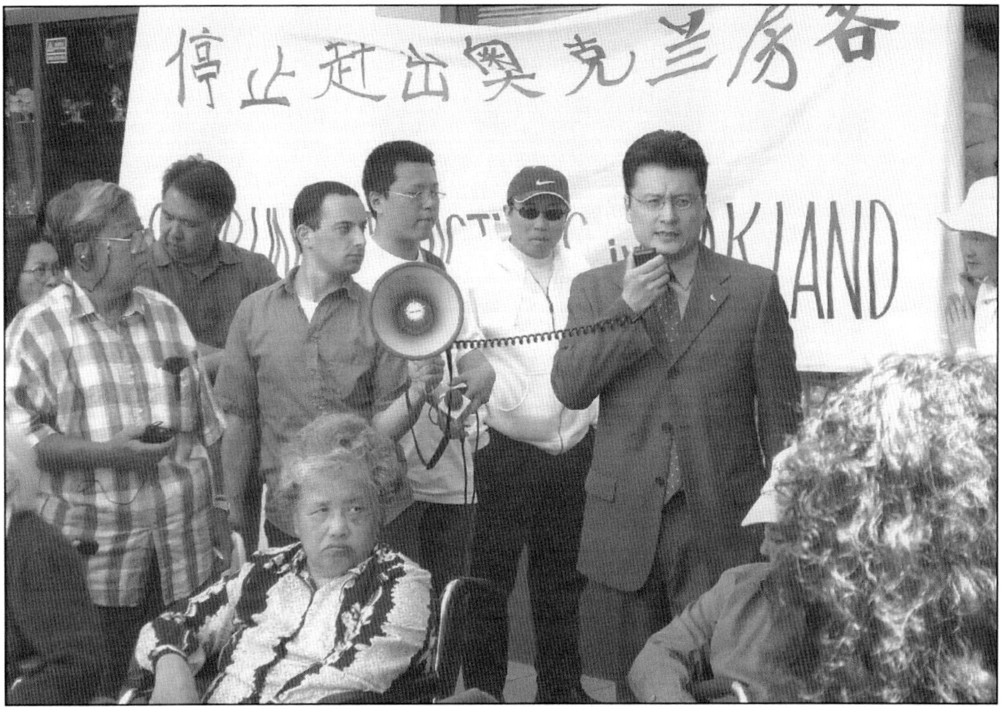

Danny Wan, speaking out here for low-income renters about to be evicted from the Pacific Renaissance Plaza, is a Taiwan immigrant who has been on the Oakland City Council since 2001, representing Chinatown and nearby neighborhoods. He has also been on the local water district's board. A former schoolteacher and attorney, Wan co-sponsored a city ordinance requiring bilingual city services. (Photo by Christopher Tom, courtesy of Danny Wan.)

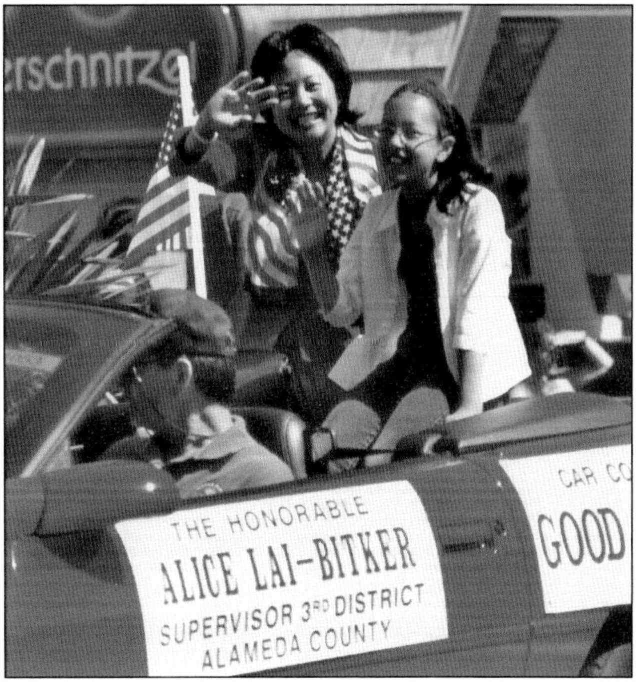

Alameda County Supervisor Alice Lai-Bitker, with her daughter Janelle, represents parts of Oakland that include Chinatown. She was appointed to the county board in 2000 and elected in 2002, after serving as an assistant to Supervisor Wilma Chan. A Hong Kong native, Lai-Bitker has been active in Oakland community and political life for more than 20 years. (Courtesy of Alice Lai-Bitker.)

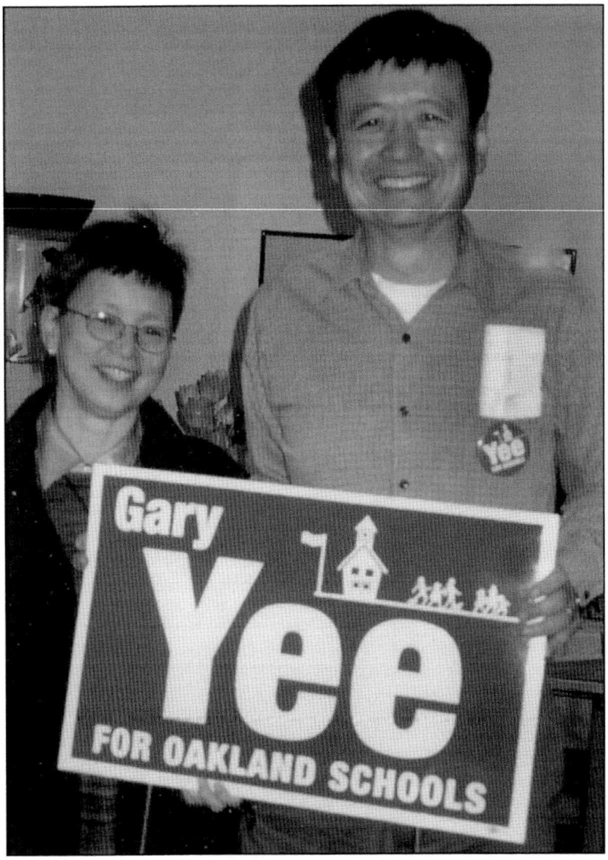

Gary Yee was elected to the Oakland school board in 2002. He has been a teacher, vice principal and principal in Oakland public schools. He has also been an education professor. His wife, Caroline Yee, is also a teacher and principal in the Oakland schools. (Courtesy of Gary Yee.)

Oakland native Jeanette Dong (fourth from the left) was a legislative assistant to Elihu Harris (to her right) when he was a state assemblyman and Oakland mayor, in the 1980s and 1990s. Dong is currently a public policy and government relations consultant. Others in this photo, taken in the 1990s in Dalian, China, where Oakland has a sister-city, are four unidentified Chinese port officials, Kathy Neal (fifth from the left), Larry Reid (behind Neal), and Mark Harris. (Courtesy of Jeanette Dong.)

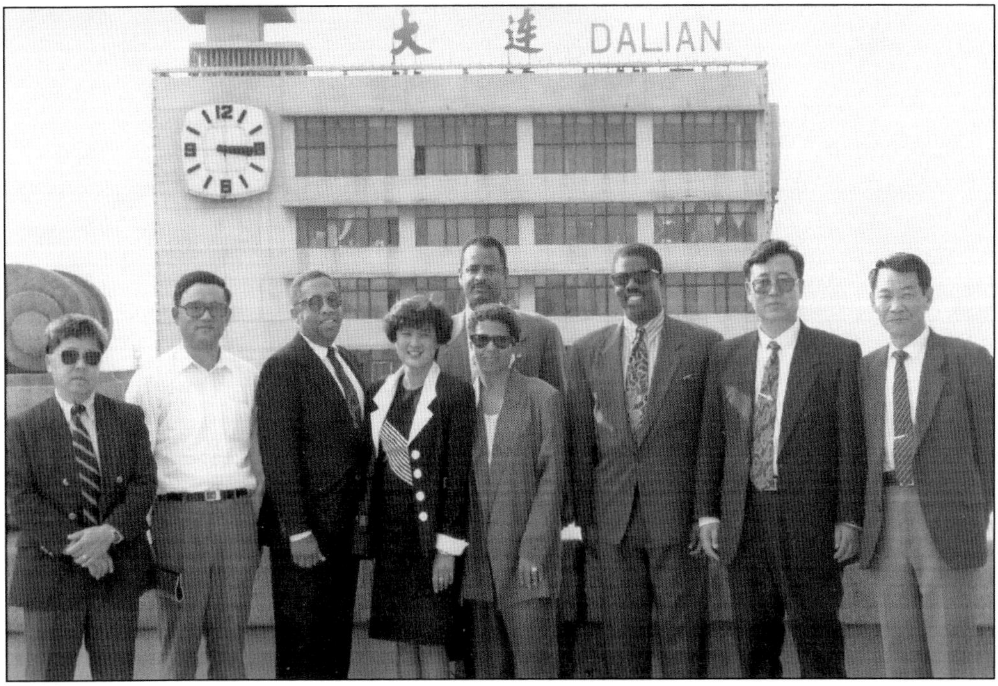

Five

HAVING FUN

Oakland Chinese are not just hard workers. They enjoy relaxing and having fun as much as anyone else. This was even so for Oakland Chinese who grew up under segregated conditions. Fun activities run the gamut, from country drives to casual strolls in a park, to dragon boat races, from mah-jongg to baseball.

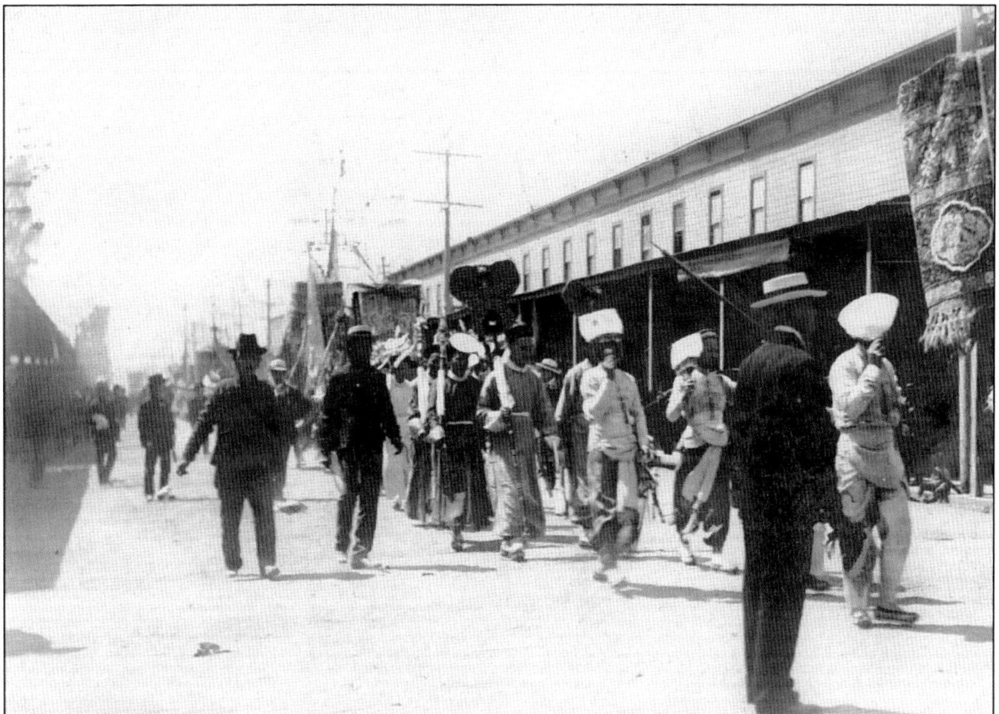

This 1907 postcard depicts an early Oakland Chinese parade on the Fourth of July. (Courtesy of Ed Clausen.)

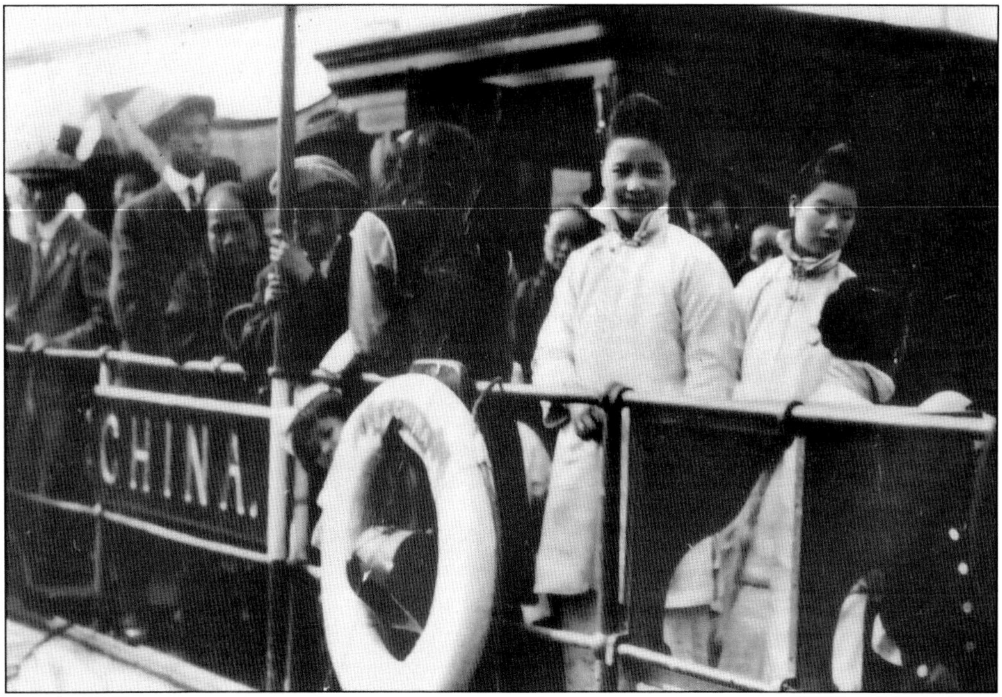

Rose Lew Moon, in a white dress facing the camera, is on a sea voyage in 1915. She was a daughter of Oakland Chinese industrialist Lew Hing. (Courtesy of Mary Mar.)

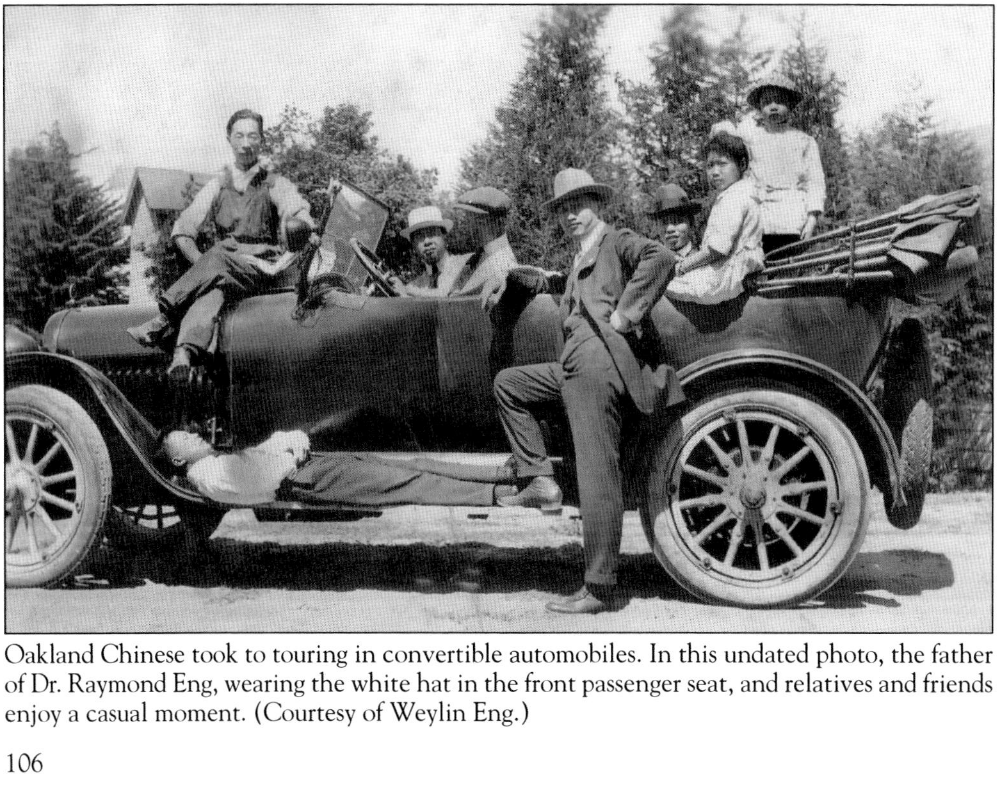

Oakland Chinese took to touring in convertible automobiles. In this undated photo, the father of Dr. Raymond Eng, wearing the white hat in the front passenger seat, and relatives and friends enjoy a casual moment. (Courtesy of Weylin Eng.)

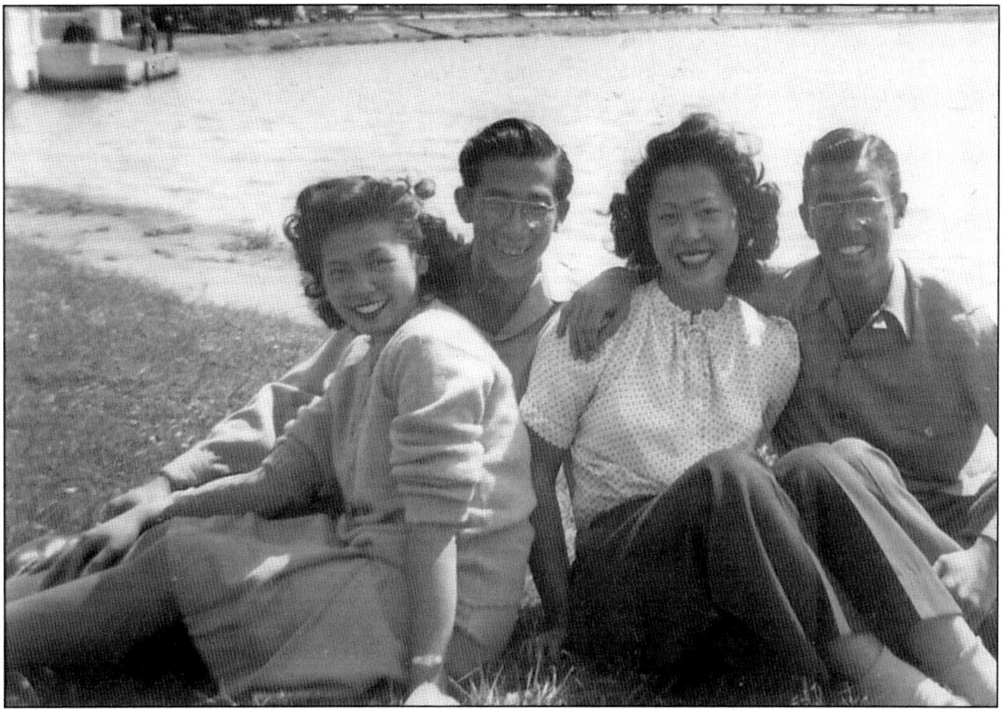

From left to right, Nancy Chin, Elwood Tom, Marie Lee, and Ben Mak relax on the shore of Lake Merritt, an Oakland landmark, in the 1940s. (Courtesy of Luella Mak.)

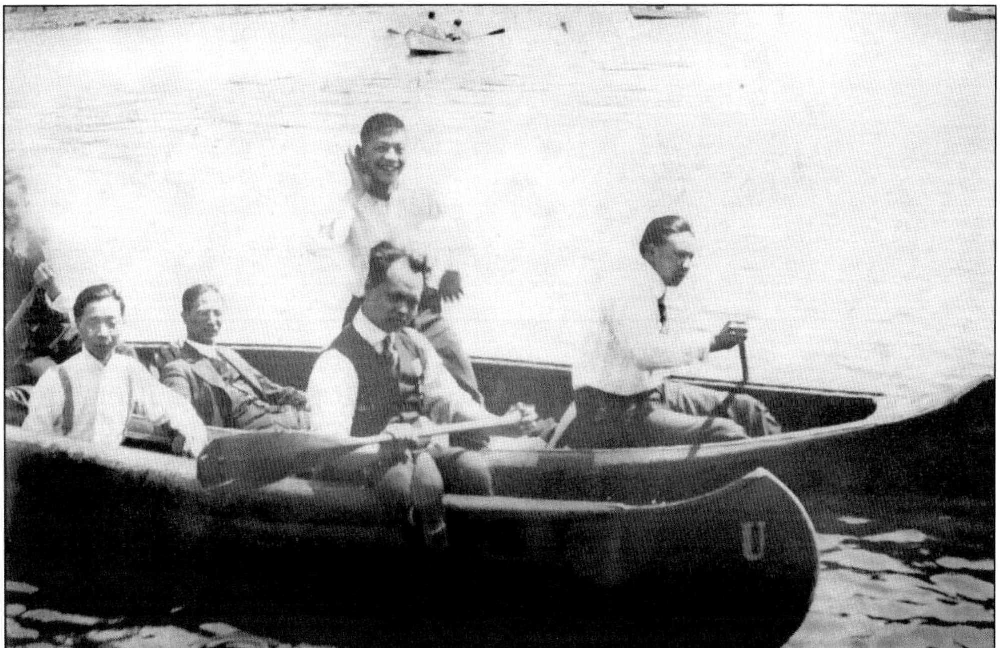

An unidentified group of Oakland Chinese canoe on Lake Merritt, in this undated photo. (Courtesy of Weylin Eng.)

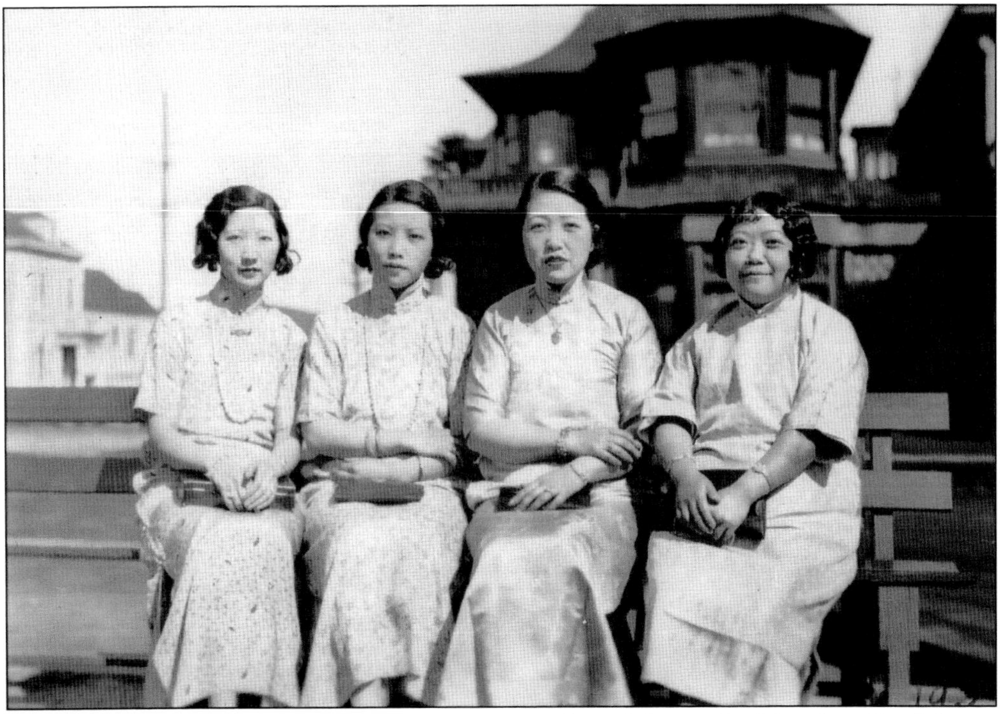

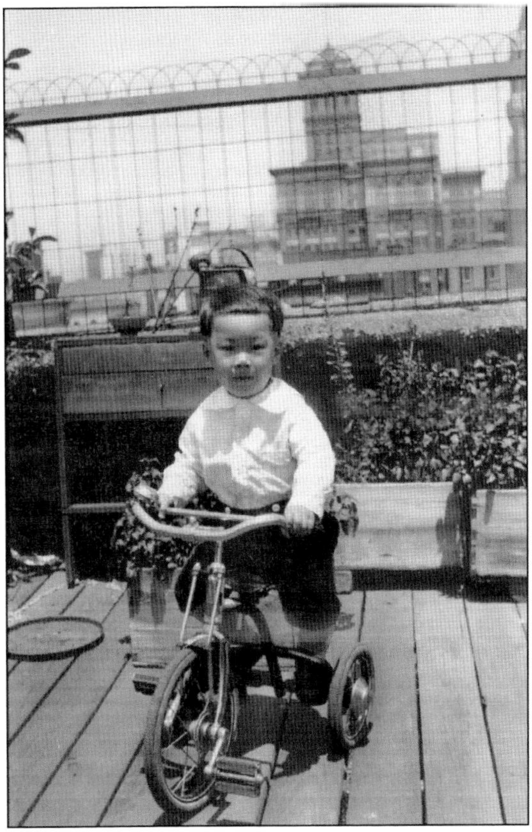

From left to right, Mary Lee, Sarah Joe, Jennie Lum, and Mary Wong take in the fresh air at Madison Square Park at Ninth and Oak Streets in 1933. The first three women are sisters and the other their cousin. (Courtesy of Darlene Lee.)

A young Art Fong rides his tricycle on the roof of his father's meat market near Chinatown in the early 1930s. He later became active in Chinatown as an organizer of Lincoln School reunions and other activities and was an assistant to the late city councilman Frank Ogawa. (Courtesy of Art Fong.)

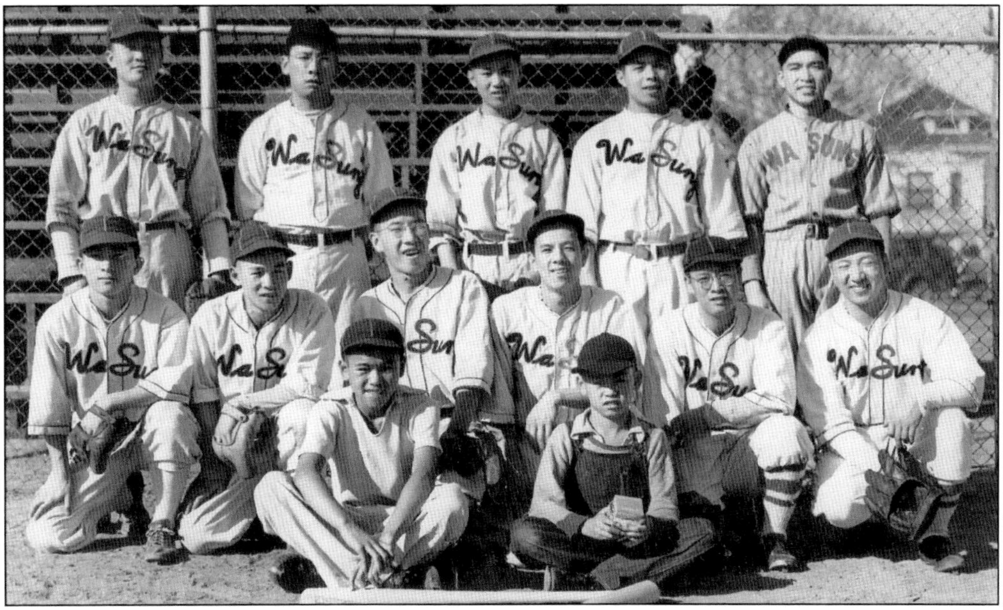

The semi-professional Wa Sung Athletic Club formed in the 1920s. Members in this 1930s photo were, from left to right, (front row) batboys Bill and Bob Chinn; (second row) Sung Wong, Key Chinn, Joe Lee, Al Bowen, Eddie Hing, and Tommy Hing; and (third row) Hector Eng, Ben Chan, Al Wong, George Bowen, and Robert Chow. The club disbanded in the late 1930s and came back in 1953 as a service club. (Courtesy of Betty Wong.)

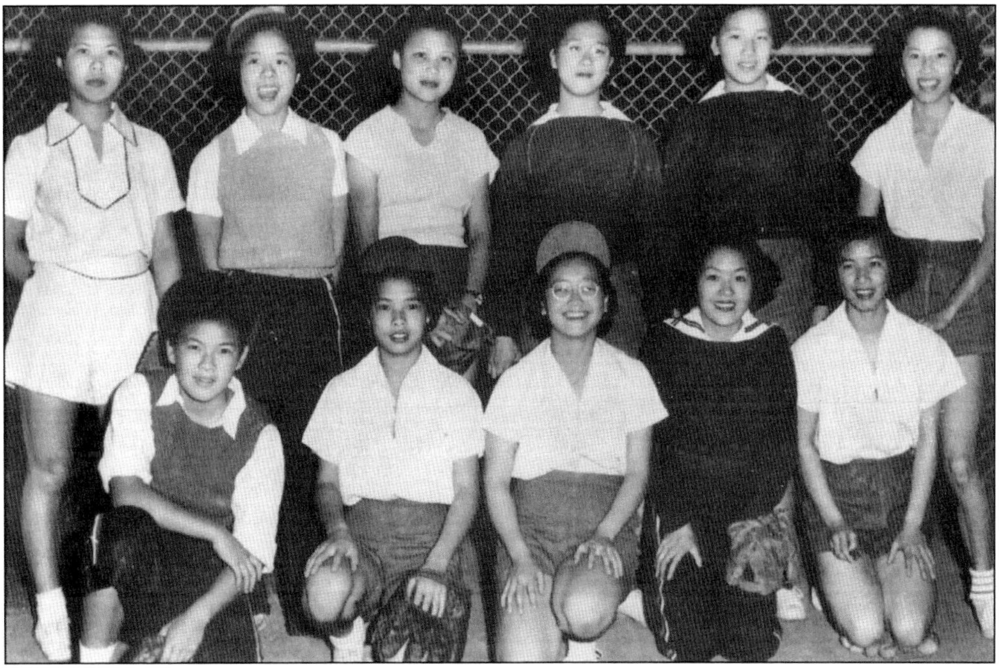

The Dragonettes were a female Chinese American softball team of mostly Oakland residents. Team members in this 1930s photo are, from left to right, (front row) Gwen Wong, Ida Lowe, Phyllis Soo Hoo, Jennie Bowen, and Ruth Chew; and (back row) Jane Lowe, Flo Bowen, Mangie Wong, Helen Eng, Inez Wong, and Dora Chew. (Courtesy of Betty Wong.)

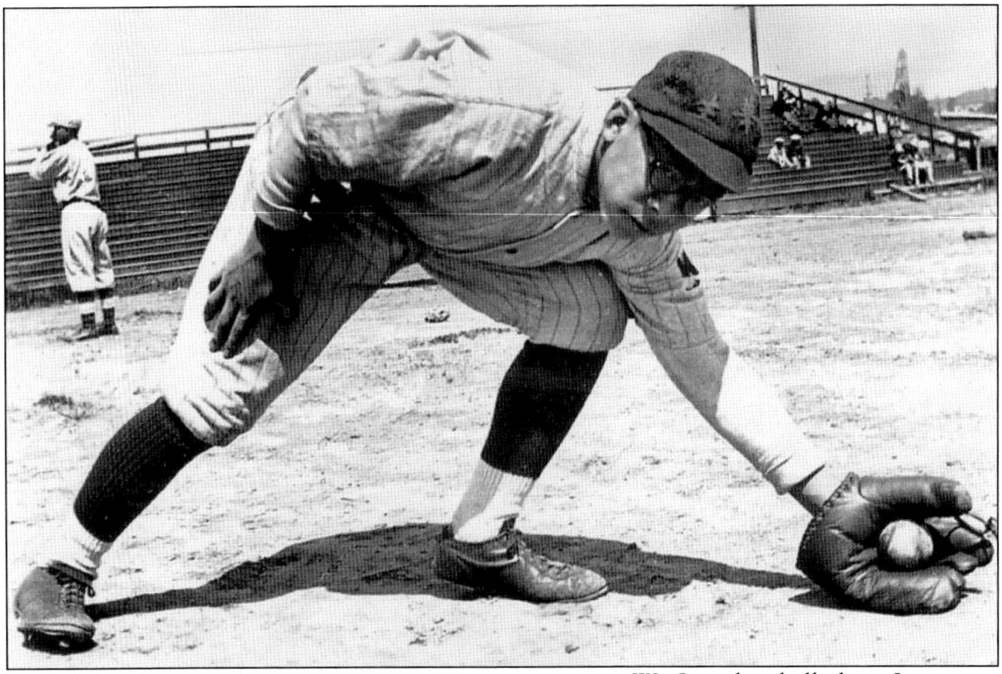

Wa Sung baseball player Lester Lee, in this 1930s photo, was born in Chinatown and became a dentist, practicing with his father, Dr. Charles Lee, the first Chinese American dentist in Oakland. His mother, Clara Chan Lee, was one of two Oakland Chinese women to be the first of their race and gender to register to vote in the United States in 1911. (Courtesy of Art Tom.)

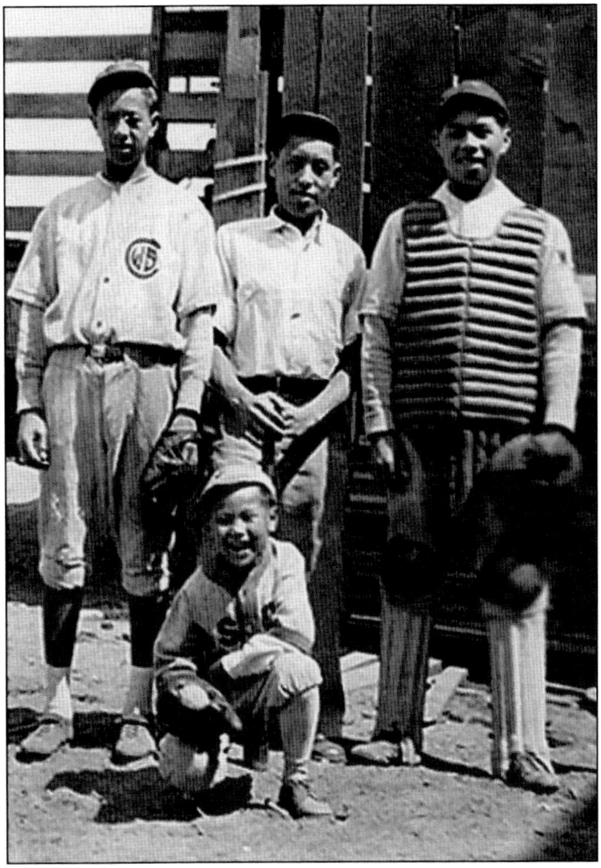

The Bowen/Wing family had many members on the Wa Sung Athletic Club and Dragonettes. The star was Al Bowen (standing, left), who became the first Chinese American professional baseball player in 1932 with the minor-league Oakland Oaks. Also pictured are Ed Bowen (standing in middle) and George Bowen. Kneeling is Allie Wong, who later became a star semi-professional player in the late 1930s. (Courtesy of Laraine C. Wing.)

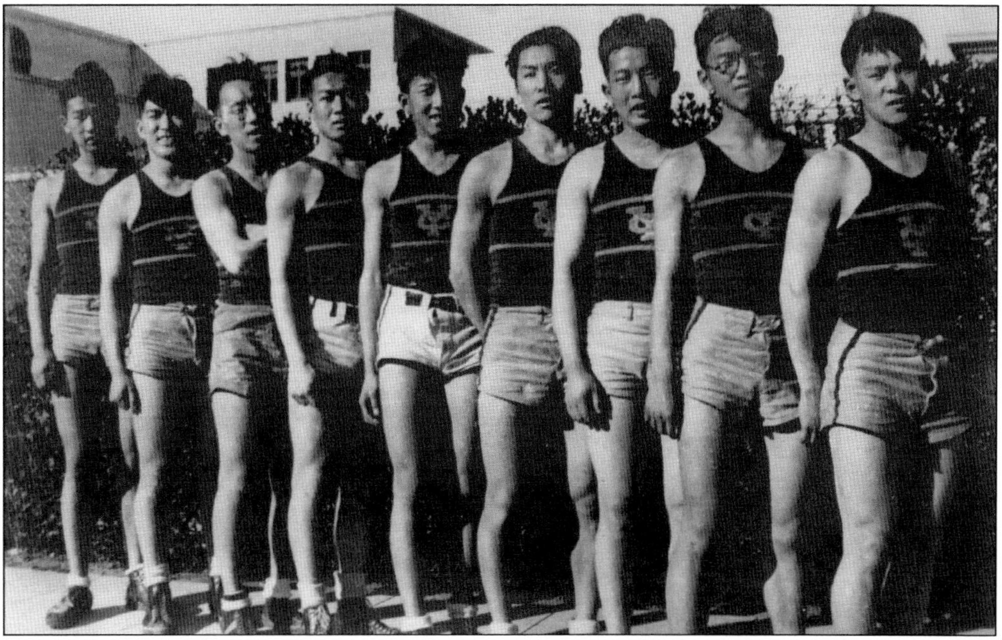

The Young Chinese Athletic Club was another Oakland Chinese sports team. Members in this undated photo are, from left to right, Edwin Chan, Robert Chow, Joseph Lee, Art Lee, Shane Lew, Louis Hong, Dave Lem, George Chan, and Key Chinn. (Courtesy of Luella Mak.)

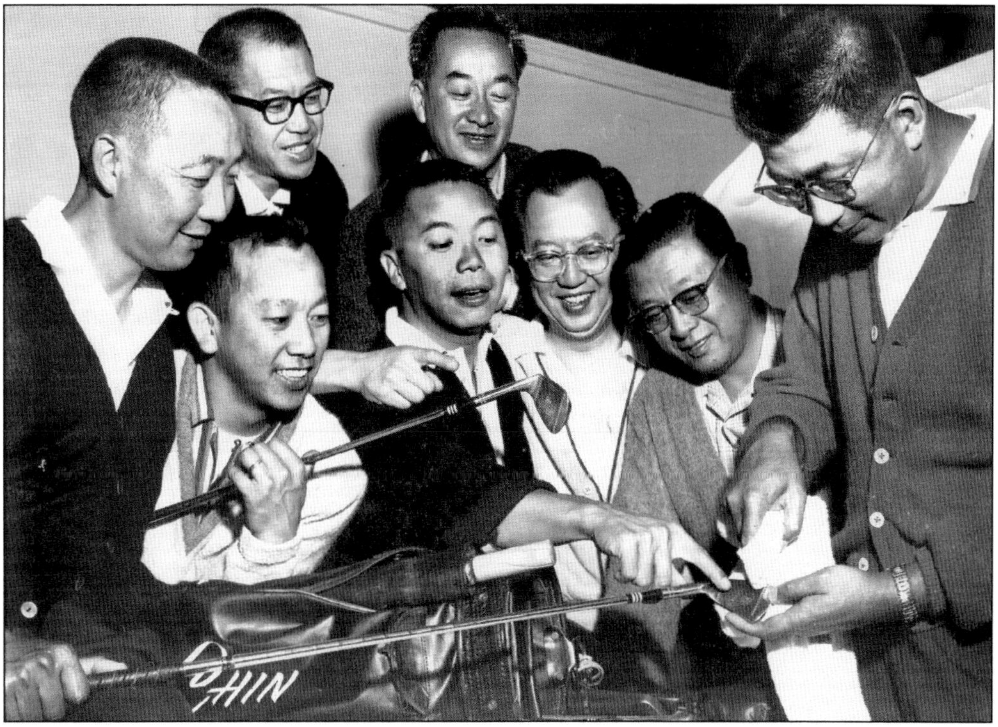

Oakland Chinese men formed a golf club in 1960. Charter members pictured here, from left to right, are (front row) Josh Fong, Lewis Chin, Francis Tom, and Ed Hing; and (standing) Augie Ong, Ray Chan, Wally Wong, and Clinton Lee. (Courtesy of Hugh Lee.)

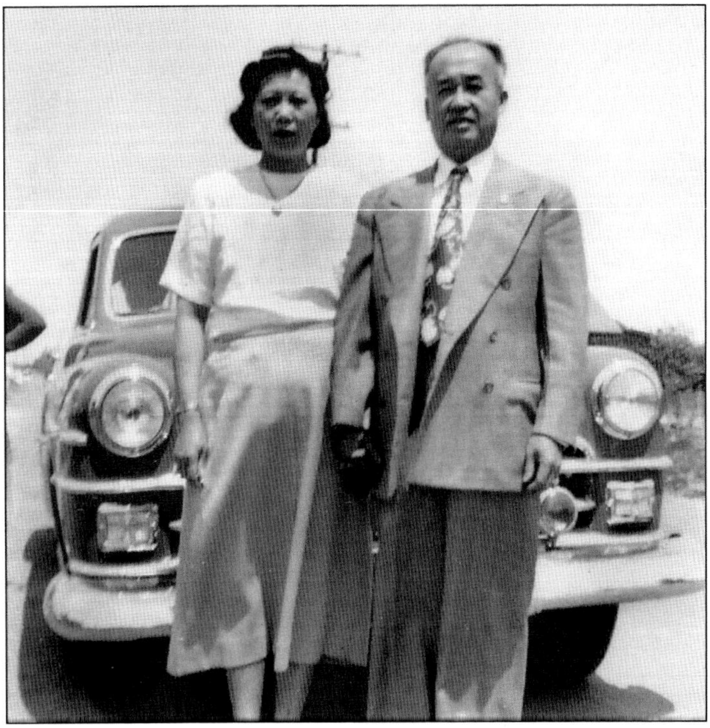

Gee Suey Ting (left) and Gee Seow Hong take a day off from their Webster Street restaurant, the Great China, in this undated photo. They were the parents of the author of this book. (Courtesy of Li Keng Wong.)

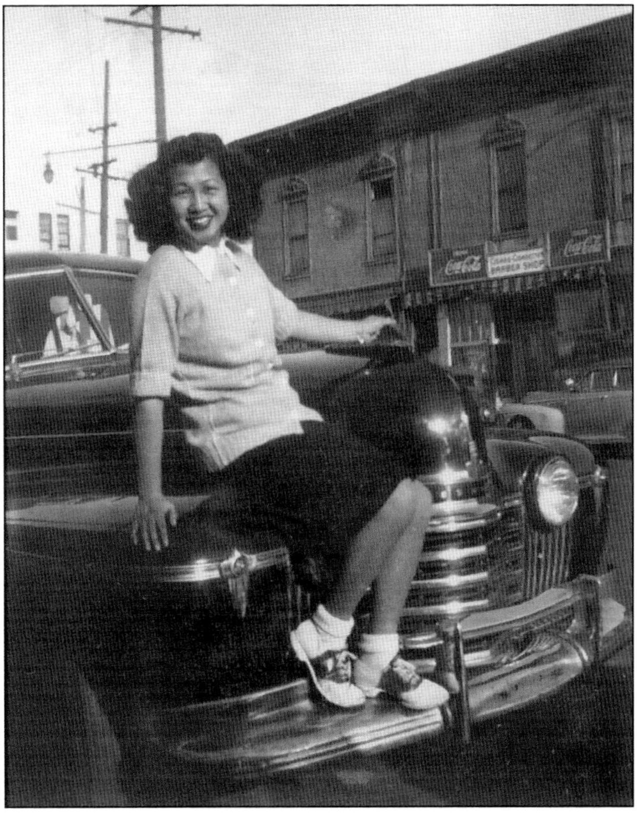

Gee Lai Wah, today known as Lai Chop Webster, frolics atop a car in front of her parents' restaurant on Webster Street between Seventh and Eighth Streets, in this late 1940s photo. She was a teenager at the time. (Courtesy of Lai Chop Webster)

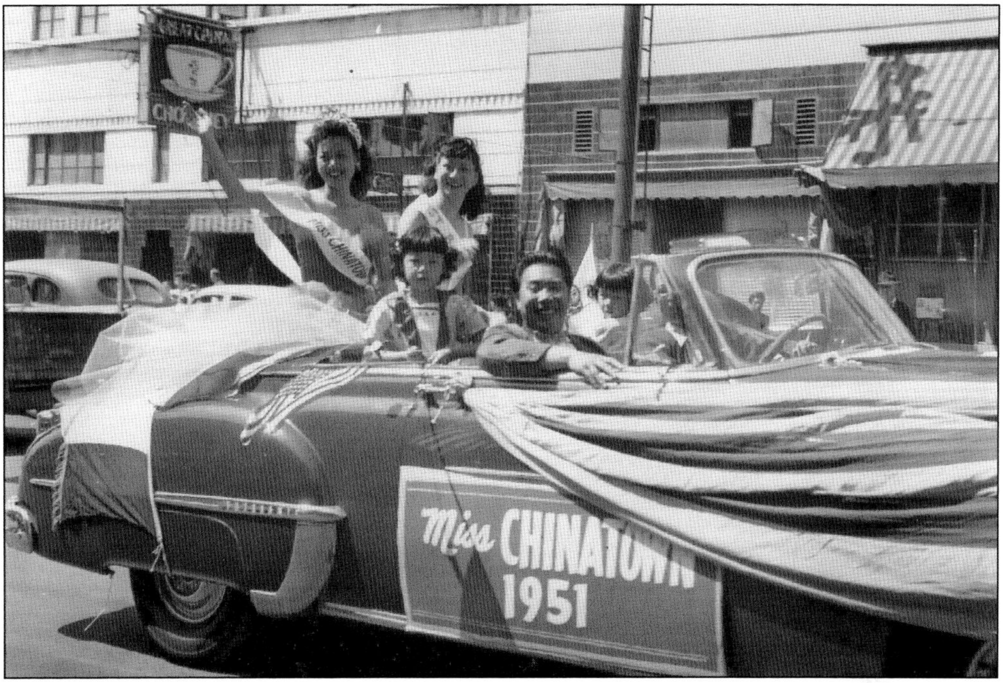

A parade featuring Miss Chinatown of 1951 moves north on Webster Street toward Eighth Street. (Photo by Barry's Studio, Gift of Bruce Quan, courtesy of Edward K. and Flo Oy Wong,)

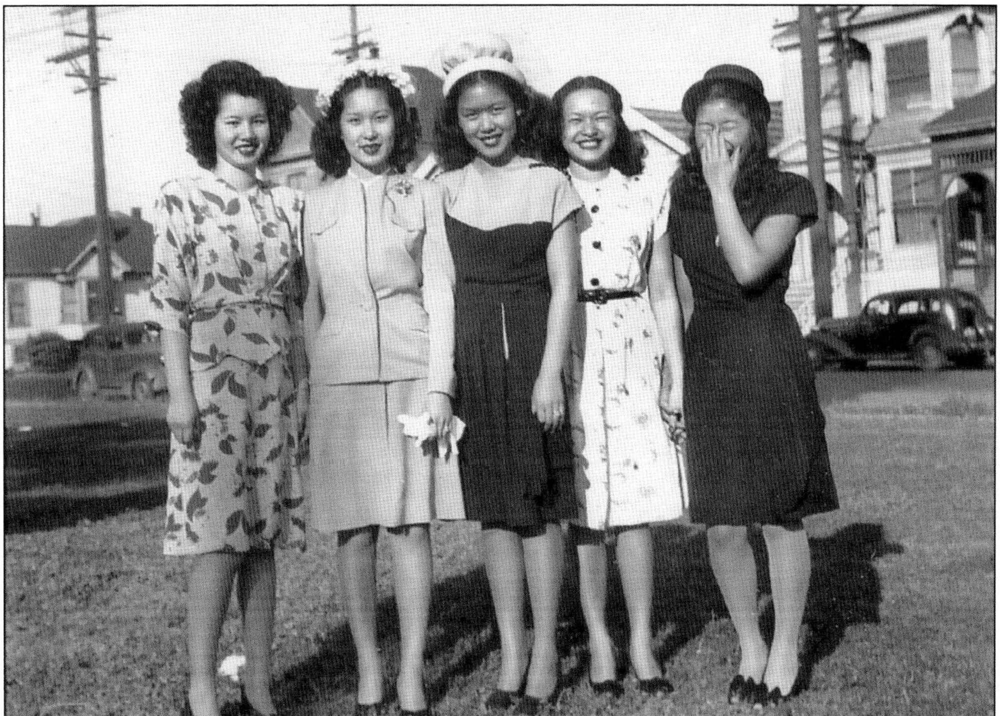

From left to right, Eva Lim, Donna Wong, Luella Wong, Maybelle Lowe, and Maribel Wong enjoy a moment in Harrison Street Park in 1946. (Courtesy of Luella Mak.)

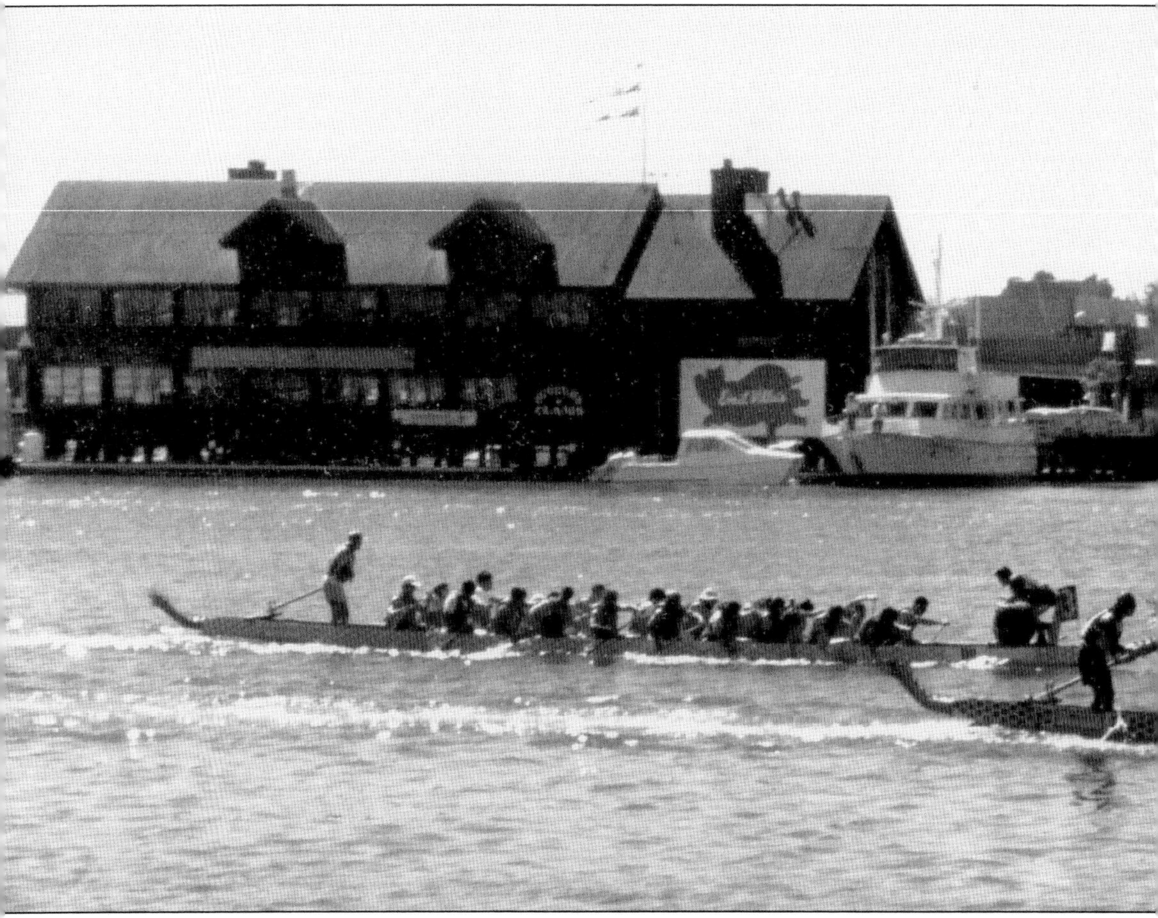

Dragon boat races, fashioned after a popular event begun in Hong Kong, have taken place on the Oakland Estuary in recent years, usually in August. Many Oakland and Bay Area Chinese

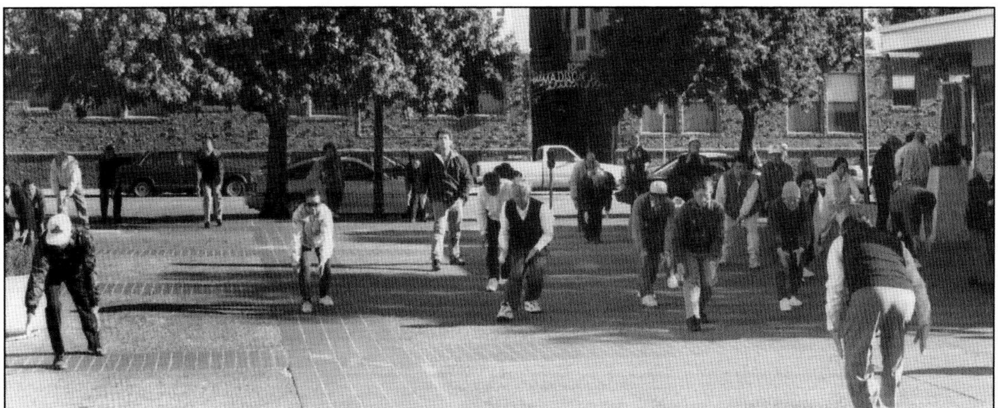

Elderly Chinese practice the ancient Chinese martial art of tai chi on the grounds of BART headquarters at Eighth and Madison Streets. BART is the Bay Area Rapid Transit, which took over Chinatown property formerly used for housing to build its system and headquarters building in the 1960s. (Courtesy of Family Bridges Inc.)

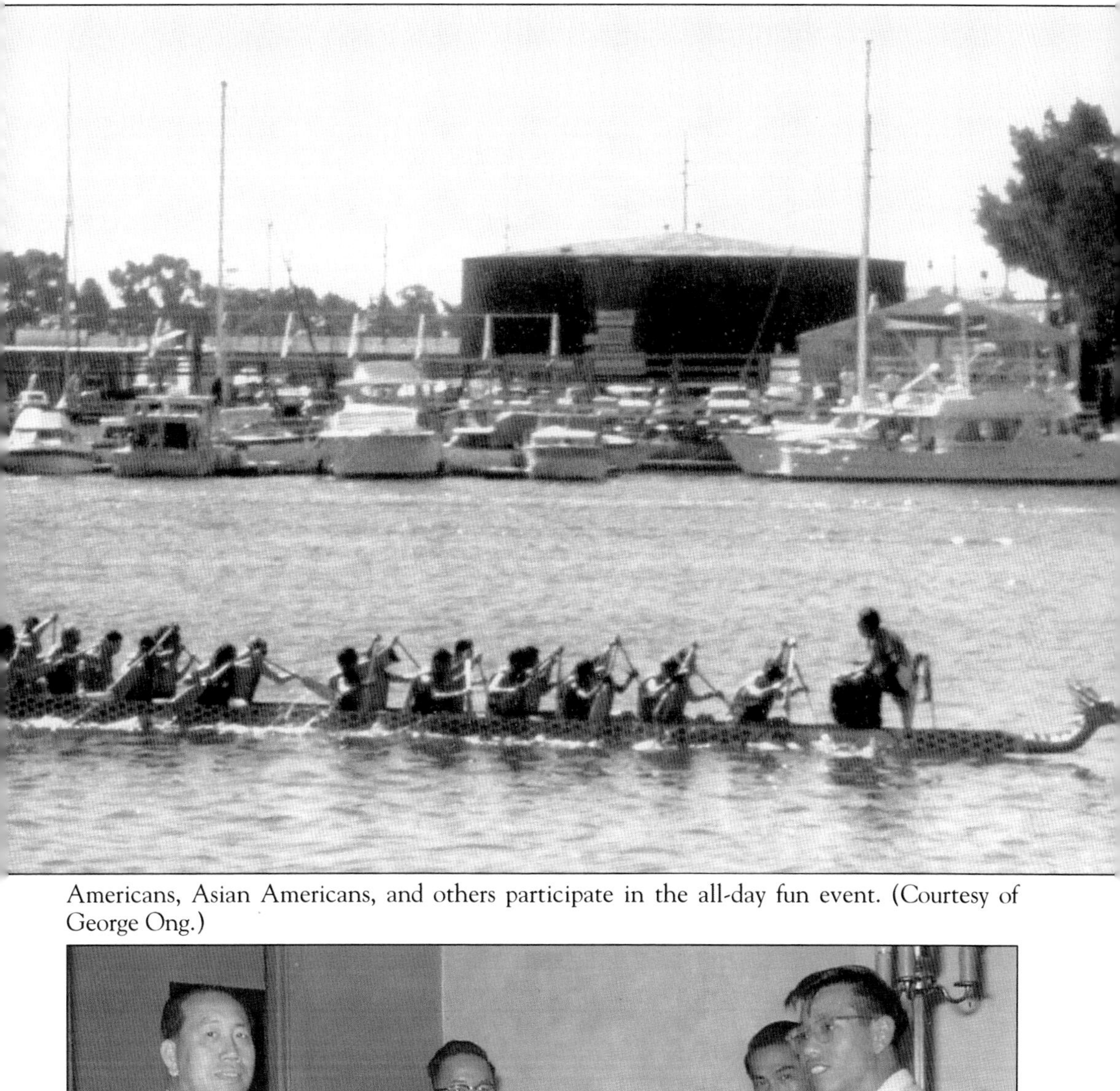

Americans, Asian Americans, and others participate in the all-day fun event. (Courtesy of George Ong.)

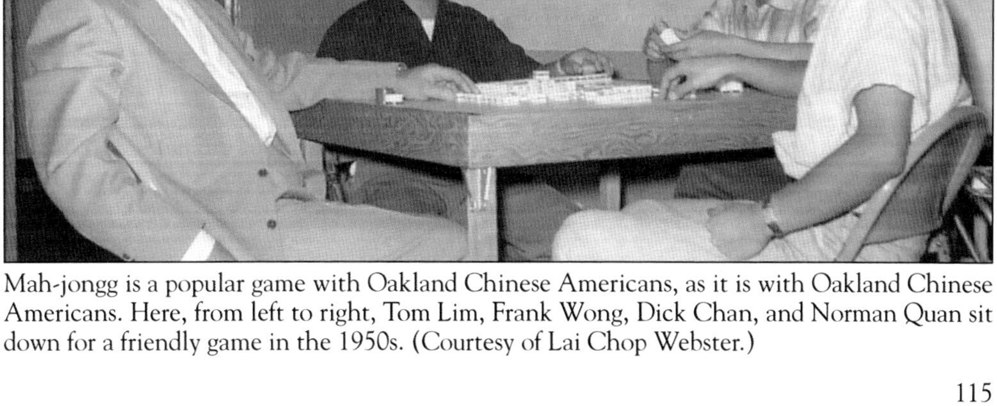

Mah-jongg is a popular game with Oakland Chinese Americans, as it is with Oakland Chinese Americans. Here, from left to right, Tom Lim, Frank Wong, Dick Chan, and Norman Quan sit down for a friendly game in the 1950s. (Courtesy of Lai Chop Webster.)

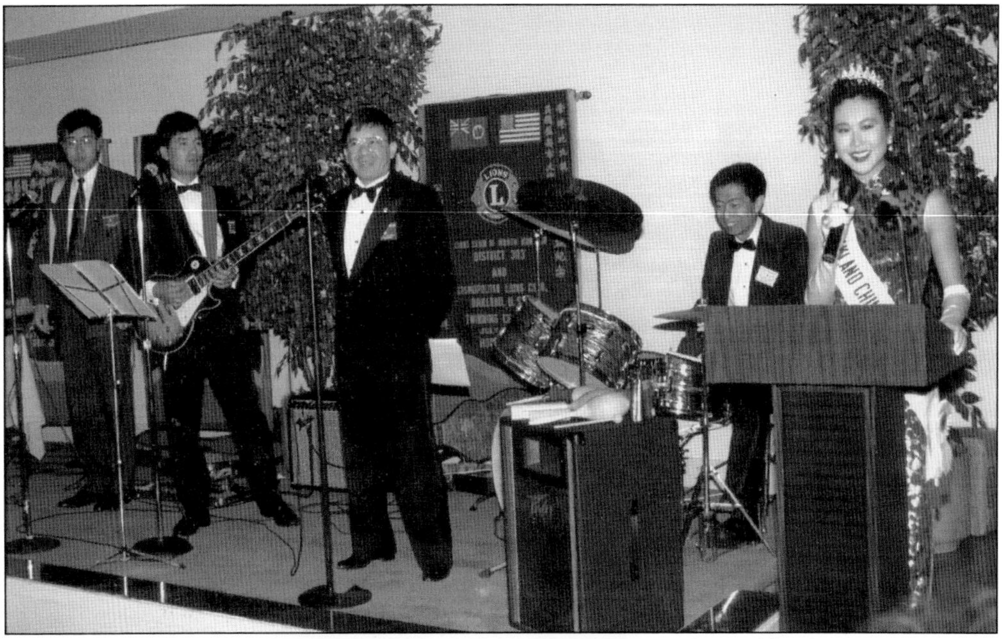

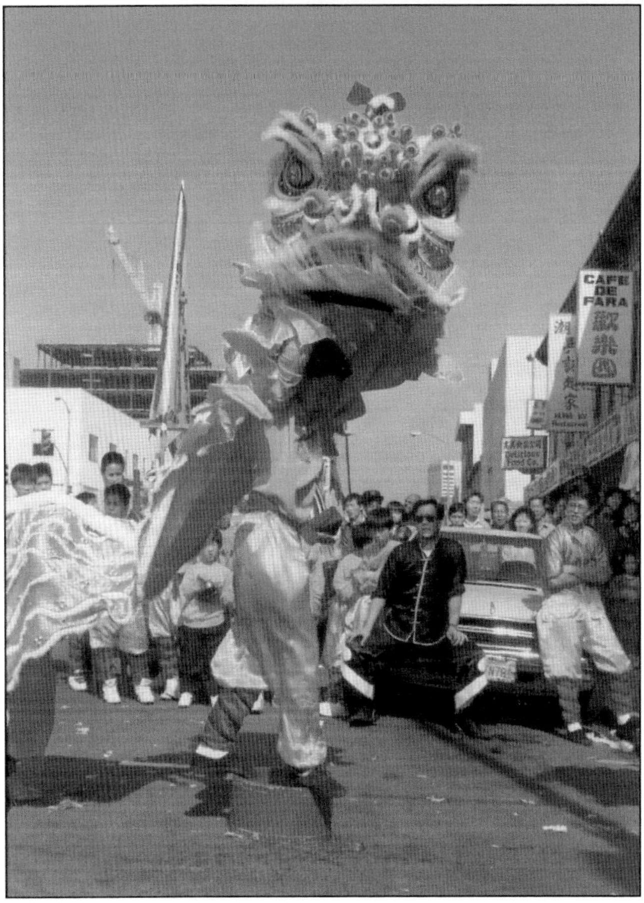

The Oakland Chinatown Lions Club began in 1954 as the Cosmopolitan Lions Club. It has sponsored numerous community activities, including a children's play area, an annual health fair, the Chinese Garden Project, and a Miss Oakland Chinatown Pageant. It also has a band, with longtime club member, community leader, and city councilman Henry Chang at the drums. Others pictured are, from left to right, unidentified, Tony Cho, Andre Leung at the microphone, and Anita Lee. (Courtesy of Henry Chang.)

The Suey Ying Lion Dance Troupe scares away evil spirits during Chinese New Year in 1989 on Webster Street, between Seventh and Eighth Streets. (Photo by and courtesy of Henry Woon.)

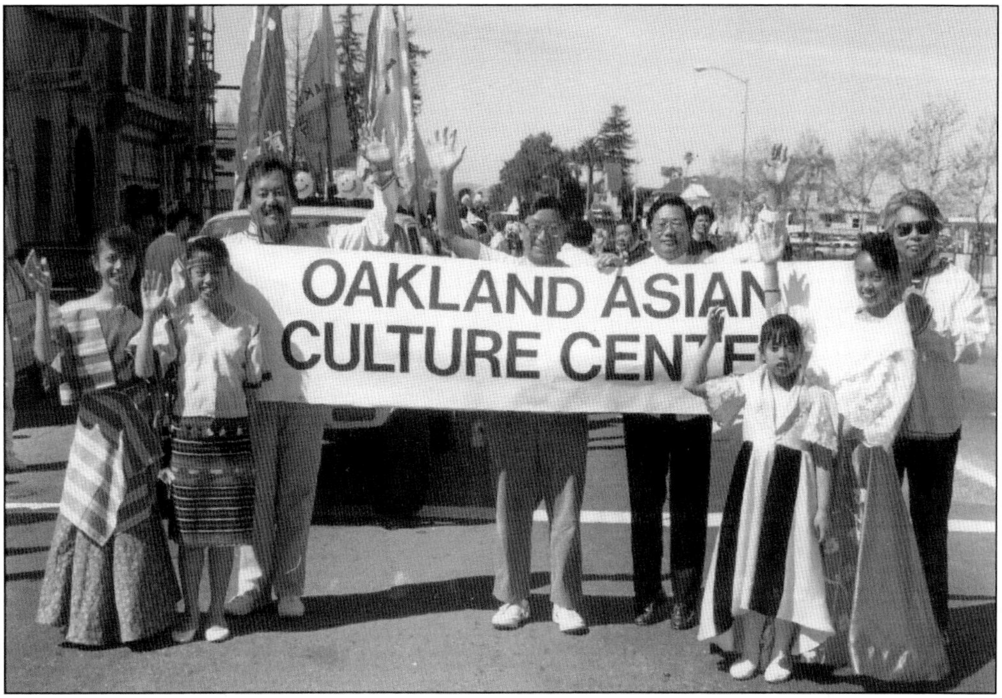

Representatives of the Oakland Asian Culture Center march in a 1988 Mid-Autumn Festival. The men are, from left to right, Bill Sato, Dick Young, Peter Eng, and Clifford Taw. The four young women are unidentified. (Photo by and courtesy of Henry Woon.)

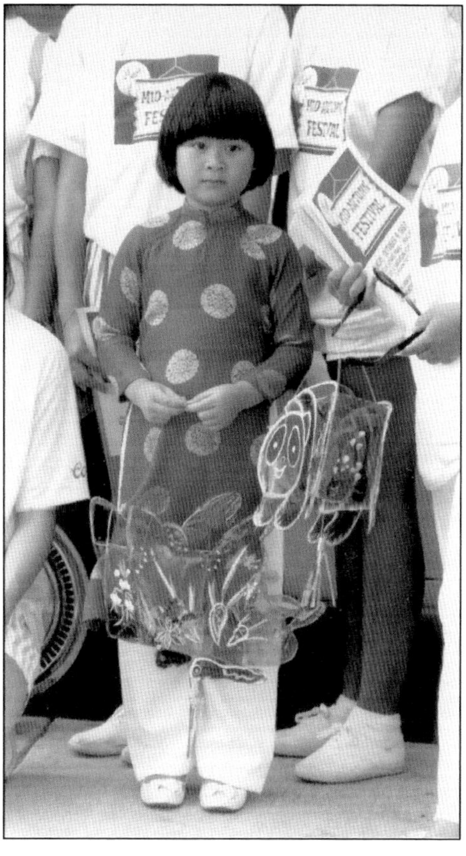

An unidentified girl enjoys the Mid-Autumn Festival in this 1980s photo. (Courtesy of Oakland Asian Cultural Center.)

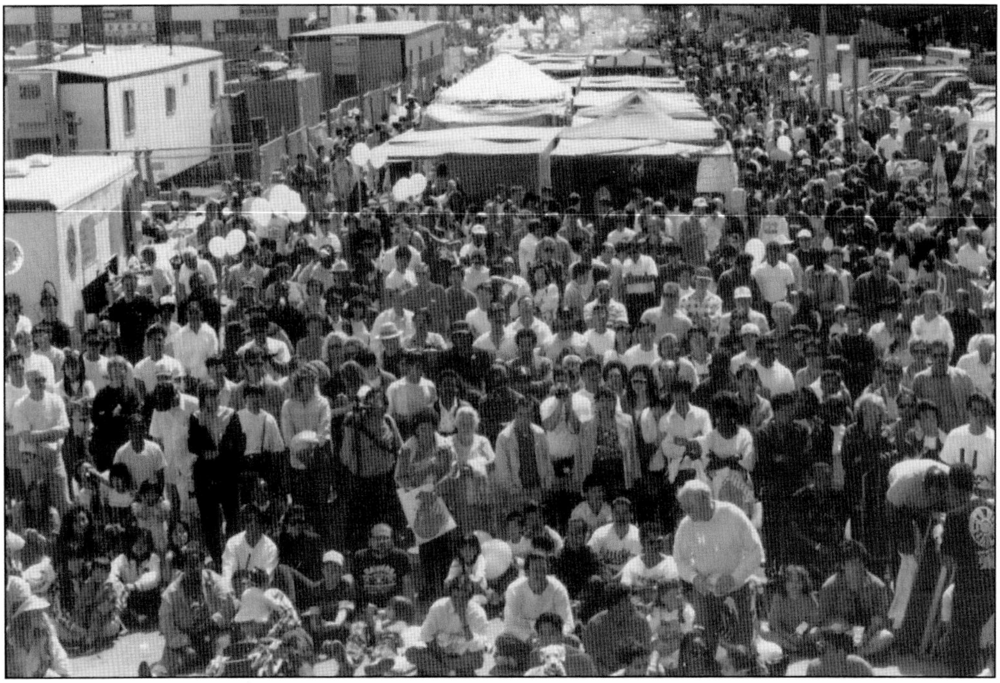

The Oakland Chinatown Chamber of Commerce started the Chinatown StreetFest in 1988 to raise Chinatown's public profile. The festival, held on the fourth weekend in August, attracts thousands of visitors to Chinatown. This is an overview of the 1991 StreetFest looking south on Franklin Street toward Ninth Street from Tenth Street. This was before the Pacific Renaissance Plaza was built, on the left. (Courtesy of George Ong.)

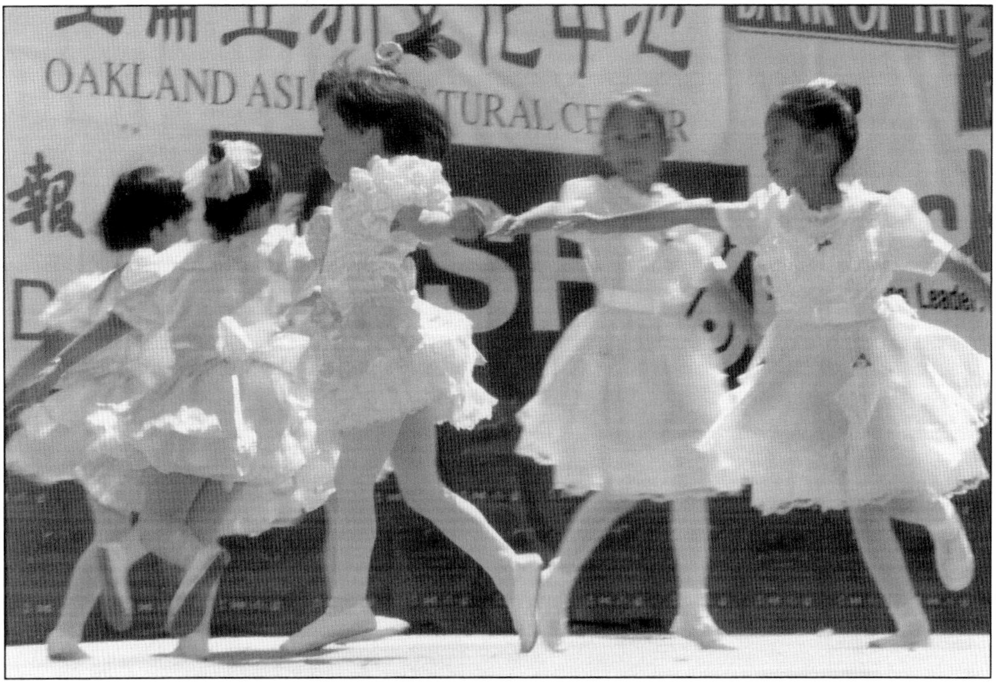

Whirling girl dancers entertain at the 1995 StreetFest. (Photo by and courtesy of Henry Woon.)

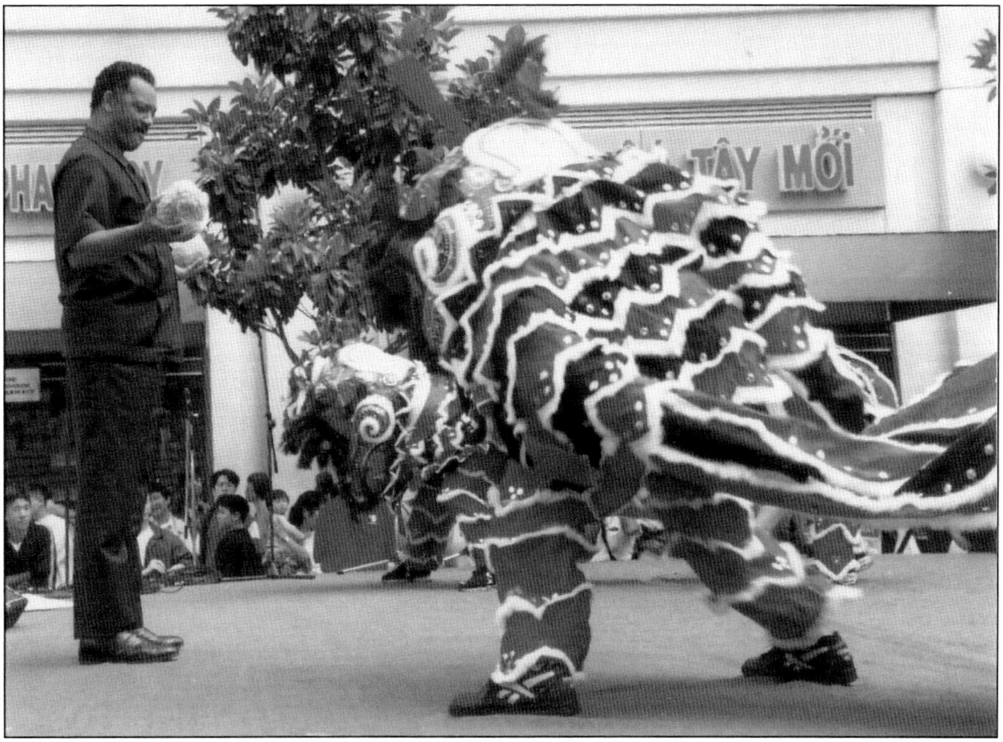

National civil rights leader and political activist Jesse Jackson faced off a hungry, dancing lion at a StreetFest in the early 1990s. He is holding a head of lettuce, a symbol for money. He fed the lion, as a sign of respect, supporting the lion's role of protecting the festival by scaring off evil spirits. (Courtesy of George Ong.)

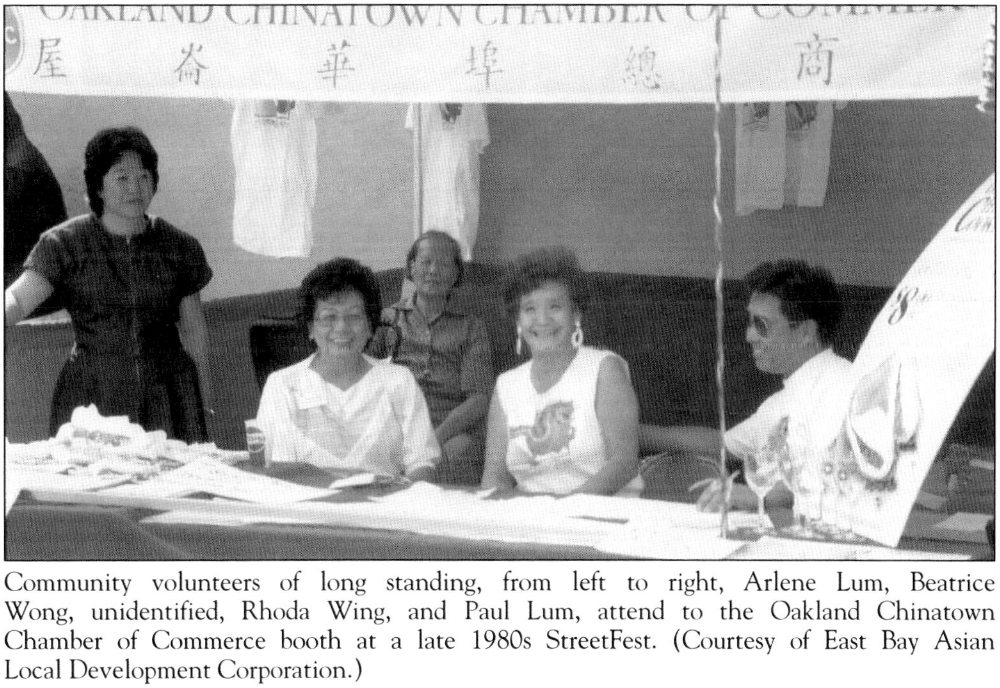

Community volunteers of long standing, from left to right, Arlene Lum, Beatrice Wong, unidentified, Rhoda Wing, and Paul Lum, attend to the Oakland Chinatown Chamber of Commerce booth at a late 1980s StreetFest. (Courtesy of East Bay Asian Local Development Corporation.)

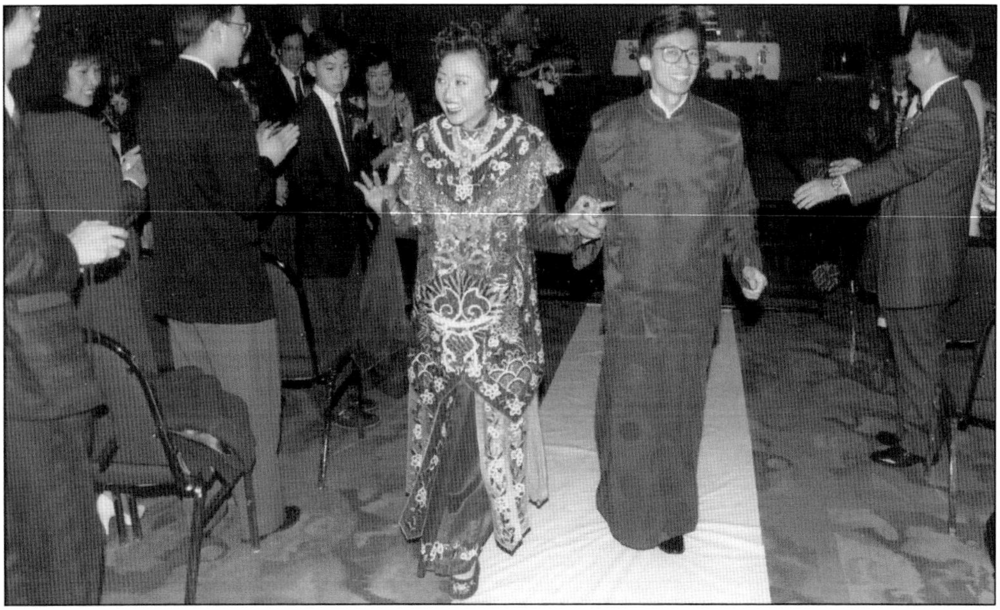

Carl and Eleanore Chan rejoice after their Buddhist wedding ceremony in 1993 near Chinatown, attended by 700 guests. A Hong Kong immigrant and real estate consultant, Carl Chan is an active volunteer with the Oakland Chinatown Chamber of Commerce and the Oakland Chinatown Lions Club, and has been on the city's convention and visitor's bureau board of directors. (Courtesy of Carl Chan.)

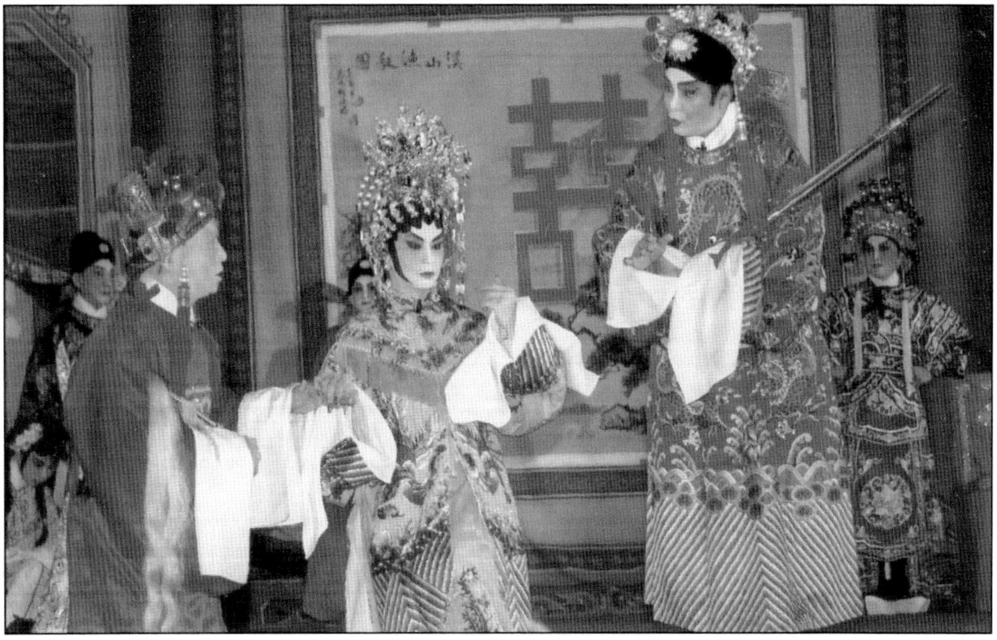

The Oakland Asian Cultural Center presented a Cantonese opera, as part of the Lunar New Year celebration in 2001. Chi Ming Wong produced the opera. The performance, and an exhibit of costumes and photographs, showed how Cantonese opera helps some overseas Chinese retain their history and culture. (Photo by Sze Kwong Wong, courtesy of Oakland Asian Cultural Center.)

Six

Artists, Writers, Media, Stars

Oakland Chinatown and the greater Chinese community have produced writers, artists, media personalities, and stars of stage and screen. Before World War II it was not easy for Oakland Chinese, or any Chinese Americans, to cross over into mainstream American cultural life. Once discriminatory barriers were lifted, however, Oakland Chinese with artistic and writing skills were better able to express themselves outside the confines of Chinatown.

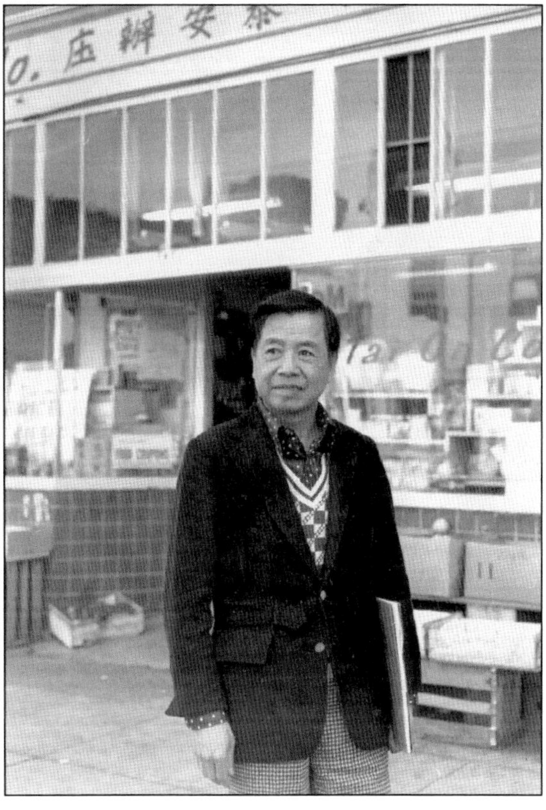

World-famous watercolorist Dong Kingman returns to his home turf near the corner of Eighth and Webster Streets in 1976. He was born in Oakland Chinatown in 1911, but received most of his education in Hong Kong, where he studied painting. At 18, he returned to Oakland to work at odd jobs and continue to study art. He got his big break in 1940 when the Metropolitan Museum of Art in New York bought one of his paintings. His art career blossomed internationally. (Courtesy of the Oakland Tribune Collection, the Oakland Museum of California, Gift of Alameda Newspaper Group.)

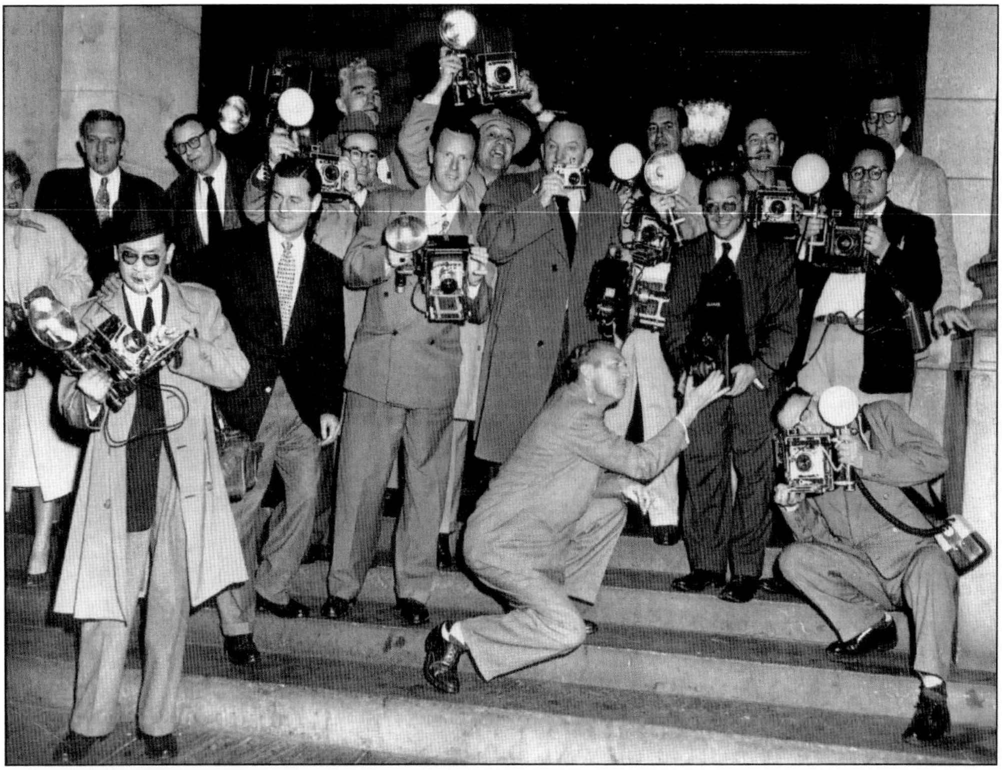

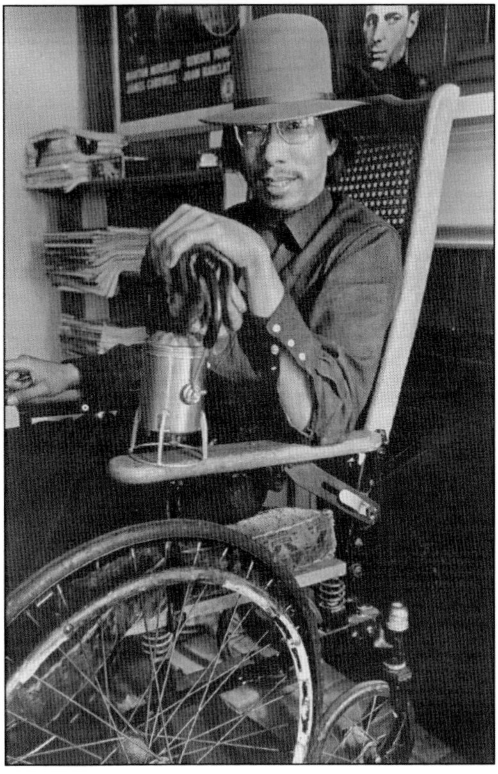

Paul Quen, shown in the left foreground in a trench coat and dark glasses, was among press photographers at an unknown event in this undated photo. He was a pioneering Chinese American press photographer. He graduated from Oakland Technical High School in 1943 and joined the *Oakland Post-Enquirer* as a photographer. After serving as a military combat photographer, he resumed his career as a local press photographer and TV news cameraman. (Courtesy of Eugene Quen.)

Writer Frank Chin, shown in this 1988 photo, went to Lincoln School and Oakland High School in the 1950s. He once worked as a brakeman for the Southern Pacific Railroad, evoking memories of Chinese railroad workers of the mid-19th century. His play, *Chickencoop Chinaman*, debuted off Broadway in 1972, a breakthrough for a Chinese American playwright. He is an avid student of Chinese literature and an unsparing critical voice of Asian American literature. (Photo by Karen Pataki, courtesy of Coffee House Press.)

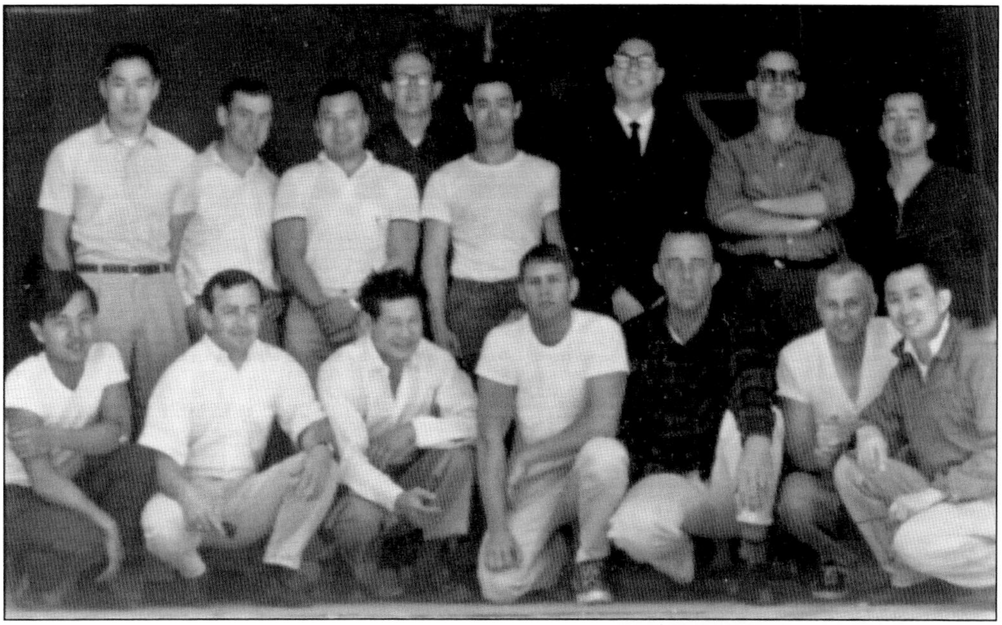

Jimmy Lee's garage in Oakland, near High Street, was where Bruce Lee (back row, fifth from left) taught martial arts for two years in the mid-1960s. Jimmy Lee is in the front row, third from the left. George Lee (back row, third from the left) was a student and designed and built Bruce's workout equipment. After teaching in Oakland, Bruce Lee went on to international TV and film fame. The three Lees weren't related. The identities of others in this photo are unknown. (Courtesy of George Lee.)

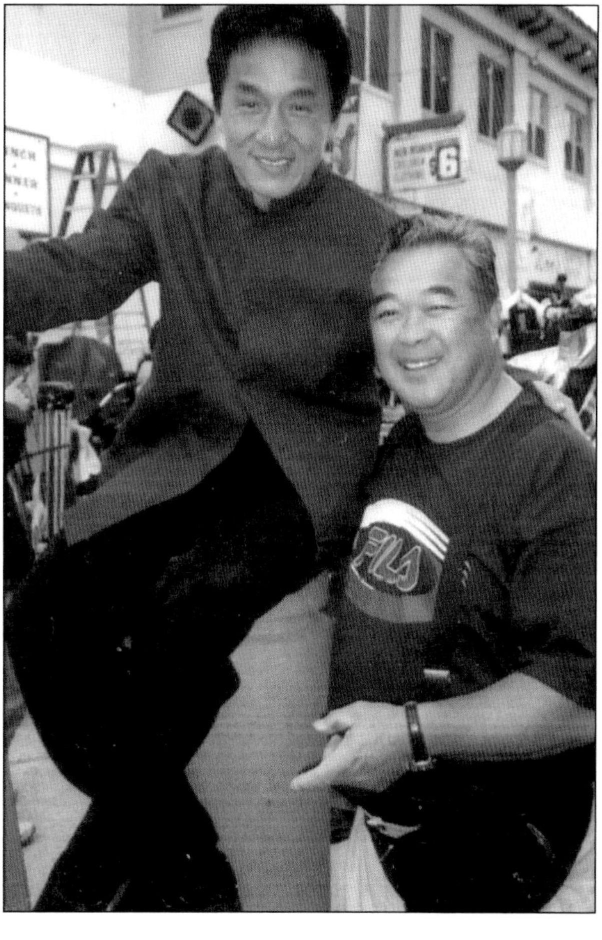

International film star Jackie Chan is shown here in 1998 in Los Angeles with an unrelated Jeff Chan. Jeff Chan, an Oakland Chinatown native, became interested in Chinese lion dancing when he visited China. When he wasn't working as a draftsman, he organized lion dance troupes in Oakland and Los Angeles. His Los Angeles troupe performs in Hollywood films, including Jackie Chan's *Rush Hour*. (Courtesy of Janet Lem.)

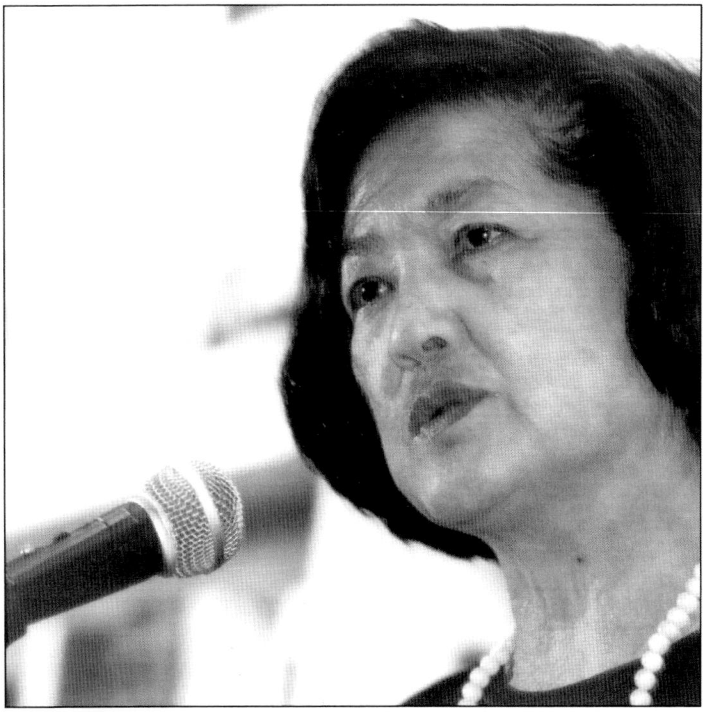

Nellie Wong, a Chinatown native, has three volumes of poetry in print. She is well known in college and women's writing circles. While working as a secretary and administrative assistant, she wrote poetry and became active with Radical Women and the Freedom Socialist Party. She and five other Asian American women formed an artist's group, Unbound Feet. She reads her poetry throughout the country. (Photo by Steven C. Wilson, courtesy of Nellie Wong.)

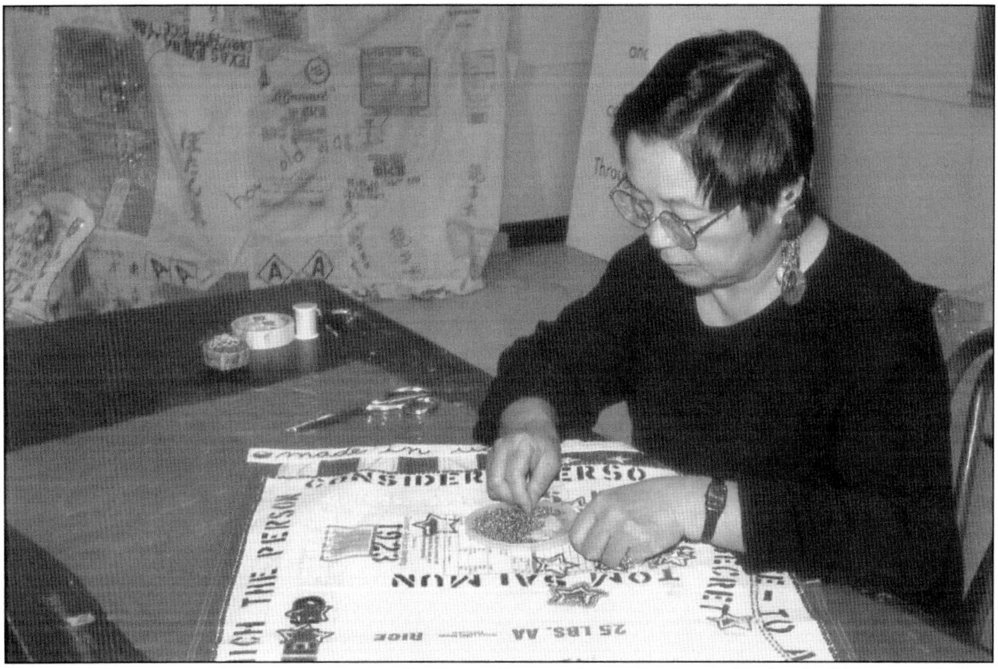

Chinatown native Flo Oy Wong, working on her *made in usa: Angel Island Shhh* art exhibit, specializes in installation pieces that use rice sacks and other Chinese cultural artifacts. Her Angel Island exhibit pays homage to Chinese immigrants detained at the immigration station from 1910 to 1940. Her work has been widely exhibited locally and at the Smithsonian and Ellis Island Immigration Museum. (Photo by James Dewrance; courtesy of Flo Oy Wong.)

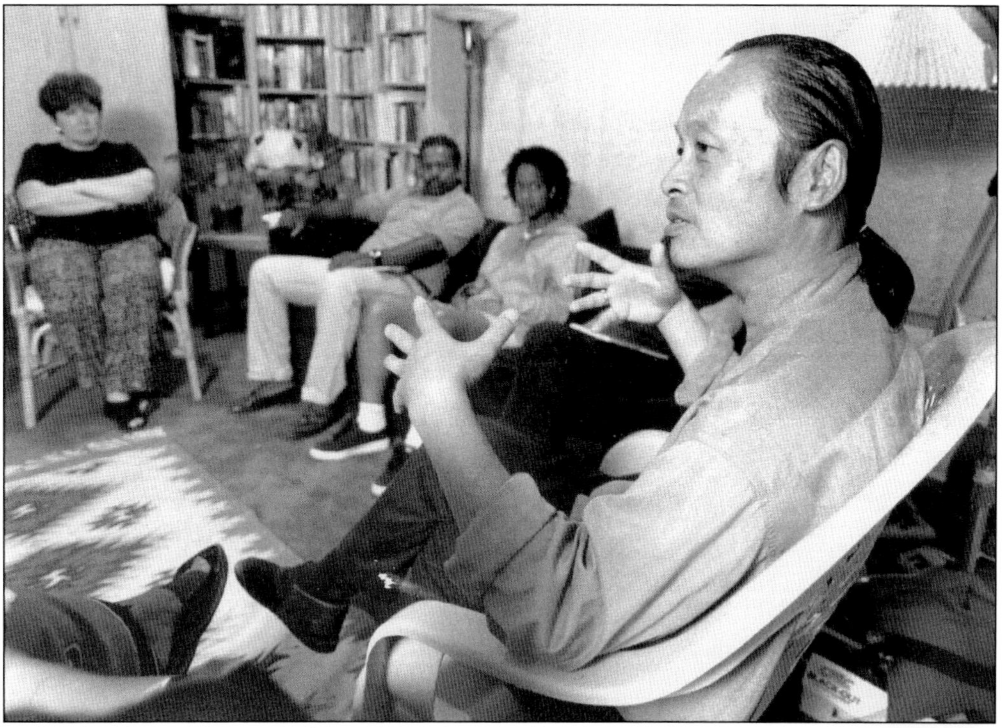

Oakland native Lee Mun Wah conducts a multicultural seminar. Born Gary Lee, he was a teacher and poet before the murder of his mother in 1985 traumatized him, necessitating therapy. He became a therapist specializing in countering racism and anger. He also produces documentary films about multicultural relations and speaks widely on the subject. Major corporations hire his company for diversity training. (Photo by Scott Braley, courtesy of Lee Mun Wah.)

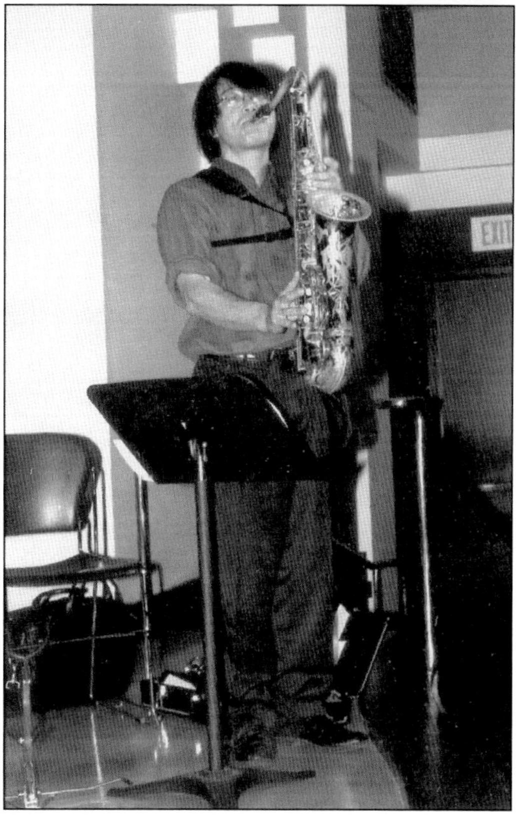

Francis Wong was co-director of the Oakland Asian Cultural Center in the late 1990s. A saxophonist and flutist, he is an activist leader in the Asian American jazz movement, along with Bay Area musicians Jon Jang, Mark Izu, Anthony Brown, and poet Genny Lim. (Courtesy of the Oakland Asian Cultural Center.)

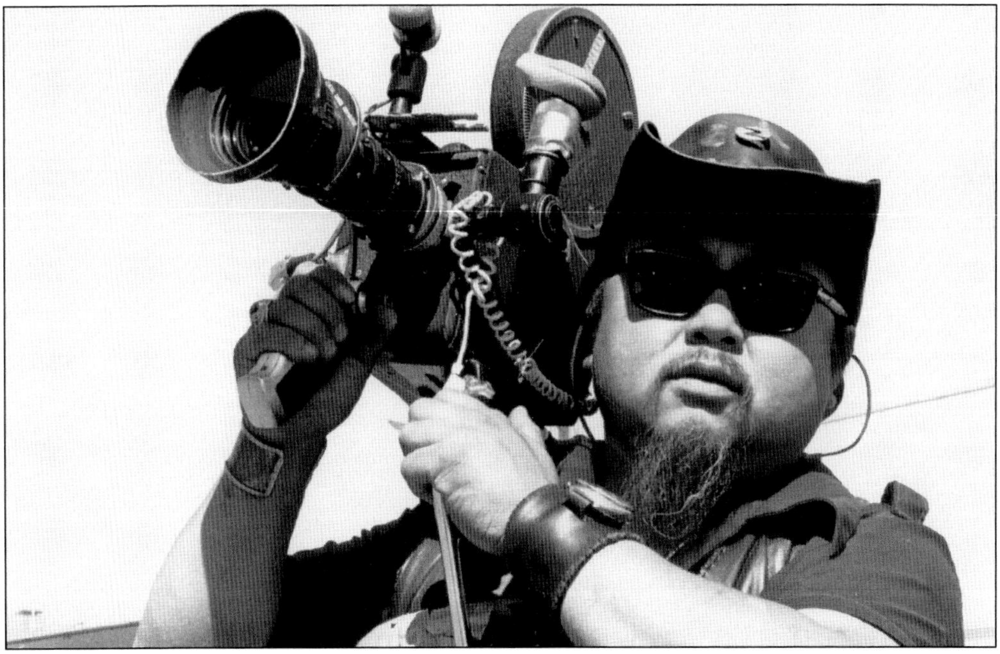

Willie Kee, shown here in his trademark black cowboy hat, was a Chinatown native and graduated from Oakland Technical High School, where he developed an interest in photography. He joined the Marines, working as a photographer, and later became a cameraman for Oakland-based KTVU-Channel 2. He won 12 Emmy Awards for his photography, producing, and writing. (Courtesy of Rosy Chu.)

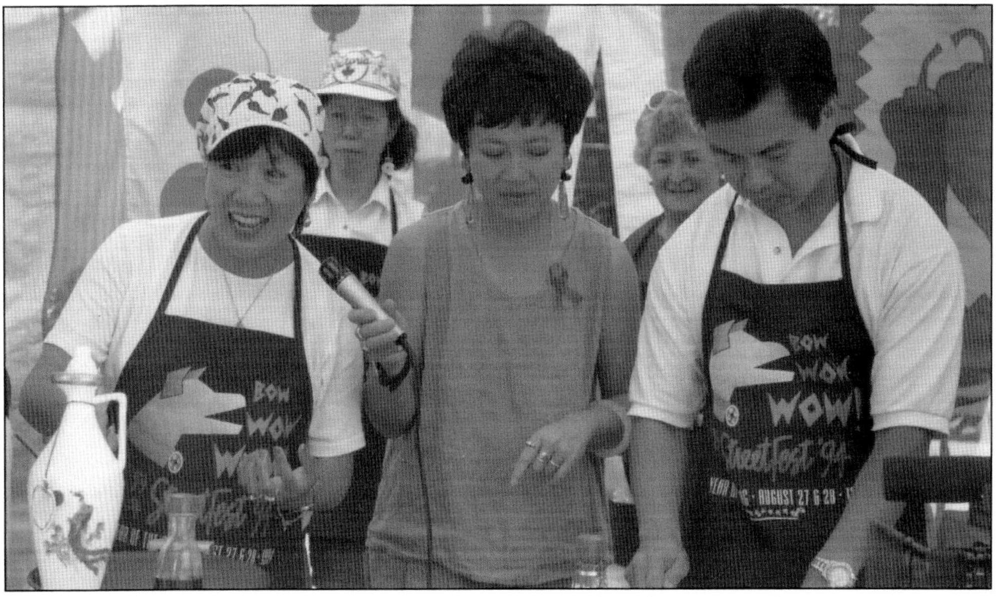

From left to right, Shirley Fong-Torres, Sherry Hu, and Rick Quan perform at a StreetFest. Fong-Torres, a Chinatown native, is a professional chef and operator of Wok Wiz Tours and Cooking Company in San Francisco. Hu grew up in Oakland and is an Oakland-based reporter for CBS5-TV, San Francisco. Quan, a sports reporter for CBS5, is originally from Houston, but now resides in Oakland. (Photo by and courtesy of Henry Woon.)

Sue Li-Jue is the founder, artistic director, and choreographer of Oakland-based Facing East Dance and Music. An Oakland resident since 1986, Li-Jue got her master of fine arts degree at Mills College in Oakland. Her most recent work, *Held So Close . . . remembering the poets of Angel Island*, pays tribute to Chinese immigrants who carved poems into the walls of the Angel Island Immigration Station. (Photo by Matt Haber, courtesy of Sue Li-Jue.)

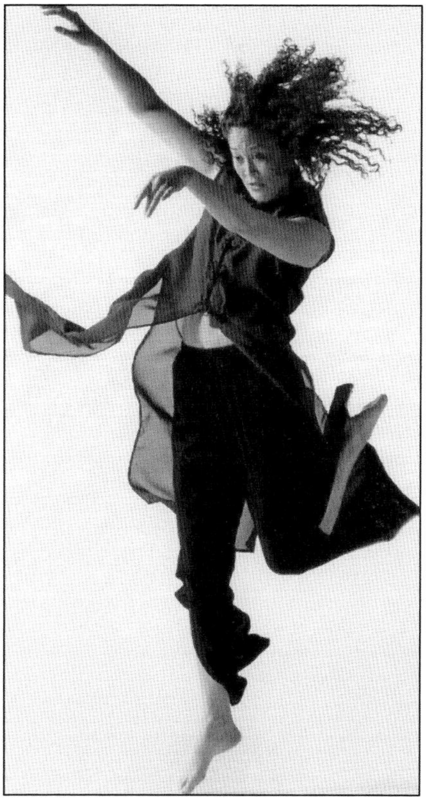

Ben Fong-Torres, seen here in 1997 with *Rolling Stone* magazine founder Jann Wenner, at left, and actor Michael Douglas at the Rock and Roll Hall of Fame in Cleveland, Ohio, grew up in Chinatown where his parents operated several restaurants. Fong-Torres is a journalist, author, radio personality, and Elvis impersonator who interviewed major rock music figures for *Rolling Stone*. His memoir, *The Rice Room*, recalls his youth in Chinatown. (Courtesy of Ben Fong-Torres.)

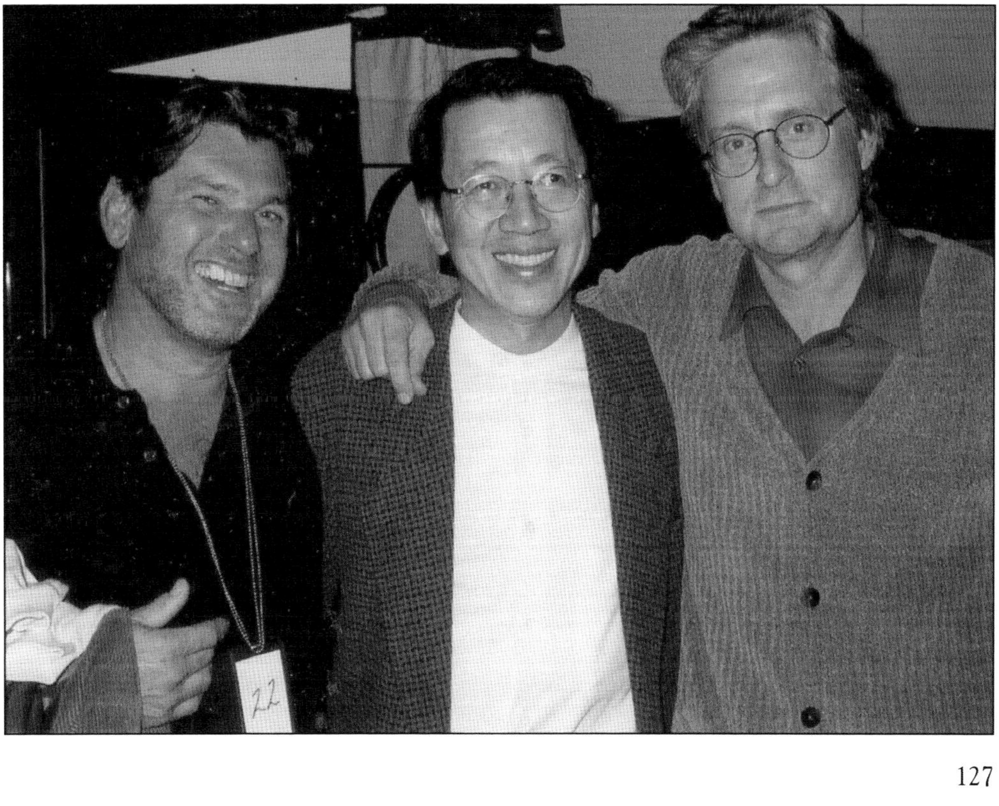

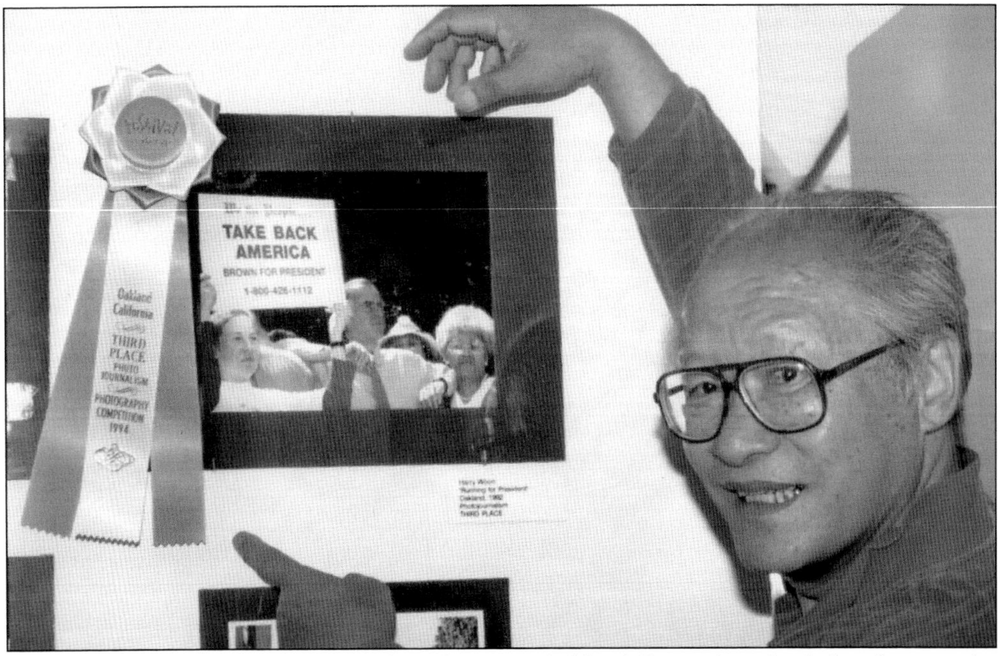

Henry Woon, pointing to his award in the 1994 Oakland Festival at the Lake photography contest, was born in Oakland's Chinatown and has been a community photographer for many decades. Not just a photographer, he is also an award-winning painter, journalist, and playwright. His play, "Now You See, Now You Don't," was performed by the East West Players in Los Angeles in 1969. Several of his photographs appear in this book. (Courtesy of Henry Woon.)

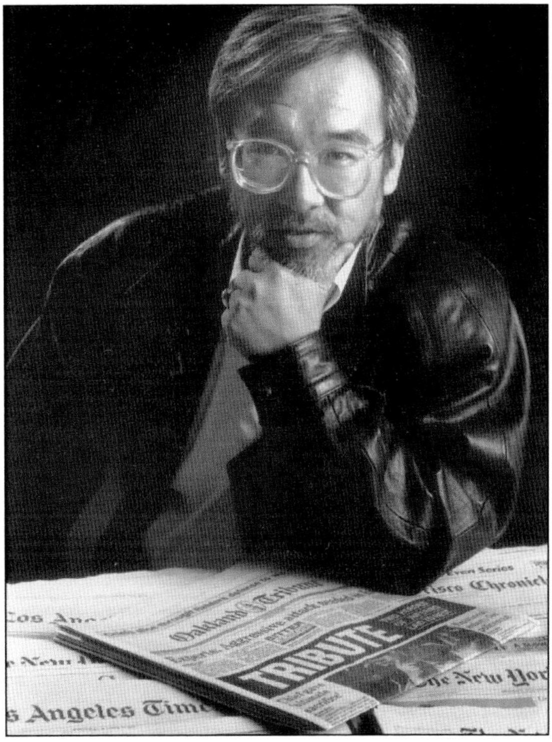

William Wong, author of this book, was born in Chinatown and worked in his parents' Great China restaurant in the 1940s and 1950s. In 1962, he became the first Asian American reporter for a mainstream San Francisco newspaper. He was a Peace Corps volunteer in the Philippines in the mid-1960s, then resumed his journalism career, writing for, among others, *The Wall Street Journal, The Oakland Tribune, the San Francisco Chronicle, San Francisco Examiner, East-West News*, and *Asian Week*. He has also been a regional commentator on *The News Hour with Jim Lehrer* on PBS. In 2001, Temple University Press published his first book, *Yellow Journalist: Dispatches from Asian America*. (Courtesy of William Wong.)